Contents

Cheese Blintzes

Serving: 5 | Prep: 15m | Ready in: 1h15m

Ingredients

Batter:

- 3 large eggs
- 1 cup all-purpose flour
- 1 cup milk
- 1/4 cup cold water
- 2 tbsps. vegetable oil
- 1 tbsp. white sugar
- 1/2 tsp. salt
- 1/4 tsp. vanilla extract

Filling:

- 1 1/2 cups ricotta cheese, strained if wet
- 1/2 cup cream cheese
- 1 lemon, zested
- 1 large egg
- 2 tbsps. confectioners' sugar
- 1 pinch salt
- 1 tbsp. butter, or as needed
- 1 tbsp. confectioners' sugar, or as needed for dusting

Direction

1. Add the following ingredients in a blender: flour, milk, 3 eggs, water, sugar, vegetable oil, salt, and vanilla extract. Blend together for 2 minutes or to a smooth texture, making sure to scrape the sides as well. Set aside for 30 minutes at room temperature.
2. In a mixing bowl, whisk in the cream cheese, ricotta cheese, egg, sugar, lemon zest, and salt.
3. Combine the contents well, then put the lid on and keep in the fridge.
4. Set the heat to medium-high, and heat a 10-inch, non-stick skillet. Lightly coat or spray vegetable oil on it. Add 1/4 cup batter into the pan and swirl it around to coat the bottom. Dry the surface by cooking for 1 minute. Flip this side and cook shortly for 30 seconds. Transfer to a plate, then do this with the rest of the batter. Stack each crepe on top of the other.
5. Prepare on oven by heating it to 165 degrees C or 325 degrees F. Lightly coat a baking dish with butter.
6. Take 3 to 4 tbsps. of filling and place on top the crepe at around one inch from the edge you are nearest to. Flatten the crepe slightly when folding the edge into the filling. Do this for both sides, and roll into a rectangle as small as you can. Make sure you place the seam on the bottom to create the blintz.
7. Set the heat to medium, then use a skillet to melt the butter. Cook each side of the blintzes for 2 minutes till golden brown on both sides. Be sure to turn them carefully. Remove to a baking dish lightly coated with butter.
8. Let it bake in the oven you prepared for 12 minutes, so the filling becomes firm. Let the blintzes cool for 10 minutes, then serve. Sprinkle with some confectioners' sugar on top.

Nutrition Information

Calories: 452 calories; Total Carbohydrate: 33.2 g Cholesterol: 207 mg Total Fat: 26.9 g Protein: 19.4 g

Chef John's Croissants

Serving: 8 | Prep: 30m | Ready in: 3h55m

Ingredients
Dough:
- 1 cup warm water (100 degrees F or 38 degrees C)
- 1 (.25 oz.) package active dry yeast
- 1/4 cup granulated white sugar
- 3 1/2 cups unbleached bread flour
- 3 tsps. kosher salt
- 6 tbsps. butter, room temperature, cut into pieces

Croissants:
- 2 sticks unsalted European-style butter
- 1 egg
- 1 tbsp. water

Direction

1. Into the bowl of a stand mixer, add warm water. Drizzle with yeast. Leave the yeast to dissolve for ten minutes. Add bread flour and sugar. Drizzle with salt; put in 6 tbsps. of butter. Attach bowl to the stand mixer. Use dough hook to mix the dough for 3 to 4 minutes just until dough forms a ball that pulls away cleanly from the bowl's sides and the butter is completely kneaded in.
2. Place the dough onto a work surface and shape to a semi-smooth ball. Return the dough into the mixer bowl and cover it. Leave it to rise in a warm place for about 2 hours until doubled.
3. Place the dough onto a work surface that is lightly floured. Deflate it by pushing and pressing the dough, then shape into a rectangle. Fold into thirds by moving one end over the middle third and fold the other side over the middle. Cover with plastic wrap. Put in a rimmed baking sheet that is lined with silicone mat. Chill for about 1 hour until chilled through.
4. Slice 2 sticks of butter lengthwise in half, then put onto a length of parchment paper that is long enough to fold over the butter, placing slightly apart from each other. Then, fold parchment paper over the butter. Push the butter down. Use a rolling pin to roll out into an 8x8-inch square. Chill for 10 to 15 minutes until just barely flexible and a little chilled.
5. Roll out the dough into a rectangle that is a bit wider than butter slab and should be just over twice as long. Put the butter onto one half of dough, leave approximately one inch margin from the edge of dough. Then, fold the other half of dough over butter. Flour dough and work surface as needed.
6. Make ridges by pushing the rolling pin down onto dough. Roll out the ridges. Repeat. Continue rolling and pressing until the dough is approximately the same size as the rectangle you had earlier when you folded it in half; dust with just a little flour as needed.
7. Fold one-third of the dough over the middle third beginning from the short side. Fold the other end on top to make a small rectangle. Use a rolling pin to flatten out just a bit. Place into the baking sheet lined with silicone; cover with plastic wrap. Chill for about 30 minutes until cold.
8. Return the dough onto a work surface and repeat the rolling and pressing technique until the dough is the size of the earlier larger rectangle. Then, fold into thirds beginning from short side. Push and roll a bit. Place back into the lined baking sheet. Cover and chill for about 15 minutes.
9. Roll back out into a big rectangle. Then, fold the dough in half. Push and roll out to make a 1/2-inch thick rectangle; add as little flour as needed to prevent the dough from sticking.
10. Use a pizza cutter or pastry wheel to slice the dough lengthwise in half. Sprinkle flour on one piece,

then roll out to make a rectangle of approximately 1/4- to 1/8-inch thick. Using pastry wheel, slice dough diagonally crosswise beginning from one corner into 8 triangles. Then, roll each up towards the tip beginning with bottom end of each triangle to make croissant, seam at the bottom. If need be, seal the tip to the rolled croissant with a little water.

11. Repeat this with the other half of dough.
12. Transfer the shaped croissants into baking sheets that are lined with silicone mats. To make the egg wash, whisk together 1 tbsp. water and egg. Coat the croissants with the egg wash. Let rise in a warm place for about 45 to 60 minutes.
13. Preheat an oven to 200 degrees C (400 degrees F). Gently but thoroughly coat the croissants with the egg wash again.
14. Bake for about 25 minutes in the oven until nicely browned. Place onto cooling rack. Let cool to room temperature before serving.

Nutrition Information

Calories: 532 calories; Total Carbohydrate: 50.1 g Cholesterol: 107 mg Total Fat: 33.3 g Protein: 8.6 g Sodium: 796 mg

Cookie Tulips

Serving: 12 | Prep: 45m | Ready in: 1h

Ingredients

- 1/4 cup butter, softened
- 1/2 cup white sugar
- 7 tbsps. all-purpose flour
- 1 tsp. vanilla extract
- 2 egg whites, beaten
- 1 (4 oz.) package cream cheese at room temperature
- 1 cup confectioners' sugar
- 1 tsp. vanilla extract
- 1/2 (8 oz.) container frozen whipped topping, thawed
- 17 large fresh strawberries, divided

Direction

1. Set the oven to 175°C or 350°F to preheat. Use a silicone sheet liner or parchment paper to line a baking sheet. Coat the outsides of twelve 2-in. baking glasses or small bowls with grease.
2. In a bowl, mash white sugar and butter together until smooth, then mix in egg whites, 1 tsp. of vanilla extract and flour to form a smooth batter. Drop on the prepped baking sheet with 2 1/2 tbsp. of mixture, then spread dough out into an extremely thin circle with the diameter of 7 inches, using a spatula or spoon. Repeat process with leftover batter.
3. In the preheated oven, bake for 7-9 minutes, until centers of cookie are set and edges are brown very slightly. Watch cookies carefully to prevent them from over-baking. Pull sheet from the oven and slip a spatula beneath each flat cookie instantly. Center and drape cookies over glasses coated with grease to harden into small wavy bowls. Let them cool fully.
4. While cookies are cooling over their molds, in a bowl, beat together confectioners' sugar and cream cheese until smooth, then blend in 1 tsp. of vanilla extract. Take off green tops and cores from five strawberries, then put them into a small bowl and mash to a somewhat lumpy and juicy texture. Mix into cream cheese mixture with mashed strawberries, then fold into strawberry cream with whipped topping gently, until mixed well.

5. Scoop 3 tbsp. of strawberry cream in every cookie bowl then place a beautiful fresh strawberry with green top on top of cream layer. Keep remaining cookies in a tightly sealed container and remaining cream in the fridge.

Nutrition Information

Calories: 199 calories; Total Carbohydrate: 26.7 g Cholesterol: 21 mg Total Fat: 9.6 g Protein: 2.1 g Sodium: 67 mg

Crab And Swiss Omelet

Serving: 2 | Prep: 10m | Ready in: 22m

Ingredients

- 2 tbsps. butter
- 1/2 cup sliced fresh mushrooms
- 4 eggs, separated
- 2 tbsps. milk
- 1 cup cooked crabmeat
- 1 cup shredded Swiss cheese

Direction

1. In a large nonstick skillet placed over medium-high heat, melt butter. Stir in mushrooms and cook for about 5 minutes until softened. Move mushrooms to a plate using a slotted spoon. Remove skillet from heat.
2. Beat together milk and egg yolks in a small bowl until well blended. Use dry beater to beat egg whites together in a separate bowl until soft peaks form. Fold yolk mixture into white mixture.
3. Return skillet to medium-high heat. When butter sizzles, pour egg mixture in. Evenly scatter crab meat and mushrooms on top. Cook for about 3 minutes until omelet starts to set. Drizzle Swiss cheese on top. Fold omelet over to form a semicircle shape using a big spatula. Cook, covered, for about 3 minutes until omelet puffs and is cooked through. Carefully slide onto a large plate and serve.

Nutrition Information

Calories: 796 calories; Total Carbohydrate: 9.7 g Cholesterol: 567 mg Total Fat: 56.6 g Protein: 61.6 g Sodium: 718 mg

Crab Omelet

Serving: 6 | Prep: 15m | Ready in: 35m

Ingredients

- 2 tbsps. olive oil
- 1 small potato, peeled and diced
- 1 onion, chopped
- 2 cloves garlic, minced
- 1/4 lb. fresh crabmeat, drained and flaked
- salt and pepper to taste
- 1 small tomato, diced
- 1 (1.5 oz.) box raisins
- 1/4 cup peas
- 1 red bell pepper, chopped

- 3 eggs, beaten

Direction
1. In a skillet set over medium heat, add olive oil. Add the potato and fry in the hot oil for 5-7 minutes until fork-tender. Place the potatoes to a plate lined with paper towels and reserve. Put the skillet back to medium heat. Cook the garlic and onion in the left oil for approximately 5 minutes until softened. Put the crab to the skillet and add pepper and salt to taste; mix. Then cover the skillet and cook for 2 minutes. Mix the tomatoes into the mixture and cook for 2 more minutes. Mix in the red bell pepper, peas, and raisins to the mixture; cook and stir for 2 more minutes.
2. Place the eggs over the mixture. And cook for 2-3 minutes until the eggs are set. Turn the omelet over and cook for 1 more minute. Place to a serving plate then serve right away.

Nutrition Information
Calories: 165 calories; Total Carbohydrate: 17.5 g Cholesterol: 104 mg Total Fat: 7.4 g Protein: 8.4 g Sodium: 104 mg

Crab Strata
Serving: 6 | Prep: 15m | Ready in: 3h

Ingredients
- 4 cups cubed firm-textured bread
- 2 (6 oz.) cans crabmeat, drained and flaked
- 4 cups shredded Swiss cheese
- 1 cup shredded Cheddar cheese
- 1/4 cup capers
- 3 green onions, chopped
- 6 eggs, lightly beaten
- 1 1/3 cups milk
- 1/4 cup dry sherry
- 1 tbsp. Dijon mustard
- 1/2 tsp. Worcestershire sauce

Direction
1. Prepare a 2-quart baking dish that is greased. Toss together the green onions, capers, Cheddar cheese, Swiss cheese, crab meat, and bread cubes in the baking dish.
2. In a bowl, combine Worcestershire sauce, mustard, sherry, milk, and eggs; stir. Then pour equally atop bread mixture. Keep in the refrigerator, tightly covered, for at least 2 hours but not more than 24 hours.
3. Prepare the oven by preheating to 350°F (175°C). Then bake strata uncovered for approximately 45 minutes, until a knife poked in the middle comes out clean. Allow it to stand for 10 minutes prior to serving. Serve immediately.

Nutrition Information
Calories: 581 calories; Total Carbohydrate: 22.4 g Cholesterol: 260 mg Total Fat: 34.8 g Protein: 43 g Sodium: 944 mg

Cream Cheese Garlic Spread
Serving: 20 | Prep: 5m | Ready in: 5m

Ingredients

- 2 (8 oz.) packages cream cheese, softened
- 1/2 tsp. garlic powder
- 1 tbsp. dried chives

Direction

1. Whip together the chives, garlic powder and cream cheese in a bowl till becoming smooth.

Nutrition Information

Calories: 78 calories; Total Carbohydrate: 0.7 g Cholesterol: 25 mg Total Fat: 7.8 g Protein: 1.7 g
Sodium: 66 mg

Creamy Curried Scrambled Eggs

Serving: 2 | Prep: 10m | Ready in: 20m

Ingredients

- 2 tsps. ghee (clarified butter)
- 2 shallots, thinly sliced
- 1 tsp. curry powder
- 1 tbsp. water (optional)
- 4 oz. cream cheese
- 4 eggs
- 1 tsp. Dijon mustard
- salt and pepper to taste

Direction

1. In a skillet, melt ghee over medium-low heat. Add the shallots; stir and wait about 3 minutes or until shallots turn tender. Put the curry powder and wait for about 5 minutes. To avoid overcooking the shallots or burning, add a tbsp. of water.
2. In a microwave-safe bowl, put cream cheese and cook on high until the cheese is soft, about 30 seconds. Beat in eggs and add the Dijon mustard. Whisk until cream cheese is well-mixed. (It's fine to see a few lumps.) Add the egg mixture into the shallots and cook slowly. Stir occasionally until the eggs are already firm. Compared to normal scrambled eggs, they still will be softer because of cream cheese. When the eggs are ready, take it out from the pan and use salt and pepper to taste.

Nutrition Information

Calories: 420 calories; Total Carbohydrate: 11.8 g Cholesterol: 445 mg Total Fat: 34.2 g Protein: 18.2 g
Sodium: 377 mg

Creme Brulee French Toast

Serving: 6 | Prep: 20m | Ready in: 9h

Ingredients

- 1/2 cup unsalted butter
- 1 cup packed brown sugar
- 2 tbsps. corn syrup
- 6 (1-inch thick) slices French bread
- 5 eggs
- 1 1/2 cups half-and-half cream
- 1 tsp. vanilla extract
- 1 tsp. brandy-based orange liqueur (such as Grand Marnier)

- 1/4 tsp. salt

Direction
1. In a small saucepan, melt butter on moderate heat, then blend in corn syrup and brown sugar while stirring until sugar dissolves. Transfer into a 13-inch x9-inch baking dish.
2. Take crusts off the bread and arrange in one single layer in the baking dish. Whisk salt, orange brandy, vanilla extract, half-and-half and eggs together in a small bowl. Drizzle mixture over bread, then place a cover and refrigerate for a minimum of 8 hours to overnight.
3. Set the oven to 175°C or 350°F to preheat. Take the dish out of fridge and bring to room temperature.
4. In the preheated oven, bake for 35-40 minutes without a cover until brown slightly and puff.

Nutrition Information
Calories: 510 calories; Total Carbohydrate: 58.7 g Cholesterol: 218 mg Total Fat: 26.9 g Protein: 10.2 g Sodium: 359 mg

Crispy Bacon And Sweet Onion Omelet
Serving: 2 | Prep: 15m | Ready in: 37m

Ingredients
- 4 strips bacon
- 1 tsp. butter
- 1/2 sweet onion, diced
- 3 jumbo eggs
- 2 tbsps. water
- 1/4 cup shredded sharp Cheddar cheese
- 1 slice process American cheese, diced
- 1/8 tsp. salt
- 1/8 tsp. crushed red pepper flakes

Direction
1. Over medium-high heat, cook the bacon in a skillet until its crisp. Lift with a slotted spoon and place onto paper towels to drain and let to cool. Then crumble the bacon and reserve.
2. Over medium heat, heat the butter in a skillet, add onions and then cook while stirring for about 10 minutes until tender.
3. Use cooking spray to coat a 10-inch non-stick skillet and then put atop a cold burner. Mix water and eggs together. Add egg mixture into the cold skillet. Cover the skillet and switch on the burner to medium-low heat. Let it cook until the steam starts to vent from skillet. Take out the lid. Drizzle the red pepper, salt, American cheese, crumbled bacon, and Cheddar cheese, atop the eggs. Scatter the onions atop the eggs. Slowly swirl skillet in a circular motion in order to release the omelet and then place it onto a plate. Roll the omelet in half. Let the cheese melts for about 2 minutes.

Nutrition Information
Calories: 380 calories; Total Carbohydrate: 4.1 g Cholesterol: 417 mg Total Fat: 28.7 g Protein: 26.2 g Sodium: 1030 mg

Croissants
Serving: 12 | Prep: 40m | Ready in: 11h15m

Ingredients

- 1 1/4 tsps. active dry yeast
- 3 tbsps. warm water (110 degrees F/45 degrees C)
- 1 tsp. white sugar
- 1 3/4 cups all-purpose flour
- 2 tsps. white sugar
- 1 1/2 tsps. salt
- 2/3 cup warm milk
- 2 tbsps. vegetable oil
- 2/3 cup unsalted butter, chilled
- 1 egg
- 1 tbsp. water

Direction

1. Mix 1 tsp. of sugar, warm water and yeast. Rest till foamy and creamy.
2. Into one mixing bowl, measure the flour. In warm milk, melt salt and 2 tsps. of sugar. Mix into the flour together with oil and yeast. Combine thoroughly; knead till smooth. Put a cover and allow to rise for 3 hours till more than triple in size. Gently punch dough down and allow to rise once more till doubled for 3 hours longer. Punch down and refrigerate for 20 minutes.
3. Massage butter till flexible, yet not oily and soft. Press dough into a rectangle, 14x8 inches in size. Spread the top 2/3 with butter, keeping a quarter-inch border on edges. Fold the unbuttered 1/3 over center third and the buttered top 1/3 down on top of that. Rotate 90° to make folds to left and right. Unroll into a rectangle, 14x6 inches in size. Fold in 3 once more. Lightly dust with flour and place dough in one plastic bag. Chill for 2 hours. Remove wrap, dust with flour, and gently punch down. Roll into a rectangle, 14x6 inches in size and fold once more. Rotate 90° and repeat. Put on wrap and refrigerate for 2 hours.
4. To form, unroll dough into a rectangle, 20x5 inches in size. Half crosswise and refrigerate 1/2 while forming the other 1/2. Unroll into a rectangle, 15x5 inches in size. Slice into 3 squares, 5x5 inches in size. Diagonally slice every square in 1/2. To make the point longer, roll every triangle lightly and turn it to 7 inches long. Get the 2 other points and as you roll it up, expand them slightly. Put on baking sheet, bending slightly. Allow the formed croissants to rise till light and puffy. Whip 1 tbsp. of water and egg together in small bowl. Using egg wash, coat the croissants.
5. In the prepped 245°C or 475°F oven, bake for 12 to 15 minutes.

Nutrition Information

Calories: 196 calories; Total Carbohydrate: 15.8 g Cholesterol: 46 mg Total Fat: 13.4 g Protein: 3.1 g Sodium: 304 mg

Dessert For Breakfast - Red Velvet Pancakes

Serving: 4 | Prep: 20m | Ready in: 35m

Ingredients
Pancakes:
- 2 cups milk
- 2 tbsps. white vinegar
- 2 cups all-purpose flour
- 1/2 cup white sugar
- 1/4 cup unsweetened cocoa powder
- 2 tsps. baking powder

- 1/2 tsp. baking soda
- 1/2 tsp. salt
- 1/3 cup unsalted butter, melted
- 2 large eggs
- 2 1/4 tsps. red food coloring
- 2 tsps. vanilla extract
- cooking spray

Cream Cheese Glaze:
- 6 oz. cream cheese, softened
- 3 tbsps. butter, softened
- 1 cup confectioners' sugar
- 1/4 cup milk, plus more if needed
- 1/2 tsp. vanilla extract
- 2 tbsps. confectioners' sugar for dusting

Direction
1. Prepare the oven by preheating to 200°F (95°C).
2. In a bowl, beat vinegar and 2 cups milk; allow it to rest for approximately 2 minutes until milk sours.
3. Sift salt, baking soda and powder, cocoa powder, white sugar, and flour in a large bowl; stir to blend.
4. In a bowl, combine 2 tsps. vanilla extract, red food coloring, eggs, melted unsalted butter, and milk mixture.
5. Add the milk mixture into the flour mixture and whisk until just blended; you'll have a lumpy batter.
6. Heat a cast-iron skillet coated with cooking spray over medium-low heat. Pour batter by 1/4 cup onto the skillet then cook for 3-4 minutes until the edges are dry and bubbles appear. Turn and cook for 2-3 minutes until the second side turned brown. Continue with the rest of the batter. Put the cooked pancakes to a baking sheet and place in the preheated oven to keep it warm.
7. In a bowl, whisk softened butter and cream cheese for approximately 2 minutes until fluffy and light. Add 1/2 tsp. vanilla extract, 1/4 milk, and 1 cup confectioner's sugar; whisk until smooth, putting more milk to achieve desired consistency. Put the cream cheese glaze over pancakes and sprinkle with the rest of the confectioner's sugar.

Nutrition Information
Calories: 949 calories; Total Carbohydrate: 119.6 g Cholesterol: 214 mg Total Fat: 45.5 g Protein: 18.6 g Sodium: 975 mg

Egg-white Crepes
Serving: 2 | Prep: 10m | Ready in: 15m

Ingredients
- 1/2 cup whole wheat flour
- 2 egg whites
- 1/2 cup skim milk
- 1 pinch salt
- 1 tbsp. vegetable oil
- 1/2 cup mixed frozen berries, thawed and drained
- 1 tbsp. confectioners' sugar for dusting

Direction
1. In a large bowl, beat oil, salt, milk, egg whites and wheat flour until smooth.

2. Use cooking spray to lightly coat a skillet and set medium heat. Drop 1/4 cup of the batter into the skillet. Slant the pan in a circular movement to let the middle to spread to the edges. Then cook for about 2 minutes until the bottom is light brown. Turn the crepe and put 2 tbsps. of the mixed berries in the middle of the crepe; then cook for 2 more minutes. Turn the crepe in half and use a spatula to take to serving plate. Sprinkle with confectioners' sugar then serve.

Nutrition Information

Calories: 228 calories; Total Carbohydrate: 33 g Cholesterol: 1 mg Total Fat: 7.6 g Protein: 10.1 g Sodium: 83 mg

Eggs Benedict

Serving: 4 | Prep: 25m | Ready in: 30m

Ingredients
- 4 egg yolks
- 3 1/2 tbsps. lemon juice
- 1 pinch ground white pepper
- 1/8 tsp. Worcestershire sauce
- 1 tbsp. water
- 1 cup butter, melted
- 1/4 tsp. salt
- 8 eggs
- 1 tsp. distilled white vinegar
- 8 strips Canadian-style bacon
- 4 English muffins, split
- 2 tbsps. butter, softened

Direction
1. Preparing the Hollandaise: Pour water to fill the bottom of a double boiler halfway. Ensure that the water doesn't touch the top of the pan. Simmer the water gently. Whisk together 1 tbsp. water, Worcestershire sauce, white pepper, lemon juice and egg yolks in the top of the boiler.
2. While whisking the yolks continuously, add the melted butter to the yolk mixture, 1-2 tbsp. at a time. Add 1-2 tsp of hot water if the hollandaise starts to become too thick. Keep on whisking until all the butter is integrated. Whisk in the salt and take it out of the heat. To keep the sauce warm, cover the pan with the lid.
3. Set an oven to preheat on broiler setting. Making the poach eggs: Pour water to fill up a big saucepan to 3 inches. Gently simmer the water then add vinegar. Crack the eggs carefully into the simmering water and let it cook for 2 1/2-3 minutes. The yolks must be soft in the middle. Use a slotted spoon to take out the eggs from the water and place it on a warm plate.
4. While the eggs are poaching, cook the bacon in a medium frying pan on medium-high heat until it browns and let the English muffins toast on a baking tray underneath the broiler.
5. Spread softened butter on toasted muffins and put a bacon slice on top of each one, succeeded by 1 poached egg. On each plate, put 2 muffins and drizzle hollandaise sauce on top, then sprinkle it with chopped chives and serve right away.

Nutrition Information

Calories: 879 calories; Total Carbohydrate: 29.6 g Cholesterol: 742 mg Total Fat: 71.1 g Protein: 31.8 g Sodium: 1719 mg

Eggs Benedict With Salmon

Serving: 8 | Prep: 30m | Ready in: 1h

Ingredients

- 3/4 cup plain low-fat yogurt
- 2 tsps. lemon juice
- 3 egg yolks
- 1/2 tsp. prepared Dijon-style mustard
- 1/4 tsp. salt
- 1/4 tsp. white sugar
- 1 pinch ground black pepper
- 1 dash hot pepper sauce
- 8 eggs
- 8 slices rye bread
- 8 oz. smoked salmon, cut into thin slices
- 1 tbsp. chopped fresh parsley, for garnish
- 1 tsp. capers, for garnish

Direction

1. For the sauce: whip hot sauce, pepper, sugar, salt, mustard, egg yolks, lemon juice and yogurt together in the top of a double boiler. Put it over the simmering water and cook while stirring continuously for 6-8 minutes or until the sauce is thick enough that you can coat the back of a spoon with the sauce.
2. Heat to a boil 2 quarts of salted water in a big stock pot. Break 1 egg at a time carefully into the boiling water. After adding all the eggs, lower the heat to medium. Use a slotted spoon to take the eggs out when they float to the top, let them drain briefly.
3. For final dish assembling: Toast slices of bread and arrange on warm plates. Put a hot poached egg and a slice of smoked salmon on top of each toast piece. Sprinkle yogurt sauce over, decorate with capers and parsley.

Nutrition Information

Calories: 223 calories; Total Carbohydrate: 18.1 g Cholesterol: 271 mg Total Fat: 9.3 g Protein: 16.4 g Sodium: 617 mg

French Ham Cheese And Egg Fondue Casserole

Serving: 12 | Prep: 30m | Ready in: 10h

Ingredients

- 2 tbsps. butter, softened
- 3 tbsps. all-purpose flour
- 1 tbsp. mustard powder
- 3 cups cubed fully cooked ham
- 8 oz. Cheddar cheese, cubed
- 3 cups cubed day old French bread
- 4 eggs, beaten
- 3 cups milk
- 1 dash hot pepper sauce
- 3 tbsps. butter, melted

- 1/2 cup freshly grated Parmesan cheese

Direction

1. Use softened butter to grease 9x13-inch glass baking dish generously. Mix mustard powder and flour; put Cheddar cubes and ham in big mixing bowl. Sprinkle flour mixture; toss till coated evenly. Add bread cubes; toss till mixed. Whisk hot pepper sauce, milk and eggs in another bowl.
2. Put 1/3 of the bread mixture in the prepared baking dish. Make a layer by smoothing out. Drizzle 1 tbsp. of butter; sprinkle 1/3 of Parmesan cheese on. Repeat twice to get 3 layers. Put egg mixture on top; use plastic wrap to cover and refrigerate for 8 hours to overnight.
3. Remove casserole from the fridge the next day and remove plastic wrap. Let stand for 30 minutes at room temperature. Preheat an oven to 175°C/350°F.
4. In the preheated oven, uncovered, bake for 1 hour till top is crispy and golden brown and eggs set.

Nutrition Information

Calories: 357 calories; Total Carbohydrate: 19.8 g Cholesterol: 121 mg Total Fat: 21.9 g Protein: 19.9 g Sodium: 857 mg

Fresh Grapefruit Juice Smoothie

Serving: 2 | Prep: 15m | Ready in: 15m

Ingredients

- 1 1/3 cups fresh red grapefruit juice
- 8 large strawberries
- 2 medium bananas, sliced
- 1 (8 oz.) container strawberry-banana yogurt
- 2 tbsps. honey
- 1 cup crushed ice

Direction

1. In a blender, add ice, honey, yogurt, bananas, strawberries and grapefruit juice. Cover and blend until smooth.

Nutrition Information

Calories: 361 calories; Total Carbohydrate: 85 g Cholesterol: 5 mg Total Fat: 1.8 g Protein: 7.2 g Sodium: 76 mg

Ginger's Shrimp And Grits

Serving: 8 | Prep: 30m | Ready in: 1h10m

Ingredients

- 3 1/2 cups skim milk
- 2 tsps. sea salt
- 1 tsp. ground cayenne pepper
- 1 tsp. ground black pepper
- 1 cup stone-ground white grits
- 1 1/2 cups shredded sharp Cheddar cheese
- 2 tbsps. bottled hot pepper sauce
- 1/2 cup olive oil
- 1 large onion, chopped
- 2 tbsps. garlic, chopped

- 2 lbs. shrimp, peeled and deveined
- 1 tsp. garlic powder
- 2 (10 oz.) cans diced tomatoes with green chile peppers, drained
- 1 cup shredded sharp Cheddar cheese

Direction

1. Boil black pepper, cayenne pepper, salt and milk in big saucepan on medium heat, constantly mixing to avoid scorching. Sprinkle grits in; cover. Simmer, occasionally mixing till thick, for 20-25 minutes.
2. Uncover grits. Add hot pepper sauce and 1 1/2 cups shredded Cheddar cheese; beating mixture with spoon till mixture is smooth and cheese melts. Cover cheese grits. Put aside so it firms up.
3. Heat olive oil in saucepan on medium heat; mix and cook garlic and onion till onion is translucent for 5 minutes. Add shrimp; toss in hot oil for 3 minutes till shrimp are opaque and just turn pink. Mix diced tomatoes with chile peppers in; put aside shrimp mixture.
4. Preheat an oven to 175°C/350°F. Spray cooking spray on a 7x11-in. baking dish. In bottom of dish, put 1 cup shrimp mixture then 1 cup cheese grits in a layer. Keep layering girts and shrimp, then put final layer of 1 cup Cheddar cheese on top.
5. In preheated oven, bake till cheese topping starts to brown and is bubbly for 30 minutes. Let casserole set before serving for 10 minutes.

Nutrition Information

Calories: 422 calories; Total Carbohydrate: 13.9 g Cholesterol: 212 mg Total Fat: 26.4 g Protein: 32.2 g Sodium: 1321 mg

Grandma Irena's Palacsinta (hungarian Crepes)

Serving: 5 | Prep: 40m | Ready in: 9h10m

Ingredients

Pancakes:
- 2 cups all-purpose flour
- 2 eggs
- 1 cup milk
- 1 cup soda water
- 1/2 cup vegetable oil
- 1 pinch salt

Almond Filling:
- 1 cup chopped almonds
- 1/2 cup white sugar
- 1/4 cup milk
- 1/4 tsp. vanilla extract
- 1 1/2 tsps. rum (optional)

Chocolate Topping:
- 1/4 cup water
- 1/2 cup white sugar
- 1/2 cup chopped bittersweet chocolate
- 2 tbsps. margarine

Direction

1. Mix together eggs and flour until smooth. Stir in salt, milk, vegetable oil, and soda water until well

blended. Place the batter in the refrigerator overnight.

2. On medium heat, heat a lightly oiled frying pan. Take the batter out of the refrigerator and stir. Scoop a quarter cup of batter into the heated pan and cook for a minute. Turn and cook for another minute until golden brown. Take the pancake out of the pan and put on top of waxed paper. Repeat with the leftover batter. Stack the pancakes and place a waxed paper in between each cake to separate them.
3. Make the filling by mixing together rum (optional), chopped almonds, vanilla extract, half a cup of sugar, and milk in a saucepan. On low heat, cook and mix until the mixture is creamy and the sugar is dissolved. Let the mixture cool for a bit before using as a pancake filling.
4. Make the chocolate topping by mixing together chocolate, half a cup of sugar, and water in a saucepan. On low heat, cook the mixture until the chocolate is melted. Take off heat and stir in margarine until melted and well blended.
5. Slather a heaping tbsp. of almond filling over each pancake. Roll the pancakes and put in a platter. You should have a total of 10-15 pancakes depending on the size. Drizzle the chocolate topping over the rolled pancakes. Warm the pancake platter for half a minute in a microwave before serving if desired.

Nutrition Information

Calories: 873 calories; Total Carbohydrate: 98.7 g Cholesterol: 71 mg Total Fat: 47.4 g Protein: 15.1 g Sodium: 104 mg

Ham, Basil, And Feta Scrambled Eggs

Serving: 2 | Prep: 10m | Ready in: 15m

Ingredients

- 4 eggs, lightly beaten
- 1/2 cup diced cooked ham
- 1/4 cup crumbled feta cheese
- 1 tbsp. dried basil
- salt and pepper to taste
- 1 1/2 tsps. butter

Direction

1. Put a skillet over medium heat setting. In a bowl, combine the lightly beaten eggs, pepper, salt, basil, ham and feta cheese.
2. Put the butter into the skillet and let it melt. Add in the egg mixture and let it cook. Stir the eggs for about 5 minutes until the eggs are no longer runny and has already set.

Nutrition Information

Calories: 328 calories; Total Carbohydrate: 3.4 g Cholesterol: 424 mg Total Fat: 25 g Protein: 22.7 g Sodium: 878 mg

Heart-shaped Pancakes With Chocolate

Serving: 4 | Prep: 10m | Ready in: 25m

Ingredients

- 2 tbsps. butter
- 1 egg, separated
- 1 3/4 cups all-purpose flour
- 1 tsp. baking powder

- 1 tbsp. white sugar
- 3/4 cup buttermilk
- 2 tbsps. buttermilk, or more as needed
- 1 tsp. butter
- 1 (4 oz.) bar milk chocolate, coarsely chopped
- 1 tbsp. confectioners' sugar, or to taste

Direction

1. In a microwave-safe dish, melt 2 tbsps. butter for 10 seconds. Allow cooling. Use a fork to beat yolk into cooled butter. Sift baking powder and flour into a large bowl. Mix in sugar. Beat in 3/4 cup plus 2 tbsps. buttermilk and egg-butter mixture until a thick, smooth batter forms. Put additional buttermilk, 1 tbsp. at a time, if the batter is too thick.
2. In a nonstick skillet, add 1 tsp. butter to melt over high heat. Lower heat and drop batter onto the hot skillet using a ladle. Then cook for 3-4 minutes until bubbles appear and edges are dry. Turn and cook for 2-3 minutes until the opposite side turned brown. Place to a warm plate. Continue with the rest of the batter. Cut out hearts using a large heart-shaped cookie cutter. Top 1 warm pancake with a few chocolate pieces and sandwich another pancake on top. Continue with the rest of the pancakes. Dust with confectioner's sugar.

Nutrition Information

Calories: 450 calories; Total Carbohydrate: 65.6 g Cholesterol: 67 mg Total Fat: 16.8 g Protein: 10.1 g Sodium: 258 mg

Holiday Waffles

Serving: 8 | Prep: 10m | Ready in: 20m

Ingredients

- 2 1/4 cups all-purpose flour
- 4 tsps. baking powder
- 1/4 tsp. salt
- 1 1/2 tbsps. white sugar
- 2 eggs, beaten
- 2 1/4 cups milk
- 3/4 cup vegetable oil
- 3 drops food color
- 2 tbsps. confectioners' sugar for dusting (optional)

Direction

1. Following the manufacturer's instructions to preheat a waffle iron.
2. Whisk sugar, salt, baking powder and flour together then set aside. In a mixing bowl, beat together vegetable oil, food color, milk and eggs, then stir into the egg mixture with the flour until just slight lumps are existed.
3. Transfer the batter into waffle iron in batches and cook until turn golden brown and crisp. Sprinkle over with confectioners' sugar to serve.

Nutrition Information

Calories: 378 calories; Total Carbohydrate: 35 g Cholesterol: 52 mg Total Fat: 23.4 g Protein: 7.5 g Sodium: 363 mg

Honeymoon Eggs Benedict

Serving: 2 | Prep: 10m | Ready in: 30m

Ingredients

- 12 fresh asparagus spears
- 4 eggs
- 1 tsp. distilled white vinegar
- 1 tsp. salt
- 2 large croissants, split
- 4 slices Canadian-style bacon
- 1 cup grated Asiago cheese
- 1/2 cup prepared hollandaise sauce

Direction

1. Put steamer insert in saucepan; fill using water to right below steamer's bottom. Cover pan; boil water. Put asparagus and cover; steam for 2-6 minutes, varies on thickness, till just tender
2. Fill big saucepan with 2-3-in. water; boil. Lower heat to medium low; put vinegar in. Keep water at gently simmer. Mix salt in till melted. Crack egg in small bowl; slip egg gently into simmering water, holding bowl right above water's surface. Repeat with leftover eggs. Poach eggs for 3-5 minutes till yolks are thick yet not had and white are firm. Use slotted spoon to remove eggs from water; drain on kitchen towel-lined plate to remove extra water. Put on warm plate.
3. Preheat an oven broiler; put oven rack 6-in. away from heat source.
4. Put croissant halves on baking sheet; put 1/4 cup Asiago cheese, 3 asparagus spears, 1 Canadian bacon slice and 1 poached egg on top.
5. In preheated oven, broil for 2-3 minutes till starting to crisp and cheese is melted.
6. Heat hollandaise sauce in saucepan for 5 minutes on medium heat till hot and bubbly. Serve sauce over baked croissants.

Nutrition Information

Calories: 859 calories; Total Carbohydrate: 36.5 g Cholesterol: 625 mg Total Fat: 60 g Protein: 44.5 g Sodium: 3302 mg

Leftover Champagne Pancakes

Serving: 12 | Prep: 10m | Ready in: 25m

Ingredients

- 1 cup buttermilk
- 2 eggs
- 2 tbsps. butter, melted
- 1 1/2 cups all-purpose flour
- 2 tbsps. white sugar
- 2 tsps. baking powder
- 1/4 tsp. salt
- 3/4 cup Champagne

Direction

1. In a bowl, beat butter, eggs, and buttermilk. In another bowl, combine salt, baking powder, sugar, and flour. Stir flour mixture into buttermilk mixture until smooth. Reserve the batter for 10-15 minutes until bubbling. Add champagne into batter; mix gently.
2. Heat a lightly greased non-stick skillet over medium-high heat. Drop 1/3 cup batter onto the skillet;

cook for 2-3 minutes until the edges are dry and bubbles appear. Turn and cook for 1-2 more minutes until the opposite side is browned. Continue with the rest of the batter.

Nutrition Information
Calories: 109 calories; Total Carbohydrate: 15.3 g Cholesterol: 37 mg Total Fat: 2.9 g Protein: 3.3 g Sodium: 177 mg

Lynzzpaige's Kaiserschmarrn (emperor's Pancakes)

Serving: 2 | Prep: 15m | Ready in: 35m

Ingredients
- 1/2 cup all-purpose flour
- 5 tbsps. white sugar
- 1/2 tsp. salt
- 1 cup milk
- 5 eggs, separated
- 2 tbsps. butter
- confectioners' sugar

Direction
1. In a mixing bowl, sift together salt, sugar and flour, then add milk to flour mixture gradually while stirring. Put in 1 egg yolk at a time while beating until well-mixed prior to putting in the next yolk.
2. In a separate bowl, add egg whites and beat until stiff peaks form. Stir gently into batter with a third of the egg whites, then fold in the rest of egg whites.
3. In an 8-inch skillet, melt 1 tbsp. of butter on moderate heat, then put in 1/2 of the batter and cook until bottom turns brown, about 4 minutes. Loosen edges and slip pancake on a plate with a spatula. Flip pancake back to the skillet and cook for 2 minutes, until both sides turn brown. Transfer to a warm platter and keep warm.
4. Make another pancake in the same manner, then sprinkle confectioners' sugar over top and serve.

Nutrition Information
Calories: 591 calories; Total Carbohydrate: 65.5 g Cholesterol: 505 mg Total Fat: 26.7 g Protein: 23.1 g Sodium: 889 mg

Mel's Eclairs

Serving: 6 | Prep: 35m | Ready in: 2h

Ingredients
Eclair Shells (Pate a Choux):
- 2 tbsps. water
- 1/4 cup butter
- 1/2 cup all-purpose flour
- 2 eggs
Custard:
- 6 1/2 tbsps. white sugar
- 5 tbsps. all-purpose flour
- 1 tsp. salt
- 1 1/2 cups milk
- 1 egg, lightly beaten

- 2 tsps. almond extract (optional)

Chocolate Icing:

- 1 (1 oz.) square unsweetened chocolate
- 1 tbsp. butter
- 2 tbsps. water
- 1/2 cup confectioners' sugar

Direction

1. Heat the oven to 200°C or 400°F. Grease or line a baking sheet using parchment paper.
2. In saucepan, boil quarter cup butter and 2 tbsps. of water. Turn heat to low and put in half cup flour, mixing forcefully till mixture shapes into a ball. Turn mixture into stand mixer or mixing bowl; whip in eggs, one by one.
3. Pipe mixture on baking sheet with plastic zipper bag corner snipped off, pastry bag, or just forming it using spatula. You must get 6 four-inch fingers or a dozen smaller eclairs. Let pastries bake in hot oven till golden and puffed approximately 30 - 50 minutes, will be based on the sizes. Take out of the oven and cool shells.
4. To prep custard, combine five tbsps. flour, salt and six and a half tbsps. white sugar in saucepan. Mix in milk; boil the mixture on moderate heat. Add hot mixture of milk in beaten egg in steady stream, mixing continuously. Pour mixture back to saucepan and let come barely to a boil, mixing continuously. Take off from heat and turn onto a mixing bowl to cool down. Mix in almond extract; place a plastic wrap tight on the surface to cover and chill till ready to stuff the eclairs.
5. To make glaze, in saucepan, mix a tbsp. butter, 2 tbsps. water and chocolate. Slowly heat till mixture melts. Take off from heat and mix in half cup confectioners' sugar. Put in a small amount of extra water in case icing turns very thick. For creamier glaze, replace 2 tbsps. of water with milk.
6. Trim tops from cooled shells and fill with custard. Put tops back, and coat them in chocolate icing.

Nutrition Information

Calories: 329 calories; Total Carbohydrate: 41.3 g Cholesterol: 112 mg Total Fat: 15.6 g Protein: 7.2 g Sodium: 513 mg

Orange Sunrise Smoothie

Serving: 2 | Prep: 15m | Ready in: 15m

Ingredients

- 1/2 cup orange juice
- 1 banana, frozen and chunked
- 1 peach, peeled and sliced
- 1/2 cup honeydew melon, cubed
- 1 (8 oz.) container orange yogurt
- 1 tsp. white sugar
- 1/2 cup ice

Direction

1. In a blender, mix together ice, sugar, yogurt, honeydew melon, peach, banana and orange juice. Blend until chunky or smooth as you wanted. Transfer into 2 glasses and serve.

Nutrition Information

Calories: 239 calories; Total Carbohydrate: 52 g Cholesterol: 9 mg Total Fat: 1.3 g Protein: 5.8 g Sodium: 69 mg

Oven-baked Caramel French Toast

Serving: 8 | Prep: 9h | Ready in: 10h

Ingredients
- 1 cup brown sugar
- 1/2 cup butter
- 2 tbsps. light corn syrup
- 1 cup chopped pecans, divided
- 12 slices French or Italian-style bread
- 6 eggs
- 1 1/2 cups milk
- 1 tsp. vanilla extract
- 1 tsp. ground nutmeg
- 1 1/2 tsps. ground cinnamon
- 1/4 tsp. salt
- Caramel Sauce
- 1/2 cup brown sugar
- 1/4 cup butter
- 1 tbsp. light corn syrup

Direction
1. Mix 2 tbsps. of corn syrup, 1/2 cup of butter and 1 cup of brown sugar in a small saucepan. Cook the mixture on moderate heat while stirring continuously, until thicken
2. Put sauce into a 9-inch by 13-inch baking dish and sprinkle 1/2 cup of pecans over. Top sauce with 6 slices of bread, then sprinkle bread with leftover pecans and cover with leftover 6 bread slices.
3. In a blender, mix salt, cinnamon, nutmeg, vanilla, milk and eggs. Pour on bread slices with the egg mixture evenly, then cover the baking dish and chill about 8 hours to overnight.
4. In the following morning, heat the oven to 175°C or 350°F. Take the French toast out of the fridge about a half hour before baking. In the preheated oven, bake until brown slightly, about 40-45 minutes. Sprinkle toast with sauce just before serving.
5. For Caramel sauce: Mix 1 tbsp. of corn syrup, 1/4 cup of butter and 1/2 cup of brown sugar in a small saucepan, cook the mixture until thicken, while stirring continuously.

Nutrition Information
Calories: 615 calories; Total Carbohydrate: 72.5 g Cholesterol: 189 mg Total Fat: 32.5 g Protein: 12.2 g Sodium: 527 mg

Pan Dulce

Serving: 14

Ingredients
- 6 tbsps. margarine
- 1 cup milk
- 1 (.25 oz.) package active dry yeast
- 1 tsp. salt
- 1/3 cup white sugar
- 5 cups all-purpose flour
- 2 eggs

- 1/2 cup white sugar
- 2/3 cup all-purpose flour
- 3 1/2 tbsps. margarine
- 2 egg yolks
- 2 tbsps. cocoa powder (optional)
- 1 egg
- 2 tbsps. milk

Direction

1. Heat 1 cup milk and 6 tbsp. margarine/butter to 110° in a small pan.
2. Mix 2 cups flour, 1/3 cup sugar, salt and yeast in a big mixing bowl. Add warmed milk mix and beat with an electric mixer for 2 minutes on medium speed, scraping often. Blend in 1 cup flour and 2 whole eggs; beat for 2 minutes on high. Beat in enough leftover flour to make a stiff dough with a spoon.
3. Knead for 5 minutes till smooth on a floured board. Put into a greased bowl and turn to grease the top; cover. Rise till doubled.
4. Make streusel as dough rises: Mix 2/3 cup flour and 1/2 cup sugar together; stir in 3 1/2 tbsp. cold margarine or butter to get fine crumbs. Use a fork to blend in the 2 egg yolks. Mix flour and 2 tbsp. cocoa powder for chocolate streusel.
5. Punch down the dough; turn onto a floured board then divide into 14 pieces. Form each into a ball; form 7 to seashells then squeeze 1/4 cup streusel to a firm ball. Press over top of every round. With slightly curved parallel lines, score to look like a scallop shell. Roll leftover dough to 4x8-in. ovals. Put 3 tbsp. streusel on each top. Make horns: From short end, roll oval; stop halfway and fold in sides then finish rolling. To make a crescent, curl the ends; put bunds on the greased baking sheet, 2-in. apart. Lightly cover; rise for 45 minutes till doubled. Beat 2 tbsp. milk and 1 egg together in a small bowl.
6. Brush egg mixture on buns; bake for 15-17 minutes at 190°C/375°F till lightly browned.

Nutrition Information

Calories: 331 calories; Total Carbohydrate: 52.3 g Cholesterol: 73 mg Total Fat: 9.9 g Protein: 8 g Sodium: 275 mg

Raspberry Cheesecake Stuffed French Toast

Serving: 6 | Prep: 20m | Ready in: 30m

Ingredients

- 1 cup milk
- 2 tbsps. vanilla extract
- 1 cup white sugar
- 2 tbsps. cinnamon
- 4 eggs, beaten
- 1 cup raspberry puree
- 4 oz. cream cheese, softened
- 1 loaf French bread, cut into 1 inch slices
- butter
- confectioners' sugar for dusting
- nutmeg, for topping

Direction

1. Whisk together cinnamon, sugar, vanilla and milk into the beaten eggs in a bowl until well combined, then set aside. Cream together cream cheese and raspberry puree in another bowl until smooth. Cut each bread slice in half and spread in the center with raspberry-cheese mixture then place another half on top to make 'sandwiches'.
2. In a big skillet or griddle, melt butter over medium heat. Dip bread into the egg mixture to coat thoroughly and cook for 5 minutes, until well-browned on both sides. Sprinkle over with nutmeg and confectioners' sugar. Serve promptly.

Nutrition Information

Calories: 622 calories; Total Carbohydrate: 96.8 g Cholesterol: 132 mg Total Fat: 18.9 g Protein: 15.8 g Sodium: 661 mg

Roesti

Serving: 6 | Prep: 10m | Ready in: 9h10m

Ingredients

- 2 1/4 lbs. potatoes, scrubbed
- 3 tbsps. butter
- 1 tsp. salt
- 2 tbsps. milk

Direction

1. Pour enough water into a large pot to cover potatoes. Bring to a boil over medium-high heat. Cook potatoes for about 15 minutes until fork-tender. Drain off water and chill potatoes overnight.
2. Remove potato skins and grate into a large bowl.
3. In a skillet, melt butter over medium heat; add grated potatoes, add salt to taste. Use a spatula to press potatoes into a round loaf. Drizzle milk over them. Put a lid on the skillet. When potatoes start to sizzle in about 5-10 minutes, turn heat down to low. Cook for about 30 minutes until a brown crust has formed on the bottom. Place a large plate to cover skillet, flip to transfer the roesti onto the plate. Serve right away.

Nutrition Information

Calories: 186 calories; Total Carbohydrate: 31.1 g Cholesterol: 15 mg Total Fat: 5.9 g Protein: 3.1 g Sodium: 436 mg

Romantic Lemon Cheesecake Pancakes

Serving: 4 | Prep: 10m | Ready in: 20m

Ingredients

- 8 oz. cream cheese, softened
- 2 eggs, beaten
- 5 tsps. all-purpose flour
- 1 1/2 tsps. white sugar
- 2 tsps. butter, melted - divided
- confectioners' sugar for dusting
- 1 tsp. lemon juice
- 1/2 lemon, cut into wedges

Direction

1. Use an electric mixer to beat cream cheese until smooth, then mix in eggs.

2. Stir in 1 tsp. of melted butter, sugar and flour to create a batter.
3. Heat on a griddle or in a heavy frying pan with leftover 1 tsp. of butter on moderate heat.
4. Drop silver dollar-sized dollops of batter on the griddle and cook for 3 minutes, until golden brown slightly. Flip over pancakes and cook for 2 more minutes.
5. To serve, sprinkle confectioners' sugar on top and drizzle with lemon juice, then serve together with lemon wedges.

Nutrition Information

Calories: 288 calories; Total Carbohydrate: 11.3 g Cholesterol: 161 mg Total Fat: 24.4 g Protein: 8 g Sodium: 218 mg

Heart Shaped Whole Wheat Mini Calzones

Serving: 10 | Prep: 30m | Ready in: 1h30m

Ingredients

Dough:

- 1 1/2 cups white whole wheat flour
- 1 1/2 cups whole wheat pastry flour
- 2 tsps. baking powder
- 1 tsp. salt
- 1 1/4 cups warm water
- 1/4 cup extra-virgin olive oil
- 2 tbsps. honey
- 4 tsps. active dry yeast
- cooking spray

Filling:

- 1 cup chopped broccoli
- 1 cup shredded cooked chicken breast
- 1 cup light cream cheese, softened

Direction

1. In the bowl of a stand mixer, mix together salt, baking powder, whole wheat pastry flour, and white whole wheat flour; form a well in the middle of the flour mixture.
2. In another bowl, combine honey, olive oil, and water; sprinkle the water mixture with yeast. Let sit without whisking for 10 minutes until the yeast starts to have creamy foam and gets tender.
3. In the well of the flour mixture, pour the yeast mixture; stir on a low setting with the paddle beater for 2-3 minutes until blended. Change the paddle beater into a dough hook and whisk the dough for 10 minutes on low setting.
4. Spray cooking spray over the inside of a big bowl.
5. Remove the dough to the prepared bowl, put a towel onto the bowl to cover and put in a warm place to rise for a minimum of 30 minutes (60 minutes for better texture).
6. Separate the dough into 2 balls; use your hands to knead each for approximately 1 minute.
7. Spray cooking spray over 2 cookie sheets.
8. Use a rolling pin to roll each dough ball onto the prepared cookie sheets until the thickness is 1/4-inch. With heart-shaped cookie cutters, cut the dough into hearts with an even number.
9. Turn the oven to 400°F (200°C) to preheat.
10. In a microwave-safe bowl, put broccoli; cook in the microwave on high for 1-2 minutes until partially soft.

11. In a bowl, combine cream cheese, chicken and cooked broccoli. In the middle of 1 heart, put 1-2
    tbsps. of the filling; put another heart on top. Press a fork around the heart to seal the edges together.
    Continue with the rest of the hearts and filling.
12. Put in the preheated oven and bake for 20 minutes until the hearts turn golden brown.

Nutrition Information
Calories: 264 calories; Total Carbohydrate: 31.6 g Cholesterol: 21 mg Total Fat: 11.4 g Protein: 10.4 g
Sodium: 416 mg

Lollipop Cookie Valentines
Serving: 6

Ingredients
- 12 craft sticks
- 1/2 cup semisweet chocolate chips
- 1/2 cup butter, softened
- 1/3 cup packed light brown sugar
- 1/2 tsp. vanilla extract
- 1 egg
- 2 cups all-purpose flour
- 1/4 cup unsweetened cocoa powder
- 1/4 tsp. salt
- 12 (1 oz.) squares white chocolate
- 1 egg white
- 1 1/4 cups confectioners' sugar
- 3 drops red food coloring

Direction
1. In a bowl of cold water, steep craft sticks for an hour.
2. Stir chocolate chips in a small heavy saucepan on very low heat, until smooth and melted. Take
   away from the heat and allow to cool.
3. Beat together vanilla, brown sugar and butter in a big bowl using an electric mixer at medium speed
   until fluffy. Beat egg in well, whip in cooled chocolate. Beat in salt, cocoa powder and flour using a
   mixer at low speed until smooth. Halve the dough.
4. Set the oven to 190°C or 375°F to preheat. Coat 2 big cookie sheets with grease.
5. Between two wax paper sheets, roll out each half of dough to the thickness of 1/8 inch. Freeze dough
   for 5 minutes in wax paper. Peel top sheets of wax paper off dough, then use a 3-inches heart-shaped
   cutter to cut out dough. Reroll scraps and freeze once more for 5 minutes, then cut out. Put 1/2 of
   the hearts on prepped cookie sheet, spacing 1-inch apart.
6. Drain sticks and pat dry. Put on each heart with a stick to create 2 1/2-in. handle, press into dough
   slightly. Top with leftover hearts, then gently press edges together to seal. Bake until firm to touch,
   for 12 minutes, then allow to cool on wire racks.
7. Stir white or milk chocolate in a 2-qt. heavy saucepan on extremely low heat or in the top of a
   double boiler placed over barely simmering water until smooth and melted. If you will use both kind
   of chocolate, melt in 2 different 1-qt. pans. Take away from the heat.
8. Hold the handle of each lollipop and dunk in chocolate to coat both sides, allowing excess chocolate
   to drip back to pan. Put each lollipop once coated on cookie sheet lined with wax paper and chill
   until chocolate sets, about 20 minutes.

9. For icing: Beat confectioners' sugar and egg white together on high speed of an electric mixer in a big bowl until extremely smooth. Transfer a small amount of icing to a separate bowl if you want and tint with drops of food coloring. Scoop colored icing in decorating bag with small writing tip and pipe preferred patterns over lollipops. Use decors and assorted candies to garnish using dots of icing to attach.

Nutrition Information
Calories: 838 calories; Total Carbohydrate: 111.2 g Cholesterol: 84 mg Total Fat: 41 g Protein: 11.3 g Sodium: 293 mg

Maraschino Cherry Almond Cookies

Serving: 48 | Prep: 1h | Ready in: 1h30m

Ingredients
- 1 cup unsalted butter, at room temperature
- 2/3 cup sifted confectioners' sugar
- 1 1/2 tsps. almond extract
- 2 eggs, at room temperature
- 1/8 tsp. salt
- 2 cups all-purpose flour
- 2/3 cup chopped drained maraschino cherries
- Royal Icing:
- 2 egg whites
- 2 tsps. lemon juice
- 1/2 tsp. vanilla extract
- 3 cups sifted confectioners' sugar

Direction
1. In a mixing bowl, beat butter on high speed with an electric mixer, about 2 minutes, until creamy and smooth. Slowly beat in 2/3 cup of confectioners' sugar; beat in salt, eggs and almond extracts, about 3 minutes longer, until mixture is well incorporated and fluffy. Adjust speed to medium, and slowly beat in flour, about 1 minutes, until dough becomes smooth. Gently mix in maraschino cherries.
2. Shape dough into two 1-inch diameter logs; roll each log in waxed paper or plastic wrap, and chill for a minimum of 2 hours until completely chilled.
3. Set oven to 350°F (175°C) to preheat. Line parchment paper over several baking sheets.
4. Slice each dough log into twenty-five of 1/2-inch-thick slices; arrange them by 1/2 inch apart on the prepared baking sheets.
5. Bake cookies for 12 to 14 minutes in the preheated oven until firm but not browned. Transfer to cooling racks, and allow to cool to room temperature, approximately 15 minutes.
6. For icing, beat egg whites and lemon juice together for about 1 minutes until frothy; whisk in vanilla extracts and 1 cupful of confectioners' sugar at a time until icing is spreadable and smooth. Spread over the top of each cookie with about 1 tsp. icing; allow icing to harden before stacking.

Nutrition Information
Calories: 98 calories; Total Carbohydrate: 14.6 g Cholesterol: 18 mg Total Fat: 4 g Protein: 1 g Sodium: 12 mg

Mary's Sugar Cookies

Serving: 30 | Prep: 15m | Ready in: 2h25m

Ingredients
- 1 cup butter, softened
- 1 1/2 cups sifted confectioners' sugar
- 1 egg
- 1 tsp. vanilla extract
- 1/2 tsp. almond extract
- 2 1/2 cups all-purpose flour
- 1 tsp. baking soda
- 1 tsp. cream of tartar
- 1/4 cup granulated sugar for decoration

Direction
1. Cream confectioners' sugar and butter together in a large bowl until smooth. Beat in egg and stir in almond extract and vanilla. Mix together cream of tartar, baking soda and flour; mix into the creamed mixture. Cover up and allow to chill for at least 2 hours.
2. Preheat the oven to 375°F (190°C). Separate the dough in two. On a lightly floured surface, roll each half out to the thickness of 3/16 inch. Use cookie cutter to cut into desired shapes. On greased cookie sheets, place the cookies 1 1/2 inches apart. Sprinkle plain or colored granulated sugar over the cookies.
3. Bake in the preheated oven for 8 minutes, until browned lightly. Cool on baking sheet for 5 minutes, then transfer to a wire rack for cooling completely.

Nutrition Information
Calories: 126 calories; Total Carbohydrate: 16 g Cholesterol: 22 mg Total Fat: 6.4 g Protein: 1.4 g Sodium: 88 mg

No-bake Chocolate Peanut Butter Bars
Serving: 60 | Prep: 15m | Ready in: 1h15m

Ingredients
- 2 cups peanut butter, divided
- 3/4 cup butter, softened
- 2 cups powdered sugar
- 3 cups graham cracker crumbs
- 1 (12 oz.) package NESTLE TOLL HOUSE Semi-Sweet Chocolate Mini Morsels, divided

Direction
1. Grease 9x13-in. baking pan.
2. In a big mixer bowl, whip butter and 1 1/4 cups of peanut butter till become creamy. Slowly whip in one cup of powdered sugar. Work in the half cup morsels, graham cracker crumbs and leftover powdered sugar using a wooden spoon or your hands. Press equally to the prepped baking pan. Using a spatula to smoothen the top.
3. In a medium-sized and heavy-duty saucepan on the lowest possible heat, melt leftover morsels and leftover peanut butter while mixing continuously till smooth in consistency. Spread on top of graham cracker crust in the pan. Let chill in the refrigerator till chocolate becomes firm, for no less than 60 minutes; chop into bars. Keep in the fridge.

Nutrition Information

Calories: 135 calories; Total Carbohydrate: 12.4 g Cholesterol: 8 mg Total Fat: 8.9 g Protein: 2.8 g
Sodium: 91 mg

Old Fashioned Butter Valentine Cookies Dipped In Chocolate

Serving: 24

Ingredients
- 3 cups all-purpose flour, sifted
- 1 tsp. baking powder
- 1/2 tsp. salt
- 1 cup butter, softened
- 3/4 cup white sugar
- 1 large egg
- 2 tbsps. milk
- 1 1/2 tsps. vanilla extract
- 1/2 cup seedless raspberry jam
- 4 oz. semisweet chocolate chips
- 2 tbsps. butter

Direction
1. In a bowl, sift together salt, baking powder and flour, then put aside.
2. Beat together vanilla extract, milk, egg, sugar and 1 cup of butter in a separate bowl until well combined.
3. Mix into butter mixture with flour mixture gradually.
4. Form the dough into a disk, then use plastic wrap to wrap and chill for a minimum of 2 hours.
5. Roll out a half of the dough at a time to the thickness of 1/8 inch.
6. Use a big heart-shaped cookie cutter to cut into cookies, then repeat process with the leftover half of dough.
7. Use a smaller heart-shaped cookie cutter to cut the center of half of the cookies.
8. Top a whole cookie with an open centered cookie to make a sandwich. Place cookies on grease-free baking sheet and put aside.
9. Set the oven to 200°C or 400°F to preheat.
10. Put in a microwavable bowl with raspberry jam and heat for 35 seconds on high setting, until jam is runny.
11. Use jam to fill the center of cookies and chill cookies about 10 minutes.
12. In the preheated oven, bake for 5-8 minutes, until coolies are firm to the touch. Cookies will be pale in color.
13. Remove cookies to a wire rack to cool through.
14. In a microwavable ceramic or glass bowl, melt 2 tbsp. of butter and chocolate in 30-second intervals for 1-3 minutes, depending on your microwave, stirring after each melting until smooth.
15. Scoop over half of each cookie decoratively with chocolate.
16. Put cookie on a baking sheet lined with waxed paper and chill for 15 minutes, until chocolate is set.

Nutrition Information
Calories: 202 calories; Total Carbohydrate: 25.9 g Cholesterol: 31 mg Total Fat: 10.4 g Protein: 2.2 g
Sodium: 134 mg

Pineapple Upside Down Cupcakes

Serving: 24 | Prep: 20m | Ready in: 45m

Ingredients

- cooking spray
- 1/2 cup butter, melted
- 1 1/2 cups brown sugar
- 24 maraschino cherries
- 1 (20 oz.) can crushed pineapple
- 1 (18.25 oz.) package pineapple cake mix (such as Duncan Hines Pineapple Supreme)
- 3 eggs
- 1 1/3 cups pineapple juice
- 1/3 cup vegetable oil
- 1 tbsp. confectioners' sugar for dusting, or as needed

Direction

1. Place one rack of oven to the center of oven. Preheat the oven to 175°C to 350 °F.
2. Use cooking spray to coat 2 dozen muffin cups.
3. Line waxed paper on a work counter.
4. Scoop a tsp. of liquified butter to the base of every prepped muffin cup.
5. In every muffin cup, scoop a tbsp. of brown sugar.
6. Force one maraschino cherry in the middle of brown sugar in every muffin cup.
7. Top cherry with one heaping tbsp. of crushed pineapple and use the back of spoon to compact into a smooth layer.
8. In big bowl, combine vegetable oil, pineapple juice, eggs and pineapple cake mix on low speed using an electric mixer to moisten, for half a minute. Raise speed of mixer to moderate and whip for two minutes.
9. Fill muffin cups to top with pineapple cake batter; avoid excessive filling.
10. In prepped oven, bake for 20 minutes, till an inserted toothpick into the middle of one cupcake gets out clean.
11. Cool cupcakes for not less than 5 minutes prior to flipping muffin cups over to waxed paper to loosen. Serve with cherry and pineapple sides facing up. Lightly dust confectioners' sugar on cupcakes.

Nutrition Information

Calories: 236 calories; Total Carbohydrate: 38.6 g Cholesterol: 33 mg Total Fat: 9 g Protein: 1.5 g Sodium: 174 mg

Pope's Valentine Cookies

Serving: 12

Ingredients

- 1/2 lb. butter, softened
- 2 1/2 cups sifted all-purpose flour
- 1 cup sifted confectioners' sugar
- 1 tbsp. milk
- 1 tsp. vanilla extract

Direction

1. Set the oven to 170°C or 325°F to preheat.
2. In a mixer, mix butter until light, then put in leftover ingredients.
3. Knead until velvety, then roll one half of dough at a time with the least quantity of flour possible to the thickness of 1/4 inch.
4. Cut out dough and bake on a pan coated lightly with grease about 12 minutes. Cookies will become nearly white once cooked.

Nutrition Information

Calories: 273 calories; Total Carbohydrate: 30.4 g Cholesterol: 41 mg Total Fat: 15.6 g Protein: 2.9 g Sodium: 110 mg

Raspberry Liqueur Valentine Cookies

Serving: 36 | Prep: 1h30m | Ready in: 1h40m

Ingredients
- 1/2 cup butter
- 1/2 cup vegetable shortening
- 1 cup confectioners' sugar
- 2 eggs
- 1/2 tsp. vanilla extract
- 1/2 tsp. lemon extract
- 2 3/4 cups all-purpose flour
- 1 tbsp. baking powder
- 1/2 tsp. salt
- 2 tbsps. milk

Frosting:
- 1 egg white, room temperature
- 3 cups confectioners' sugar
- 2 tbsps. milk, room temperature
- 2 tbsps. raspberry flavored liqueur
- 1 tbsp. cherry flavored Jell-O mix
- 1 pinch salt

Direction
1. Whisk 1 cup sugar, shortening, and butter together in a medium-sized bowl until creamy and smooth; and then add lemon extract, vanilla extract, and eggs. Combine baking powder, salt, and flour in a big bowl. Create a well in the center, and put the creamy mixture into it, folding the dry into the wet until blended. Mix in 2 tbsps. milk at the end. You can chill the mixture with a cover for 1 hour to a maximum of several days so that the rolling process will be easier.
2. Start preheating the oven to 350°F (175°C). Roll the dough to 1/8 inch thickness on a surface lightly scattered with flour. Cut the dough into shapes with a heart-shaped cookie cutter. Put the cookies on a cookie sheet 2" apart.
3. Put in the preheated oven and bake for 6-10 minutes. You can bake until the cookies turn light brown, but not needed. Take out of the cookie sheet and put on wire racks to cool.
4. In the meantime, use an electric mixer to whisk egg white in a medium-sized bowl until foamy but not stiff. Slowly whisk in 1 1/2 cups sugar, and then 1/8 cup milk. Stir in cherry-flavored gelatin and raspberry liqueur. Slowly mix in a pinch of salt and the rest of the 1 1/2 cups sugar, blending until the ice resembles marshmallow fluff, but not stiff enough to form peaks. Spread over the tops of the

cookies with the icing.

Nutrition Information

Calories: 147 calories; Total Carbohydrate: 22.1 g Cholesterol: 17 mg Total Fat: 5.8 g Protein: 1.6 g
Sodium: 99 mg

Real Strawberry Cupcakes
Serving: 12 | Prep: 40m | Ready in: 1h15m

Ingredients

- 8 large fresh strawberries, or as needed
- 2 eggs
- 1 cup white sugar
- 1/3 cup vegetable oil
- 1/2 tsp. vanilla extract
- 1/2 tsp. lemon zest
- 1 1/2 cups all-purpose flour
- 2 tsps. baking powder
- 1/4 tsp. salt
- 3 tbsps. instant vanilla pudding mix (optional)
- 1 drop red food coloring, or as needed (optional)
- 3/4 cup cream cheese, softened
- 2 tbsps. butter, softened
- 1/2 cup confectioners' sugar
- 1/2 tsp. vanilla extract
- 3 large fresh strawberries, sliced

Direction

1. Set oven to preheat at 165°C (325°F). Into the cupcake cups, line cupcake liners or spray cooking spray.
2. Into a blender, add 8 strawberries and blend smoothly. Run the puree through a strainer to eliminate seeds. The resulting puree should equal about 3/4 cup. Put it aside.
3. Beat lemon zest, strawberry puree, eggs, white sugar, vegetable oil and 1/2 tsp. vanilla extract together in a large bowl until well mixed. Stir in the vanilla pudding mix (for a moister cupcake), salt, baking powder, flour, and red food coloring to create a shade of pink you like. Into the prepared cupcake cups, scoop the batter to about 2/3 full each.
4. In the preheated oven, bake until the cupcakes have risen and a toothpick comes out clean when inserted into the center of the cupcake for about 23 minutes. Let them cool down for at least 10 minutes before frosting.
5. For the frosting, use an electric mixer to beat together butter and cream cheese in a mixing bowl until smooth; mix in 1/2 tsp. vanilla extract and confectioners' sugar to achieve a no lump-icing. Use about 2 tbsps. of icing to frost each cupcake, and top a strawberry slice on each.

Nutrition Information

Calories: 295 calories; Total Carbohydrate: 39 g Cholesterol: 52 mg Total Fat: 14.1 g Protein: 3.9 g
Sodium: 249 mg

Red Velvet Chocolate Chip Cookies
Serving: 15 | Prep: 20m | Ready in: 1h30m

Ingredients

- 1 1/2 cups all-purpose flour
- 1/3 cup unsweetened cocoa powder
- 1 tsp. baking soda
- 1/2 tsp. baking powder
- 1/2 tsp. salt
- 1/2 cup butter, softened
- 3/4 cup brown sugar
- 1/4 cup white sugar
- 1 egg
- 1 1/2 tbsps. milk
- 1 1/2 tsps. vanilla extract
- 2 tbsps. red food coloring
- 1 cup dark chocolate chips, or as needed

Direction

1. In a bowl, combine salt, baking powder, baking soda, cocoa powder and flour.
2. Using an electric mixer, beat butter for 2 minutes until fluffy; beat in white sugar and brown sugar for 1 minute, until the mixture is smooth. Beat vanilla extract, milk, egg into butter mixture; beat in food coloring until evenly tinted.
3. Using an electric mixer on low speed, beat flour mixture little by little into butter mixture until blended; mix in a cup of chocolate chips. Use plastic wrap to cover the bowl and refrigerate for an hour or overnight.
4. Set oven to 175°C (350°F) and start preheating. Use parchment paper to line baking sheets.
5. Form dough into balls of 2 inches; slightly flatten onto lined baking sheets.
6. Bake at 175°C (350°F) for 10 minutes until edges turn light brown. Sprinkle with several additional chocolate chips; wait until fully cool.

Nutrition Information

Calories: 205 calories; Total Carbohydrate: 28.9 g Cholesterol: 29 mg Total Fat: 9.9 g Protein: 2.8 g Sodium: 232 mg

Red Velvet Cupcakes

Serving: 20 | Prep: 30m | Ready in: 50m

Ingredients

- 1/2 cup butter
- 1 1/2 cups white sugar
- 2 eggs
- 1 cup buttermilk
- 1 fluid oz. red food coloring
- 1 tsp. vanilla extract
- 1 1/2 tsps. baking soda
- 1 tbsp. distilled white vinegar
- 2 cups all-purpose flour
- 1/3 cup unsweetened cocoa powder
- 1 tsp. salt

Direction

1. Set oven to preheat at 350°F (175°C). Put 20 paper baking cups into pans, or grease two 12-cup muffin pans.
2. Beat sugar and butter in a bowl, using an electric mixer, until fluffy and light. Beat in the eggs, vanilla, buttermilk and red food coloring. Mix in the vinegar and baking soda. Mix salt, flour, and cocoa powder together, then mix it into the batter. Stir well. Pour batter into the muffin cups, spooning evenly.
3. Bake for 20-25 minutes, until they spring back when you touch them. Let it cool on a wire rack. Once cooled, arrange the cakes on a platter. Apply frosting as desired.

Nutrition Information

Calories: 160 calories; Total Carbohydrate: 26 g Cholesterol: 31 mg Total Fat: 5.5 g Protein: 2.7 g Sodium: 264 mg

Romance Bars

Serving: 32 | Prep: 15m | Ready in: 55m

Ingredients

- 1 cup all-purpose flour
- 1/2 cup butter, melted
- 1 tbsp. white sugar
- 1 cup brown sugar
- 2 tbsps. all-purpose flour
- 1 tsp. baking powder
- 2 eggs, beaten
- 1 tsp. vanilla extract
- 2/3 cup chopped walnuts
- 1 cup flaked coconut
- 1/2 cup chopped maraschino cherries
- 3 tbsps. butter, softened
- 1 cup confectioners' sugar
- 1 tbsp. boiling water
- 1 tbsp. milk
- 1/2 tsp. almond extract
- 1/2 tsp. vanilla extract

Direction

1. Start preheating oven to 300°F (150°C). Mix one tbsp. of the white sugar and one cup of flour together in a medium bowl. Mix in the melted butter. Spread thinly over bottom of 9x13 in. pan.
2. Bake in oven preheated for 20 mins or until firm. Stir baking powder, 2 tbsps. of the flour, and brown sugar together in a medium bowl. Mix in one tsp. of vanilla and eggs until well blended. Stir in maraschino cherries, coconut and walnuts. Transfer mixture over prepared crust.
3. Bake in the prepared oven for 20 to 25 mins or until top turns light brown. Before frosting, cool completely. Making frosting, mix confectioners' sugar and 3 tbsps. of the butter together. Beat in vanilla extract, almond extract, milk and water until they become smooth. Spread over the cooled bars. Allow to stand until firm. Cut into squares.

Nutrition Information

Calories: 131 calories; Total Carbohydrate: 17.2 g Cholesterol: 22 mg Total Fat: 6.6 g Protein: 1.4 g Sodium: 53 mg

So Pink Cereal Bars

Serving: 24 | Prep: 20m | Ready in: 35m

Ingredients

- 2 tbsps. butter
- 1 (10 oz.) package large marshmallows
- 1/2 (3 oz.) package cranberry flavored Jell-O mix
- 3 cups crispy rice cereal squares (such as Rice Chex)
- 3 cups toasted oat cereal rings (such as Cheerios)
- 2/3 cup mini candy-coated chocolate pieces (such as mini M&M's)
- 1/2 cup sweetened dried cranberries

Direction

1. Coat a 12-inch x9-inch baking dish with butter.
2. In a big nonstick pot, melt 2 tbsp. of butter on low heat.
3. Mix in cranberry gelatin mix and marshmallows until the mixture is smooth and marshmallows melt.
4. Stir in dried cranberries, mini candy-coated chocolate pieces, oat cereal rings and rice squares until mixed well.
5. Pat the mixture quickly into prepped baking dish and let it cool.
6. Slice into 2-inches squares.

Nutrition Information

Calories: 98 calories; Total Carbohydrate: 19.3 g Cholesterol: 3 mg Total Fat: 2.3 g Protein: 1 g Sodium: 51 mg

Strawberry-chocolate Mini Cupcakes With White Chocolate Ganache

Serving: 48 | Prep: 30m | Ready in: 1h20m

Ingredients

- 2 cups all-purpose flour
- 1/4 tsp. baking soda
- 1 tbsp. baking powder
- 1 cup unsweetened cocoa powder
- 5 tbsps. unsweetened cocoa powder
- 1 (0.13 oz.) package unsweetened strawberry-flavored drink mix
- 1/4 tsp. salt
- 5 tbsps. butter
- 2 1/2 cups white sugar
- 4 eggs
- 2 1/2 tsps. vanilla extract, or to taste
- 1 3/4 cups milk
- 1/4 cup heavy cream
- 2 cups heavy cream
- 2 (0.13 oz.) packages unsweetened strawberry-flavored drink mix

- 36 oz. white chocolate, chopped

Direction

1. Preheat an oven to 150°C/300°F; line paper liners on cups of 4 24-cup mini cupcake pans. Sift salt, 1 strawberry drink mix package, all cocoa powder, baking powder, baking soda and flour in mixing bowl.
2. Use electric mixer to beat white sugar and butter on medium speed till fluffy and light in another bowl; one by one, beat eggs in, adding each egg after last one is incorporated fully. Beta vanilla extract in; in 4 additions, mix flour-cocoa mixture, alternating each time using milk. Lower mixer speed to low; beat cream in. Fill cupcake cups to 1/2-3/4 full.
3. In preheated oven, bake for 10-15 minutes till an inserted toothpick in cupcake's middle exits clean. Transfer to racks; cool cupcakes.
4. Put 2 cups cream to almost boiling in saucepan on medium high heat; melt 2 strawberry drink mix packets in cream. Mix white chocolate in till chunks melt and mixture is shiny, smooth and melted. Put aside; cool ganache to warm temperature, about 35°C/95°F; use ganache to frost each cupcake.

Nutrition Information

Calories: 238 calories; Total Carbohydrate: 29 g Cholesterol: 39 mg Total Fat: 13 g Protein: 3.3 g Sodium: 85 mg

Strufoli I

Serving: 8

Ingredients

- 4 eggs
- 2 1/2 cups all-purpose flour
- 16 oz. honey
- 1/2 vanilla bean, halved lengthwise
- 4 tbsps. chopped semisweet chocolate
- 1/2 cup blanched slivered almonds
- 1 (1.75 oz.) package multicolored sprinkles (jimmies)
- 1 cup vegetable oil for frying
- 1/3 cup confectioners' sugar for decoration

Direction

1. In a bowl, add eggs and beat until triple in volume. Gradually put in flour until well mixed without using all of the flour. The dough should be still somewhat sticky.
2. Remove to a board coated with flour. Cut off a piece of dough at a time. Roll piece of dough between your hands to make pencil shapes, using a little flour if necessary.
3. Cut into 1/4 inch pieces and arrange each piece on a cloth dusted with flour. Heat oil in a big pan on top of the stove to 190°C or 375°F. Deep-fry about 1/2 cup pieces at a time while turning continuously until golden. Drain pieces and put aside. Dough will start to turn brown rapidly after a few batches, this is the time to replace oil.
4. Bring honey with vanilla bean in a big pan to a boil, then get rid of bean. Into hot honey, put deep-fried pieces and toss to coat all. Allow to cool and stir in multi-colored jimmies, nuts and chocolate. Put on a plate while shaping firmly into tall cone, then sprinkle confectioners' sugar over top.

Nutrition Information

Calories: 492 calories; Total Carbohydrate: 90.8 g Cholesterol: 93 mg Total Fat: 12 g Protein: 9.2 g

Sodium: 40 mg

Ultimate Double Chocolate Cookies

Serving: 42 | Prep: 25m | Ready in: 1h40m

Ingredients

- 1 lb. semisweet chocolate, chopped
- 2 cups all-purpose flour
- 1/2 cup Dutch process cocoa powder
- 2 tsps. baking powder
- 1 tsp. salt
- 10 tbsps. unsalted butter
- 1 1/2 cups packed brown sugar
- 1/2 cup white sugar
- 4 eggs
- 2 tsps. instant coffee granules
- 2 tsps. vanilla extract

Direction

1. On a double boiler or in the microwave, melt chocolate while stirring sometimes until smooth. Sift salt, baking powder, cocoa and flour together, then put aside.
2. Cream brown and white sugars and butter together in a medium bowl until smooth. Beat in 1 egg at a time, then stir in vanilla and coffee crystals until well combined. Stir in melted chocolate. Stir in dry ingredients with a wooden spoon just until everything is blended. Place a cover and allow to stand about 35 minutes to help chocolate set up.
3. Set the oven to 175°C or 350°F to preheat. Use parchment paper to line 2 cookie sheets. Form dough into balls with walnut size, or drop dough onto prepped cookie sheets by rounded tablespoonfuls, spaced 2 inches between.
4. In the preheated oven, bake for about 8-10 minutes. Cookies will be set yet the centers are still extremely soft due to chocolate. Let cookies cool on baking sheet about 10 minutes prior to removing to wire racks to cool thoroughly.

Nutrition Information

Calories: 148 calories; Total Carbohydrate: 21.4 g Cholesterol: 25 mg Total Fat: 6.8 g Protein: 2.2 g
Sodium: 88 mg

Valentine's Day Cookies

Serving: 18 | Prep: 15m | Ready in: 1h

Ingredients

- 1 1/4 cups all-purpose flour
- 1/4 cup white sugar
- 1/2 tsp. baking soda
- 2 pinches salt
- 1/2 cup honey (optional)
- 1/3 cup milk
- 1/4 cup butter, softened
- 1/4 tsp. vanilla extract
- 1/2 cup semisweet chocolate chips (optional)

- 1/2 cup vanilla chips
- 1/2 cup confectioners' sugar

Direction

1. Set the oven to 175°C or 350°F to preheat.
2. In a bowl, whisk salt, baking soda, white sugar and flour together.
3. In a big bowl, beat together vanilla extract, butter, milk and honey until smooth.
4. Stir into honey mixture with flour mixture until just mixed.
5. Fold chocolate and vanilla chips in.
6. Roll into walnut-sized balls and arrange on nonstick baking sheets, spacing 2 inches apart.
7. In the preheated oven, bake about 15-18 minutes, until golden brown.
8. Let cookies cool and sprinkle confectioners' sugar over top.

Nutrition Information

Calories: 170 calories; Total Carbohydrate: 28 g Cholesterol: 7 mg Total Fat: 6 g Protein: 1.8 g Sodium: 70 mg

Wednesday Cookies

Serving: 60

Ingredients

- 1/2 cup butter
- 1 1/2 cups white sugar
- 2 eggs
- 1 cup sour cream
- 1 tsp. vanilla extract
- 2 3/4 cups all-purpose flour
- 1/2 tsp. baking powder
- 1/2 tsp. salt
- 1/2 tsp. baking soda
- 1 cup shortening
- 1/4 cup milk
- 2 egg whites
- 1/4 cup all-purpose flour
- 2 tsps. vanilla extract
- 1 lb. confectioners' sugar

Direction

1. Cream sugar and butter together in a medium bowl, then stir in vanilla and eggs, followed by the sour cream. Sift together baking soda, salt, baking powder and flour, then mix into creamed mixture. Place a cover and refrigerate for a minimum of an hour.
2. Set the oven to 175°C or 350°F to preheat.
3. Drop on cookie sheets with heaping teaspoonfuls of cookies. In the preheated oven, bake about 10-12 minutes, then transfer to wire racks to cool. Use icing to frost the flat side once cool.
4. For icing, in a medium bowl, mix together confectioners' sugar, vanilla, 1/4 cup flour, egg whites, milk and shortening using an electric mixer on high speed until fluffy. The icing will be fluffier if you mix it longer.

Nutrition Information

Calories: 128 calories; Total Carbohydrate: 17.6 g Cholesterol: 12 mg Total Fat: 6 g Protein: 1.1 g
Sodium: 52 mg

Angel Hair With Walnuts

Serving: 4 servings. | Prep: 10m | Ready in: 20m

Ingredients

- 8 oz. uncooked angel hair pasta
- 1-1/2 to 2 tsps. minced garlic
- 1/4 cup olive oil
- 1/2 cup chopped walnuts
- 1/8 to 1/4 tsp. crushed red pepper flakes
- 1/8 tsp. salt
- 2 tbsps. minced fresh parsley
- 1/2 cup shredded Romano cheese

Direction

1. Following the package instructions, cook the pasta. At the same time, sauté the garlic in oil in a large skillet until tender. Stir in the salt, pepper flakes, and walnuts. Cook until the walnuts get toasted for 2-3 minutes.
2. Take away from the heat; add parsley and stir. Let the pasta drain; transfer to the skillet. Add cheese; toss to coat.

Artichokes With Tarragon Butter

Serving: 2 servings. | Prep: 10m | Ready in: 20m

Ingredients

- 2 medium artichokes
- 4 tsps. lemon juice, divided
- 1/4 cup butter, melted
- 1/4 tsp. dill weed
- 1/4 tsp. dried oregano
- 1/4 tsp. dried tarragon

Direction

1. Level each artichoke's bottom and cut off 1 inch from the top with a sharp knife. Snip off tips of outer leaves with kitchen scissors. Use 1 tsp. of lemon juice to brush the cut edges.
2. In a deep 8-inch microwavable dish, arrange artichokes, then put in 1 inch of water. Cover and place in the microwave to cook on high until it is easy to pull out leaves near the center, about 10 to 12 minutes. Allow to stand about 5 minutes.
3. In the meantime, mix together leftover lemon juice, tarragon, oregano, dill and butter in a small bowl. Serve along with artichokes.

Nutrition Information

Calories: 265 calories Total Carbohydrate: 15 g Cholesterol: 60 mg Total Fat: 23 g Fiber: 7 g Protein: 5 g Sodium: 276 mg

Bacon, Cremini & Brie Potatoes For Two

Serving: 2 servings. | Prep: 10m | Ready in: 60m

Ingredients
- 2 medium potatoes
- 2 tsps. olive oil
- 1/4 tsp. salt
- 3 bacon strips, chopped
- 1/4 lb. sliced baby portobello (cremini) mushrooms
- 2 oz. Brie cheese, sliced
- 1 tbsp. minced fresh chives

Direction
1. Scrub potatoes and pierce them. Use oil to rub over skins of potato, then sprinkle with salt. Bake at 400 degrees until soften, about 50 to 60 minutes.
2. Cook bacon in a skillet on moderate heat until crispy. Transfer to paper towels using a slotted spoon, then drain and save 1 tbsp. of drippings. Sauté mushrooms in drippings.
3. Cut in tops of potatoes with a 2-inch X, then insert slices of cheese. Put chives, bacon and mushrooms on top.

Nutrition Information
Calories: 531 calories Total Carbohydrate: 41 g Cholesterol: 58 mg Total Fat: 34 g Fiber: 4 g Protein: 16 g Sodium: 781 mg

Basil Cheese Butterfly Pasta
Serving: 4 servings. | Prep: 5m | Ready in: 20m

Ingredients
- 3 cups uncooked bow tie pasta
- 1 garlic clove, minced
- 1 tbsp. olive oil
- 1 tbsp. lemon juice
- 1 tsp. dried basil
- 1/2 tsp. salt
- 1/4 tsp. pepper
- 1/2 cup grated Parmesan cheese

Direction
1. Cook pasta following the package directions in a large saucepan. Let the pasta drain and put aside.
2. Sauté garlic in oil for one minute in the same saucepan. Stir in pepper, salt, basil, and lemon juice. Return the pasta to the pan. Then, add cheese and toss to coat.

Broccoli-cauliflower Cheese Bake
Serving: 16 servings. | Prep: 35m | Ready in: 55m

Ingredients
- 7 cups fresh cauliflowerets
- 6 cups fresh broccoli florets
- 3 tbsps. butter
- 1/3 cup all-purpose flour
- 1-1/2 tsps. spicy brown mustard
- 3/4 tsp. salt

- 1/4 tsp. ground nutmeg
- 1/4 tsp. cayenne pepper
- 1/4 tsp. pepper
- 3-3/4 cups fat-free milk
- 1-1/2 cups shredded part-skim mozzarella cheese, divided
- 1-1/2 cups shredded Swiss cheese, divided

Direction

1. Add the broccoli and cauliflower into the Dutch oven; pour in 1 inch of water. Boil. Lower the heat; keep covered and let simmer till tender-crisp or for 3 to 5 minutes. Drain off; move into the 13x9-inch baking dish that is coated using the cooking spray.
2. In the small-sized sauce pan, melt the butter. Whisk in the pepper, cayenne, nutmeg, salt, mustard and flour till becoming smooth; slowly pour in the milk. Boil; cook and stir till becoming thick or for 1 to 2 minutes.
3. Whisk in 1.25 cups of each of the Swiss cheeses and mozzarella till melted. Add on top of the vegetables. Bake, while uncovered, at 400 degrees till bubbling or for 15 to 20 minutes. Drizzle with the rest of the cheeses. Bake till turning golden brown or for 5 more minutes.

Nutrition Information

Calories: 132 calories Total Carbohydrate: 9 g Cholesterol: 22 mg Total Fat: 7 g Fiber: 2 g Protein: 9 g Sodium: 252 mg

Cheddar Cheese Mashed Potatoes

Serving: 12 servings (3/4 cup each). | Prep: 35m | Ready in: 45m

Ingredients

- 3-3/4 lbs. Yukon Gold potatoes, peeled and cubed
- 1 large sweet potato, peeled and cubed
- 6 garlic cloves, halved
- 1 cup (8 oz.) reduced-fat sour cream
- 1 tsp. minced fresh thyme or 1/4 tsp. dried thyme
- 1-1/2 tsps. salt
- 1/2 tsp. pepper
- 2 cups shredded reduced-fat cheddar cheese, divided

Direction

1. Add the garlic and potatoes into the big sauce pan and cover with the water. Boil. Lower the heat; keep covered and cooked till the potatoes soften or for 10 to 15 minutes. Drain off.
2. In the big bowl, smash the potatoes. Whisk in 1 cup of the cheese, pepper, salt, thyme, and sour cream. Move into the 3-quart baking dish that is coated using the cooking spray. Drizzle with the rest of the cheese. Bake, while uncovered, at 350 degrees till thoroughly heated or for 10 to 15 minutes.

Nutrition Information

Calories: 179 calories Total Carbohydrate: 25 g Cholesterol: 19 mg Total Fat: 6 g Fiber: 2 g Protein: 8 g Sodium: 434 mg

Creamy Parmesan Rice

Serving: 4 servings. | Prep: 5m | Ready in: 30m

Ingredients

- 2 cans (14-1/2 oz. each) chicken broth
- 1 cup uncooked long grain rice
- 1/4 tsp. salt
- 1/8 tsp. garlic powder
- 1/4 cup grated Parmesan cheese
- 2 tsps. minced fresh parsley

Direction

1. Heat 2 cups broth (saving remainder) in a big saucepan over medium heat. Heat to a boil. Mix in garlic powder, salt, and rice. Lower heat and simmer 20 minutes, covered, till almost liquid is absorbed.
2. Mix in Parmesan cheese. Pour in reserved broth, 2 tbsps. each time, mixing continuously, till liquid is absorbed before another addition. Cook 5-10 minutes just until creamy and the rice is nearly tender. Mix in parsley. Serve right away.

Nutrition Information

Calories: 221 calories Total Carbohydrate: 42 g Cholesterol: 9 mg Total Fat: 2 g Fiber: 1 g Protein: 6 g Sodium: 1128 mg

Creamy Poppy Seed Fettuccine

Serving: 2 servings. | Prep: 10m | Ready in: 25m

Ingredients

- 4 oz. uncooked fettuccine
- 1/4 cup butter, cubed
- 1 garlic clove, minced
- 2 tbsps. all-purpose flour
- 3/4 cup water
- 1/2 cup half-and-half cream
- 1/2 cup shredded Parmesan cheese
- 2 tsps. dried parsley flakes
- 1/2 tsp. poppy seeds
- 1/2 tsp. pepper
- 1/4 tsp. salt
- 4 fresh basil leaves, thinly sliced or 1/2 tsp. dried basil

Direction

1. Follow the directions on the package to cook fettuccine. In the meantime, melt butter over medium heat in a small skillet. Sauté garlic in melted butter for 1 minute. Mix in flour until well combined. Slowly stir in cream and water. Cook, stirring, until mixture thickens for 1 to 2 minutes.
2. Mix in salt, pepper, poppy seeds, parsley, and Parmesan cheese until incorporated. Drain pasta; add to the cream sauce and mix well. Scatter basil on top.

Crumb-topped Baked Tomatoes

Serving: 2 servings. | Prep: 10m | Ready in: 20m

Ingredients

- 1 large ripe tomato

- 1/8 tsp. salt
- Dash pepper
- 1/4 cup crushed saltines
- 1 tbsp. butter, melted
- 1/4 tsp. minced fresh basil or dash dried basil

Direction

1. Halve the tomato widthwise, then arrange in a shallow baking dish with cut-side facing up. Use pepper and salt to sprinkle over. Mix together basil, butter and cracker crumbs, then sprinkle over tomatoes.
2. Bake at 375 degrees without a cover until crumbs turn golden brown, about 10 to 12 minutes.

Festive Rice Medley

Serving: 5 servings. | Prep: 10m | Ready in: 15m

Ingredients

- 1-1/2 cups uncooked instant rice
- 1/4 cup chopped sweet red pepper
- 1/4 cup chopped sweet yellow pepper
- 2 tsps. canola oil
- 2 tbsps. minced fresh cilantro
- 2 tbsps. chopped green onion
- 1/2 tsp. minced garlic
- 1/4 tsp. salt
- 1/4 tsp. paprika, optional

Direction

1. Follow package directions to cook rice. Sauté peppers in a big skillet with oil until softened, about 2 to 3 minutes. Put in salt, garlic, onion and cilantro, then stir in paprika, if you want, and rice. Cook until heated through, about 2 to 3 minutes.

Nutrition Information

Calories: 130 calories Total Carbohydrate: 25 g Cholesterol: 0 mg Total Fat: 2 g Fiber: 1 g Protein: 2 g Sodium: 121 mg

Fontina Potatoes Au Gratin

Serving: 2 servings. | Prep: 20m | Ready in: 60m

Ingredients

- 2 tbsps. butter
- 2 tsps. all-purpose flour
- 1/2 tsp. salt
- 1/8 tsp. pepper
- 2/3 cup milk
- 3 medium potatoes, peeled and cut into 1/4-inch slices
- 1/4 cup shredded fontina cheese
- 2 tbsps. minced chives
- 1 tbsp. grated Parmesan cheese

Direction

1. Melt butter in a small saucepan. Mix in pepper, salt and the flour until smooth. Slowly mix in milk. Bring to a boil; cook while stirring until thickened, about 2 minutes.
2. Layer 1/2 of the potatoes, fontina cheese, white sauce and chives in a 3-cup baking dish coated with grease. Add the rest of potatoes, chives, sauce and fontina on top.
3. Put in an oven and bake with a cover at 400° for 30 minutes. Remove the cover; sprinkle with Parmesan cheese. Put back in the oven and bake 10-15 minutes more or until potatoes get tender and the top is lightly browned. Let sit for 5 minutes before serving.

Nutrition Information

Calories: 357 calories Total Carbohydrate: 37 g Cholesterol: 57 mg Total Fat: 19 g Fiber: 2 g Protein: 10 g Sodium: 859 mg

Garlic & Chive Mashed Red Potatoes

Serving: 10 servings. | Prep: 15m | Ready in: 30m

Ingredients

- 3-1/2 lbs. medium red potatoes, cubed
- 2 cups (16 oz.) sour cream
- 1/2 cup 2% milk
- 1/3 cup minced chives
- 3 garlic cloves, minced
- 1 tsp. salt
- 1/2 tsp. pepper

Direction

1. In a Dutch oven, put potatoes and add water to cover. Boil it. Lower the heat, put a cover on and cook until soft, or about 10-15 minutes.
2. Strain, mash the potatoes with milk and sour cream. Mix in pepper, salt, garlic, and chives.

Nutrition Information

Calories: 218 calories Total Carbohydrate: 28 g Cholesterol: 33 mg Total Fat: 8 g Fiber: 3 g Protein: 5 g Sodium: 268 mg

Garlic-roasted Sweet Potatoes

Serving: 2 servings. | Prep: 10m | Ready in: 35m

Ingredients

- 2 cups cubed peeled sweet potatoes
- 1 garlic clove, minced
- 1 tbsp. olive oil
- 1/8 tsp. salt
- Pinch pepper

Direction

1. Mix garlic and sweet potatoes together in a small baking dish. Drizzle oil over and sprinkle with pepper and salt. Bake at 425 degrees without a cover until soft while stirring after each 10 minutes, about 25 to 30 minutes.

Nutrition Information

Calories: 202 calories Total Carbohydrate: 33 g Cholesterol: 0 mg Total Fat: 7 g Fiber: 4 g Protein: 2 g Sodium: 165 mg

Ginger Beets And Carrots

Serving: 4 servings. | Prep: 10m | Ready in: 25m

Ingredients
- 1-1/2 cups thinly sliced fresh carrots
- 1-1/2 cups thinly sliced fresh beets
- 4 tsps. olive oil
- 1-1/2 tsps. honey
- 1-1/2 tsps. ground ginger
- 3/4 tsp. soy sauce
- 1/2 tsp. sea salt
- 1/2 tsp. chili powder

Direction
1. Turn oven to 400° to preheat. Arrange vegetables in an oiled 15x10x1-inch baking pan. Stir together remaining ingredients; spoon over vegetables and stir until evenly coated. Bake for 15 to 20 minutes in the preheated oven until beets and carrots are crisp-tender.

Nutrition Information
Calories: 92 calories Total Carbohydrate: 12 g Cholesterol: 0 mg Total Fat: 5 g Fiber: 3 g Protein: 1 g Sodium: 379 mg

Ginger Veggie Stir-fry

Serving: 6 | Prep: 25m | Ready in: 40m

Ingredients
- 1 tbsp. cornstarch
- 1 1/2 cloves garlic, crushed
- 2 tsps. chopped fresh ginger root, divided
- 1/4 cup vegetable oil, divided
- 1 small head broccoli, cut into florets
- 1/2 cup snow peas
- 3/4 cup julienned carrots
- 1/2 cup halved green beans
- 2 tbsps. soy sauce
- 2 1/2 tbsps. water
- 1/4 cup chopped onion
- 1/2 tbsp. salt

Direction
1. Blend 2 tbsp. vegetable oil, 1 tsp. ginger, garlic and cornstarch in a big bowl, until the cornstarch dissolves. Stir in green beans, carrots, snow peas and broccoli, then toss until lightly coated.
2. In a wok or a big skillet, heat the leftover 2 tbsp. of oil on medium heat. Cook the vegetables in oil for 2 minutes, mixing continuously, to avoid burning. Mix in water and soy sauce. Stir in the leftover 1 tsp. ginger, salt and onion. Let it cook until the vegetables become tender but still crisp.

Nutrition Information
Calories: 119 calories; Total Carbohydrate: 8 g Cholesterol: 0 mg Total Fat: 9.3 g Protein: 2.2 g Sodium: 903 mg

Great Green Beans

Serving: 2 servings. | Prep: 10m | Ready in: 30m

Ingredients

- 2 cups cut fresh green beans
- 1 cup chicken broth
- 1 garlic clove, minced
- 2 tbsps. butter
- 2 tbsps. minced fresh parsley
- 1 tsp. minced fresh rosemary or 1/4 tsp. dried rosemary, crushed
- 1/8 tsp. garlic salt
- 1 tbsp. shredded Parmesan cheese

Direction

1. Bring broth and beans in a small saucepan to a boil, then lower heat and simmer without a cover until crisp-tender, about 10 minutes.
2. Sauté garlic in a small skillet with butter, until soft. Stir in garlic salt, rosemary and parsley, then drain beans. Drizzle with butter mixture and toss to coat well. Sprinkle Parmesan cheese over.

Green Bean Stir-fry

Serving: 2 servings. | Prep: 10m | Ready in: 10m

Ingredients

- 1 tbsp. reduced-sodium soy sauce
- 2 garlic cloves, minced
- 1 tsp. sesame seeds, toasted
- 1 tsp. brown sugar
- 1 tsp. peanut butter
- 3/4 lb. fresh green beans, trimmed
- 4-1/2 tsps. vegetable oil

Direction

1. Mix together peanut butter, brown sugar, sesame seeds, garlic and soy sauce in a small bowl, then put aside.
2. Stir-fry green beans in a big skillet with oil until tender yet still crispy. Take away from the heat and put in soy sauce mixture, then stir to coat well.

Nutrition Information

Calories: 178 calories Total Carbohydrate: 15 g Cholesterol: 0 mg Total Fat: 12 g Fiber: 6 g Protein: 5 g Sodium: 491 mg

Green Beans And Red Peppers

Serving: 2 servings. | Prep: 5m | Ready in: 15m

Ingredients

- 1/3 lb. fresh green beans, trimmed
- 3 tbsps. chopped sweet red pepper
- 1 green onion, thinly sliced
- 1 small garlic clove, minced

- 1 tbsp. butter
- Dash salt and pepper

Direction

1. In a large saucepan, put beans and cover with water. Bring to a boil. Uncover and cook until crisp-tender, about 8-10 minutes.
2. In the meantime, sauté garlic, onion, and red pepper in butter in a small skillet until softened. Then remove from the heat; dust with pepper and salt. Allow the beans to drain and transfer to a serving plate. Add the red pepper mixture and gently stir to coat.

Nutrition Information

Calories: 79 calories Total Carbohydrate: 7 g Cholesterol: 15 mg Total Fat: 6 g Fiber: 3 g Protein: 2 g Sodium: 120 mg

Herbed New Potatoes

Serving: Makes 8 servings

Ingredients

- 3 lbs. 1 1/2-inch-diameter new potatoes, scrubbed, quartered
- 2 tbsps. olive oil
- 3 garlic cloves, minced
- 6 tbsps. mixed chopped fresh herbs (such as parsley, dill, and chives)

Direction

1. Steam potatoes for 9 minutes, until soft. You can steam potatoes 2 hours in advance. Allow to stand at room temperature.
2. In a big skillet, heat oil on medium-high heat, then add in garlic and stir for a half minute. Add in herbs and potatoes, then sprinkle pepper and salt lightly over top. Sauté for 8 minutes, until potatoes are golden and heated through. Use pepper and salt to season and transfer to a bowl. Serve.

Nutrition Information

Calories: 164 Total Carbohydrate: 30 g Total Fat: 4 g Fiber: 4 g Protein: 4 g Sodium: 12 mg Saturated Fat: 1 g

Lemon-butter New Potatoes

Serving: 4 servings. | Prep: 10m | Ready in: 30m

Ingredients

- 12 small red potatoes
- 1/3 cup butter, cubed
- 3 tbsps. lemon juice
- 1 tsp. salt
- 1 tsp. grated lemon peel
- 1/4 tsp. pepper
- 1/8 tsp. ground nutmeg
- 2 tbsps. minced fresh parsley

Direction

1. Peel a strip from around each potato. Put potatoes in a big saucepan, pour in water to cover then heat to a boil. Lower the heat, put on a cover and cook until just tender, about 15-20 minutes.
2. At the same time, melt butter in a small saucepan. Mix in nutmeg, pepper, lemon peel, salt, and

lemon juice. Drain potatoes then bring to a serving bowl. Spread butter mixture over the potatoes; gently toss to coat. Sprinkle parsley over top.

Nutrition Information

Calories: 238 calories Total Carbohydrate: 23 g Cholesterol: 40 mg Total Fat: 15 g Fiber: 3 g Protein: 3 g Sodium: 707 mg

Lemon-pepper Green Beans

Serving: 2 servings. | Prep: 5m | Ready in: 20m

Ingredients

- 1/2 lb. fresh green beans, trimmed
- 1 tbsp. olive oil
- 1-1/2 tsps. cider vinegar
- 1/4 to 1/2 tsp. Italian seasoning
- 1/4 tsp. onion salt
- 1/8 tsp. lemon-pepper seasoning

Direction

1. In a steamer basket, add beans then put in a big saucepan set over 1 inch of water. Bring water to a boil, then cover and steam beans until tender-crisp, about 8 to 10 minutes.
2. In the meantime, whisk together seasonings, vinegar and oil in a small bowl until combined. Remove beans to a serving bowl and use seasoning mixture to drizzle over top. Toss to coat.

Nutrition Information

Calories: 92 calories Total Carbohydrate: 8 g Cholesterol: 0 mg Total Fat: 7 g Fiber: 3 g Protein: 2 g Sodium: 261 mg

Marinated Asparagus With Blue Cheese

Serving: 4 servings. | Prep: 10m | Ready in: 20m

Ingredients

- 1 lb. fresh asparagus, trimmed
- 4 green onions, thinly sliced
- 1/4 cup olive oil
- 2 tbsps. white wine vinegar
- 1 garlic clove, minced
- 1/2 tsp. salt
- 1/4 tsp. pepper
- 1/2 cup crumbled blue cheese

Direction

1. Boil 6 cups water in a large saucepan. Add asparagus; uncover and cook just until crisp-tender, around 2-3 minutes. Remove the asparagus and drop into ice water immediately. Drain and pat dry.
2. Combine green onions, pepper, salt, garlic, vinegar, and oil in a large resealable plastic bag. Put in the asparagus; seal the bag and turn to coat. Chill for at least 1 hour.
3. Drain asparagus and discard the marinade. Arrange the asparagus on a serving dish and dust with cheese.

Nutrition Information

Calories: 136 calories Total Carbohydrate: 3 g Cholesterol: 13 mg Total Fat: 12 g Fiber: 1 g Protein: 5 g

Sodium: 348 mg

Mashed Cauliflower

Serving: 4 | Prep: 10m | Ready in: 55m

Ingredients

- 1 head cauliflower, cut into florets
- 2 tbsps. butter
- 1/2 cup milk
- 1/2 cup sour cream
- 1 cup Italian-seasoned bread crumbs
- salt and ground black pepper to taste

Direction

1. Set an oven to 190°C (375°F) and start preheating.
2. Boil a large pot of water. In the boiling water, cook the cauliflower for about 10 minutes until it becomes tender; drain the water and put aside.
3. In the same pot, let the butter melt on medium heat. Stir the sour cream, milk, and cauliflower into the melted butter.
4. In the pot, mash the cauliflower with a hand blender until it becomes creamy.
5. Place the cauliflower mixture to a baking dish; use breadcrumbs to cover evenly and use black pepper and salt to season.
6. Bake for about half an hour in the prepared oven until the breadcrumbs are lightly browned.

Nutrition Information

Calories: 274 calories; Total Carbohydrate: 30.3 g Cholesterol: 30 mg Total Fat: 14 g Protein: 8.8 g Sodium: 542 mg

Mushroom And Spinach Saute

Serving: 2 servings. | Prep: 5m | Ready in: 10m

Ingredients

- 2 tsps. olive oil
- 2 cups sliced fresh mushrooms
- 2 garlic cloves, minced
- 1 package (5 to 6 oz.) fresh baby spinach
- 1/8 tsp. salt
- 1/8 tsp. pepper

Direction

1. Heat oil in a big skillet on moderately high heat. Put in mushrooms and sauté for 2 minutes, until soft. Put in garlic and cook for another minute. Working in batches, put in spinach, then cook and stir for a minute until wilted. Use pepper and salt to season, then serve instantly.

Nutrition Information

Calories: 76 calories Total Carbohydrate: 6 g Cholesterol: 0 mg Total Fat: 5 g Fiber: 2 g Protein: 4 g Sodium: 208 mg

Orzo Timbales With Fontina Cheese

Serving: 6 servings. | Prep: 20m | Ready in: 50m

Ingredients

- 1 cup uncooked orzo pasta
- 1-1/2 cups shredded fontina cheese
- 1/2 cup finely chopped roasted sweet red peppers
- 1 can (2-1/4 oz.) sliced ripe olives, drained
- 2 large eggs
- 1-1/2 cups 2% milk
- 1/4 tsp. salt
- 1/8 tsp. ground nutmeg
- Minced fresh parsley, optional

Direction

1. Preheat the oven to 350 degrees. Cook the orzo based on the instruction on the package for al dente; drain. Move into the bowl. Whisk the olives, pepper and cheese. Split between six greased 10-oz. ramekins/custard cups. Add the ramekins onto the baking sheet.
2. In the small-sized bowl, stir the nutmeg, salt, milk and eggs; add on top of the orzo mixture. Bake till turning golden brown or for 30 to 35 minutes. Allow it to rest for 5 minutes prior to serving. As you want, slice the knife around the sides of ramekins and invert into the serving dish. As you wish, drizzle with parsley.

Pasta Puttanesca

Serving: 4 | Prep: 15m | Ready in: 35m

Ingredients

- 1 (12 oz.) package dried penne pasta
- 3 tbsps. olive oil
- 1 1/2 lbs. skinless, boneless chicken breast halves - cubed
- 1 cup all-purpose flour
- salt and pepper to taste
- 2 lemons
- 1/2 cup capers
- 40 kalamata olives, pitted and chopped
- 1/2 tsp. anchovy paste
- 5 roma (plum) tomatoes, diced
- 1/2 cup Parmesan cheese

Direction

1. Pour lightly salted water in a large pot then bring to a boil. Put in pasta and cook for 8-10 minutes or till al dente; drain pasta.
2. Pour oil in a skillet then heat on medium heat. Dredge cubed chicken in flour seasoned with salt and pepper then brown the floured chicken cubes in hot oil. When chicken gets brown color on all sides, squeeze lemon juice from a lemon on top of the brown chicken cubes. Add anchovy paste, olives and capers then cook for 5 minutes minimum to allow flavors to mingle then cook the chicken.
3. When chicken is not pink anymore, put in salt, pepper, the juice from the remaining lemon, diced tomatoes. Put cheese and pasta into the pan then cook, stir just till heated through.

Nutrition Information

Calories: 866 calories; Total Carbohydrate: 94.6 g Cholesterol: 106 mg Total Fat: 29.6 g Protein: 55.7 g

Portobello & Green Bean Saute

Serving: 10 servings. | Prep: 10m | Ready in: 20m

Ingredients

- 1 lb. fresh green beans, trimmed and halved
- 1 lb. baby portobello mushrooms, quartered
- 1 medium onion, finely chopped
- 1/4 cup butter, cubed
- 2 garlic cloves, minced
- 1 tsp. chicken bouillon granules
- 4 plum tomatoes, peeled and chopped
- 1 tsp. dried marjoram
- 1/4 tsp. pepper
- 1/4 cup minced fresh parsley

Direction

1. Add the beans into the big sauce pan and cover with water; boil. Keep covered and cook till tender-crisp or for 3 to 5 minutes.
2. At the same time, in the big skillet, sauté the onion and mushrooms in the butter till becoming soft. Put in the bouillon and garlic; cook for 60 seconds more. Drain off the green beans; put into the skillet and coat by tossing. Take out of the heat. Whisk in pepper, marjoram and tomatoes. Drizzle with parsley.

Nutrition Information

Calories: 77 calories Total Carbohydrate: 8 g Cholesterol: 12 mg Total Fat: 5 g Fiber: 3 g Protein: 3 g Sodium: 123 mg

Rich And Creamy Mashed Potatoes

Serving: 4 servings. | Prep: 5m | Ready in: 25m

Ingredients

- 6 medium unpeeled red potatoes (about 1-1/2 lbs.), cut into 1-inch pieces
- 1/3 to 1/2 cup heavy whipping cream, warmed
- 2 tbsps. butter
- 1/2 tsp. salt
- 1/4 tsp. pepper

Direction

1. Put potatoes in a big pot; pour in water to cover then boil. Lower the heat then cover; cook for 10-15 minutes until the potatoes are tender. Drain the potatoes then mash with pepper, salt, butter and cream.

Nutrition Information

Calories: 241 calories Total Carbohydrate: 28 g Cholesterol: 42 mg Total Fat: 13 g Fiber: 3 g Protein: 4 g Sodium: 371 mg

Roasted Garlic Twice-baked Potato

Serving: 2 servings. | Prep: 60m | Ready in: 01h25m

Ingredients

- 1 large baking potato
- 1 tsp. canola oil, divided
- 6 garlic cloves, unpeeled
- 2 tbsps. butter, softened
- 2 tbsps. 2% milk
- 2 tbsps. sour cream
- 1/4 tsp. minced fresh rosemary or dash dried rosemary, crushed
- 1/8 tsp. salt
- 1/8 tsp. pepper

Direction

1. Scrub the potato then puncture; massage with a half tsp. oil. On a double-thick heavy-duty foil, put garlic then sprinkle with the remaining oil; wrap the foil around the garlic. Arrange the garlic and potato on a baking sheet; bake for 15 minutes in 400 degrees oven. Take the garlic out then bake the potato for another 45 minutes until tender.
2. Halve the potato lengthwise once cool enough to touch; scoop the pulp out, keeping thin shells.
3. In a small bowl, squeeze the soft garlic then mash with the potato pulp; mix in the rest of the ingredients. Scoop the mixture inside the shells then arrange on an ungreased baking sheet. Bake for 25-30 minutes in 350 degrees oven, with no cover, until completely heated.

Nutrition Information

Calories: 318 calories Total Carbohydrate: 38 g Cholesterol: 41 mg Total Fat: 17 g Fiber: 3 g Protein: 6 g Sodium: 253 mg

Roasted Vegetable Risotto

Serving: 5 servings. | Prep: 10m | Ready in: 40m

Ingredients

- 3 cups chicken stock
- 3 garlic cloves, minced
- 3 tbsps. butter
- 1 cup uncooked arborio rice
- 1/4 tsp. pepper
- 1/4 cup white wine
- 2 cups Roasted Green Vegetable Medley
- 2 tbsps. grated Parmesan cheese

Direction

1. Put stock in a big saucepan then warm until heated. Maintain its warmth. Use cooking spray to coat a big non-stick skillet. Add garlic, sautéing until it tenderizes or for about 2 to 3 minutes. Insert pepper and rice, cooking and stirring for 2 to 3 minutes. Lower the heat and add the wine in, cooking and stirring until all liquids have been absorbed. Pour in the heated broth, half a cup by half a cup. Stir regularly during the process. In between every addition, give some time for the liquid to be absorbed. Continue cooking for around 20 minutes until the rice just about softens and risotto becomes rich and thick. Insert the vegetables, cooking and stirring until thoroughly heated. Scatter cheese on the top and serve at once.

Nutrition Information

Calories: 237 calories Total Carbohydrate: 33 g Cholesterol: 20 mg Total Fat: 8 g Fiber: 0 g Protein: 6 g Sodium: 386 mg

Rustic Tuscan Pepper Bruschetta

Serving: 4 dozen. | Prep: 40m | Ready in: 40m

Ingredients

- 2 tbsps. olive oil
- 2 tbsps. balsamic vinegar
- 1 tbsp. honey
- 1 tbsp. minced fresh mint
- 1 each medium sweet yellow, orange and red pepper, cut into thin 1-inch strips
- 6 oz. fresh goat cheese
- 2/3 cup whipped cream cheese
- 48 assorted crackers

Direction

1. In the big bowl, stir the mint, honey, vinegar and oil. Put in peppers; coat by tossing. Allow to sit for 15 minutes.
2. At the same time, in the small-sized bowl, whip the cream cheese and goat cheese. Spread 1 rounded tsp. on each of the cracker. Drain the peppers well. Arrange the peppers on the cheese-topped crackers.

Nutrition Information

Calories: 34 calories Total Carbohydrate: 3 g Cholesterol: 5 mg Total Fat: 2 g Fiber: 0 g Protein: 1 g Sodium: 60 mg

Seasoned Potatoes

Serving: 2 servings. | Prep: 10m | Ready in: 25m

Ingredients

- 1 tbsp. olive oil
- 1 can (14-1/2 oz.) sliced potatoes, drained
- 1 small onion, cut into thin wedges
- 2 tsps. minced fresh parsley
- 1/2 tsp. paprika
- 1/4 tsp. garlic powder
- 1/4 tsp. onion powder
- Pinch salt

Direction

1. Heat oil in a small skillet on medium heat. Add in onion and potatoes, then cook and stir until browned slightly, about 10 minutes. Mix together salt, onion powder, garlic powder, paprika and parsley, then sprinkle the mixture over potato mixture. Toss together to coat well. Cook until onion is softened, about 5 to 10 minutes more.

Nutrition Information

Calories: 157 calories Total Carbohydrate: 21 g Cholesterol: 0 mg Total Fat: 7 g Fiber: 3 g Protein: 2 g Sodium: 553 mg

Shallot & Basil Green Beans

Serving: 2 servings. | Prep: 10m | Ready in: 25m

Ingredients

- 1/2 lb. fresh green beans, trimmed
- 2 shallots, chopped
- 1 tsp. olive oil
- 1/4 tsp. sugar
- 1/4 tsp. salt
- 1/8 tsp. pepper
- 2 tbsps. minced fresh basil or 1/2 tsp. dried basil
- 1 tsp. grated lemon peel

Direction

1. Put beans in a small saucepan and pour water to cover beans; bring to a boil. Cook without a lid for 8 to 10 minutes or until beans become crisp-tender.
2. While waiting for the beans, put oil and shallot in a small skillet then sauté shallots in oil till they become soft. Put in salt and pepper, sugar.
3. Drain beans and put beans into the skillet. Put in lemon peel and basil; toss to coat.

Nutrition Information

Calories: 83 calories Total Carbohydrate: 15 g Cholesterol: 0 mg Total Fat: 2 g Fiber: 4 g Protein: 3 g Sodium: 306 mg

Shiitake & Butternut Risotto

Serving: 2 servings. | Prep: 25m | Ready in: 50m

Ingredients

- 1 cup cubed peeled butternut squash
- 2 tsps. olive oil, divided
- Dash salt
- 1-1/4 cups reduced-sodium chicken broth
- 2/3 cup sliced fresh shiitake mushrooms
- 2 tbsps. chopped onion
- 1 small garlic clove, minced
- 1/3 cup uncooked arborio rice
- Dash pepper
- 1/4 cup white wine or 1/4 cup additional reduced-sodium chicken broth
- 1/4 cup grated Parmesan cheese
- 1 tsp. minced fresh sage

Direction

1. Arrange squash in an oiled 9-inch square baking dish. Add salt and 1 tsp. oil; stir until evenly coated.
2. Bake, uncovered, for 25 to 30 minutes at 350° until tender, stirring occasionally.
3. In the meantime, heat broth in small saucepan and keep warm. Sauté garlic, onion, and mushrooms in the remaining oil in a small skillet until tender for 3 to 4 minutes. Mix in pepper and rice; sauté for 2 to 3 minutes. Lower heat; pour in wine. Cook until all of the liquid is absorbed, stirring well.
4. Pour in heated broth, a quarter cup at a time, and stir frequently. Let the liquid absorb after each

addition. Cook just until rice is almost tender and risotto is creamy. Cooking time is about 20 minutes. Mix in cheese until melted. Mix in sage and squash. Serve right away.

Nutrition Information

Calories: 282 calories Total Carbohydrate: 40 g Cholesterol: 12 mg Total Fat: 9 g Fiber: 3 g Protein: 10 g Sodium: 567 mg

Shrimp Scampi Topped Potatoes

Serving: 10 servings. | Prep: 40m | Ready in: 01h40m

Ingredients

- 10 medium potatoes
- 3 tbsps. olive oil
- 1-1/2 tsps. salt

FILLING:

- 1/2 cup sour cream
- 1/4 cup heavy whipping cream
- 4 garlic cloves, minced
- 1 tbsp. minced fresh parsley
- 1 tbsp. prepared horseradish
- 1/2 tsp. salt

TOPPING:

- 3 garlic cloves, minced
- 2 tbsps. olive oil
- 10 uncooked jumbo shrimp, peeled and deveined
- 2 tbsps. minced fresh parsley
- 2 tbsps. lemon juice
- 2 tbsps. white wine or chicken broth
- 1/8 tsp. salt

Direction

1. Scrub and pierce potatoes; use salt and oil to rub the pierced potatoes. Arrange potatoes on a baking sheet. Bake at 400 degrees for an hour or till potatoes become soft. Let potatoes cool slightly; chop a thin slice off the top of each potato then throw away those slices. Spoon out pulp, leave a thin shell.
2. Mash pulp with salt, horseradish, parsley, garlic, heavy cream and sour cream in a large bowl till everything is blended. Scoop the mixture into the potato shell, keep them warm.
3. Sauté garlic in oil for a minute in a large skillet. Put in shrimp; cook shrimp for a minute per side. Put in salt, broth or wine, lemon juice and parsley then cook for 2 to 3 minutes more or till shrimp gets pink color. Use one shrimp to top each potato, use pan drippings to drizzle.

Nutrition Information

Calories: 301 calories Total Carbohydrate: 40 g Cholesterol: 47 mg Total Fat: 12 g Fiber: 4 g Protein: 9 g Sodium: 557 mg

Snow Pea Medley

Serving: 2 servings. | Prep: 15m | Ready in: 25m

Ingredients

- 1/3 cup chopped red onion

- 2 tsps. canola oil
- 1/3 cup julienned sweet red pepper
- 1/3 cup julienned sweet yellow pepper
- 1/2 cup fresh snow peas
- 1/2 cup sliced fresh mushrooms
- 1/4 tsp. salt

Direction

1. Sauté onion in oil in a nonstick skillet coated with cooking spray for 1 to 2 minutes. Add peppers; cook for another 2 minutes.
2. Mix in mushrooms and peas; sauté until vegetables are crisp-tender, about 3 to 4 minutes more. Add salt for seasoning.

Nutrition Information

Calories: 83 calories Total Carbohydrate: 8 g Cholesterol: 0 mg Total Fat: 5 g Fiber: 2 g Protein: 3 g Sodium: 299 mg

Squash Ribbons

Serving: 2 servings. | Prep: 15m | Ready in: 15m

Ingredients

- 1 small yellow summer squash
- 1 small zucchini
- 3 tsps. butter, melted
- 1/4 tsp. onion powder
- 1/4 tsp. dried rosemary, crushed
- 1/8 tsp. salt
- 1/8 tsp. dried thyme
- 1/8 tsp. pepper

Direction

1. Cut down the length of each squash with extremely thin slices to make long ribbons, using a metal cheese slicer or vegetable peeler. Put in a steamer basket and set over 1 inch of boiling water in a saucepan. Place a cover and steam until soft, about 2 to 3 minutes.
2. Mix together pepper, thyme, salt, rosemary, onion powder and butter in a small bowl, then put in squash and toss to coat.

Nutrition Information

Calories: 55 calories Total Carbohydrate: 6 g Cholesterol: 10 mg Total Fat: 3 g Fiber: 3 g Protein: 2 g Sodium: 187 mg

Sweet-sour Green Beans

Serving: 2 servings. | Prep: 5m | Ready in: 15m

Ingredients

- 2 cups cut fresh green beans (2-inch pieces)
- 2 bacon strips, diced
- 1/4 cup chopped onion
- 4 tsps. brown sugar
- 4 tsps. cider vinegar

Direction

1. In a small saucepan, add green beans and water to cover, then bring to a boil. Cook without a cover until tender yet still crispy, about 8 to 10 minutes.
2. In the meantime, cook bacon in a small skillet on moderate heat until crispy. Transfer bacon to paper towels with a slotted spoon to drain, saving 2 tsp. of drippings. In the reserved drippings, sauté onion until soft. Stir in vinegar and brown sugar, then heat through. Drain beans and transfer them into a bowl, stir in onion mixture. Place bacon on top.

Nutrition Information

Calories: 183 calories Total Carbohydrate: 19 g Cholesterol: 15 mg Total Fat: 10 g Fiber: 4 g Protein: 5 g Sodium: 200 mg

Triple Mash With Horseradish Bread Crumbs

Serving: 12 servings (2/3 cup each). | Prep: 15m | Ready in: 30m

Ingredients

- 1-3/4 lbs. Yukon Gold potatoes, peeled and cubed
- 4 medium parsnips (about 1-1/4 lbs.), peeled and cubed
- 2-1/2 cups cubed peeled rutabaga
- 2 tsps. salt
- 1/2 cup butter, divided
- 1 cup soft bread crumbs
- 2 tbsps. prepared horseradish
- 1 cup whole milk
- 1/4 tsp. pepper

Direction

1. In a 6-quart stockpot, add salt, rutabaga, parsnips and potatoes, then put in water to cover and bring to boil. Lower the heat and cook without a cover until softened, or for 15 to 20 minutes.
2. In the meantime, heat 1/4 cup butter in a skillet on medium heat. Put in bread crumbs then cook and stir until toasted, or for 3 to 5 minutes. Stir in horseradish and take away from the heat.
3. Drain vegetables and bring back to the pot. Mash vegetables on low heat while putting in the leftover butter, pepper and milk gradually. Turn out into a serving dish and sprinkle over with bread crumbs.

Nutrition Information

Calories: 199 calories Total Carbohydrate: 28 g Cholesterol: 22 mg Total Fat: 9 g Fiber: 4 g Protein: 4 g Sodium: 240 mg

Twice-baked Creamy Sweet Potatoes

Serving: 2 servings. | Prep: 20m | Ready in: 35m

Ingredients

- 2 medium sweet potatoes
- 2 oz. cream cheese, softened
- 2 tbsps. sour cream
- 1 tbsp. butter
- 1/4 tsp. salt
- 2 tbsps. brown sugar
- 1/2 tsp. ground cinnamon

Direction

1. Scrub and pierce potatoes, then put on a microwavable plate. Microwave without a cover on high setting until softened while turning one time, or for about 12 to 14 minutes.
2. Once cool enough to handle, cut off from top of each potato with a thin slice and get rid of it, then spoon out pulp carefully to leave a thin shell. Mash the pulp in a big bowl. Put in salt, butter, sour cream and cream cheese then blend well. Scoop into potato shells.
3. Put on a baking sheet and sprinkle over with cinnamon as well as brown sugar. Bake at 425 degrees without a cover until heated through and topping turns golden brown, or for about 12 to 15 minutes.

Nutrition Information

Calories: 350 calories Total Carbohydrate: 43 g Cholesterol: 56 mg Total Fat: 18 g Fiber: 4 g Protein: 5 g Sodium: 441 mg

Twice-baked Potatoes With Bacon

Serving: 2 servings. | Prep: 01h15m | Ready in: 01h35m

Ingredients

- 2 medium baking potatoes
- 2 tbsps. reduced-fat butter
- 1/4 cup fat-free milk
- 1 bacon strip, cooked and crumbled
- 1 tbsp. finely chopped onion
- 1 tsp. minced chives
- 1/4 tsp. salt
- Dash pepper
- 1/2 cup shredded reduced-fat cheddar cheese, divided

Direction

1. Bake potatoes at 375 degrees until softened, about 60 minutes. Once they are cool enough to handle, at the top of each potato, cut a thin slice off and discard. Scoop the pulp out and leave a thin shell.
2. Mash the pulp with butter in a small bowl. Stir in 1/3 cup cheese, pepper, salt, chives, onion, bacon, and milk. Then scoop into the potato shells. Lay the remaining cheese on top.
3. Next, arrange on a baking sheet and bake at 375 degrees until the cheese is melted, about 20-25 minutes.

Nutrition Information

Calories: 328 calories Total Carbohydrate: 42 g Cholesterol: 39 mg Total Fat: 14 g Fiber: 4 g Protein: 14 g Sodium: 669 mg

White Wine Mushrooms

Serving: 6 servings. | Prep: 15m | Ready in: 45m

Ingredients

- 5 garlic cloves, minced
- 1/2 cup butter, divided
- 3/4 cup white wine
- 2 lbs. halved baby portobello mushrooms
- 1/4 tsp. salt
- 1/4 tsp. coarsely ground pepper

Direction

1. Cook garlic for 1-2 minutes in a big pan with a quarter cup of butter. Mix in wine then put in mushrooms; boil. Lower heat; let it simmer for 15-20 minutes without cover until the liquid is nearly evaporated.
2. Mix in the remaining butter, pepper, and salt; cook until the butter melts.

Nutrition Information

Calories: 200 calories Total Carbohydrate: 8 g Cholesterol: 40 mg Total Fat: 16 g Fiber: 2 g Protein: 5 g Sodium: 214 mg

Berry-almond Sandwich Cookies

Serving: 3 dozen. | Prep: 30m | Ready in: 40m

Ingredients

- 1-1/2 cups butter, softened
- 1 cup sugar
- 1 tsp. vanilla extract
- 2-3/4 cups all-purpose flour
- 1/2 tsp. salt
- 2 cups ground almonds
- 3/4 cup raspberry filling
- Edible glitter or confectioners' sugar

Direction

1. Preheat an oven to 325°. Cream sugar and butter till fluffy and light in big bowl; beat vanilla in. Mix salt and flour; add to creamed mixture slowly. Stir well; mix almonds in.
2. Roll dough out to 1/8-in. thick on heavily floured surface. Cut to desired shapes using floured 2 1/2-in. cookie cutters.
3. Put on ungreased baking sheets, 1-in. apart. Bake till edges start to brown, about 10-12 minutes. Transfer to wire racks; cool.
4. Spread 1 tsp. raspberry filling on bottoms of 1/2 of the cookies; top with leftover cookies. Sprinkle confectioners' sugar/edible glitter. Keep in airtight container.

Nutrition Information

Calories: 167 calories Total Carbohydrate: 17 g Cholesterol: 20 mg Total Fat: 10 g Fiber: 1 g Protein: 2 g Sodium: 114 mg

Butterscotch-toffee Cheesecake Bars

Serving: 2 dozen. | Prep: 15m | Ready in: 45m

Ingredients

- 1 package yellow cake mix (regular size)
- 1 package (3.4 oz.) instant butterscotch pudding mix
- 1/3 cup canola oil
- 2 large eggs, divided use
- 1 package (8 oz.) cream cheese, softened
- 1/3 cup sugar
- 1 cup brickle toffee bits, divided
- 1/2 cup butterscotch chips

Direction

1. Set oven to 350 degrees and start preheating. Mix together 1 egg, oil, pudding mix and cake mix in a big bowl until mixture forms crumbs. Set aside a cup of mixture for topping. Pat the rest into an ungreased baking pan (13x9 inches). Bake in the preheated oven for 10 minutes. Place on a wire rack until completely cool.
2. Whisk sugar and cream cheese in a small bowl until smooth. Pour in remaining eggs; on low speed, beat mixture until incorporated. Fold in half cup toffee bits. Pour onto crust. Garnish with saved crumb mixture. Bake until filling is set, about 15 to 20 minutes.
3. Garnish with the rest of toffee bits and butterscotch chips. Continue baking for another minute. Place on a wire rack for an hour to cool. Chill in the refrigerator for 2 hours. Slice into bars.

Nutrition Information

Calories: 257 calories Total Carbohydrate: 34 g Cholesterol: 31 mg Total Fat: 13 g Fiber: 0 g Protein: 2 g Sodium: 297 mg

Cannoli In A Glass

Serving: 2 servings. | Prep: 10m | Ready in: 10m

Ingredients

- 1 cup part-skim ricotta cheese
- 3 tbsps. confectioners' sugar
- 1 tsp. grated orange zest
- 1/4 tsp. vanilla extract
- 1/8 tsp. ground cinnamon
- 2 tbsps. miniature semisweet chocolate chips
- 2 tsps. pistachios, finely chopped
- 2 maraschino cherries

Direction

1. In a food processor, put the initial 5 ingredients. Put cover and process until it becomes smooth. Fold in the chocolate chips. Scoop the ricotta mixture on the 2 dessert dishes or parfait glasses and sprinkle pistachios on top of each. Put the cherry on top.

Nutrition Information

Calories: 293 calories Total Carbohydrate: 28 g Cholesterol: 38 mg Total Fat: 14 g Fiber: 1 g Protein: 15 g Sodium: 167 mg

Cappuccino Truffles

Serving: Makes about 5 dozen truffles or 30 servings, 2 truffles each. | Prep: 30m | Ready in: 2h30m

Ingredients

- 2 Tbsp. MAXWELL HOUSE Instant Coffee
- 2 Tbsp. orange juice
- 2 tsp. vanilla
- 1 jar (7 oz.) JET-PUFFED Marshmallow Creme
- 1 pkg. (9 oz.) chocolate wafer cookies , finely crushed
- 1 cup finely chopped PLANTERS Pecans
- 1 Tbsp. grated orange zest

- 2 Tbsp. unsweetened cocoa powder
- 2 Tbsp. powdered sugar

Direction

1. Melt instant coffee in mixed vanilla and juice. Add marshmallow crème slowly into small electric mixer's bowl; beat on low speed till blended well. Add zest, pecans and water crumbs; stir well.
2. Form to 1-in. balls; roll in mixed powdered sugar and cocoa till coated evenly. In 1 layer, put in shallow pan. Tightly cover.
3. Refrigerate till firm or for a few hours. Store in a tightly covered container in the fridge.

Nutrition Information

Calories: 90 Total Carbohydrate: 13 g Cholesterol: 0 mg Total Fat: 4 g Fiber: 1 g Protein: 1 g Sodium: 60 mg
Sugar: 8 g
Saturated Fat: 0.5 g

Caramel Fondue

Serving: 1-3/4 cups. | Prep: 5m | Ready in: 20m

Ingredients

- 1 cup heavy whipping cream, divided
- 3/4 cup sugar
- 1/2 cup light corn syrup
- 1/4 cup butter
- 1/4 tsp. salt
- 1/2 tsp. vanilla extract
- Pound cake and assorted fresh fruit, cut into pieces

Direction

1. Mix together corn syrup, sugar, salt, butter, and half a cup of cream in a hefty saucepan. Boil the mixture on medium heat until a candy thermometer reads 234° which is considered the soft-ball stage. Constantly stir the contents of the pan while cooking. Allow the mixture to cool up to 220° and then pour in the remaining cream. Boil again. Take off from the heat and add the vanilla; stir.
2. Pour the mixture in a fondue pot to keep it warm and serve with fruit and lb. cake.

Nutrition Information

Calories: 162 calories Total Carbohydrate: 20 g Cholesterol: 32 mg Total Fat: 10 g Fiber: 0 g Protein: 0 g Sodium: 96 mg

Cherry Cordial Cookies

Serving: 12

Ingredients

- 1 cup dried cherries
- 1/3 cup cherry liqueur
- 1/2 cup unsalted butter
- 1/2 cup white sugar
- 1/2 cup packed brown sugar
- 1 egg
- 1 1/2 tsps. vanilla extract

- 1 tsp. almond extract
- 1 1/2 cups all-purpose flour
- 1/2 tsp. baking soda
- 3/4 cup chopped white chocolate
- 1/2 cup chopped semisweet chocolate
- 1/2 cup chopped macadamia nuts

Direction

1. Dip the dried cherries for 2 to 3 minutes in boiling water. Drain then soak in a small bowl with cherry liqueur. The longer you soak dried cherries, the better you get. Heat the oven beforehand to 175°C or 350°F. Arrange parchment paper on the cookie sheets.
2. Cream the brown sugar and white sugar in butter in a medium bowl. Mix in almond extract, vanilla and egg. Sift the baking soda and the flour together then stir into the mixture that was creamed. Fold the cherries mixture in gently, with the macadamia nuts, semi-sweet chocolate, white chocolate and liqueur. The batter will become creamy and soft.
3. By tbsps., drop the cookie dough onto prepped cookie sheet, 2 to 3 inches of space between cookie sheet. Bake it in the preheated oven for 12 to 13 minutes. The cookies should turn lightly browned. Transfer to wire racks from baking sheets; allow to cool.

Nutrition Information

Calories: 394 calories; Total Carbohydrate: 49.3 g Cholesterol: 38 mg Total Fat: 18.2 g Protein: 4.5 g Sodium: 74 mg

Cherry Kisses

Serving: 6 dozen. | Prep: 10m | Ready in: 30m

Ingredients
- 4 large egg whites
- 1-1/4 cups sugar
- 1/3 cup chopped walnuts
- 1/3 cup chopped pitted dates
- 1/3 cup chopped candied cherries

Direction

1. Put egg whites in big bowl; stand for 30 minutes at room temperature. Beat till soft peaks form on medium speed. 1 tbsp. at a time, beat in sugar slowly on high till sugar melts and stiff glossy peaks form; fold cherries, dates and walnuts in.
2. Drop on lightly greased baking sheets, 2-in. apart, by teaspoonfuls. Bake for 20-30 minutes till firm to touch at 300°. Cool for 1 minute; remove onto wire rack. Keep in airtight container.

Nutrition Information

Calories: 45 calories Total Carbohydrate: 10 g Cholesterol: 0 mg Total Fat: 1 g Fiber: 0 g Protein: 1 g Sodium: 7 mg

Cherry-nut Brownie Bars

Serving: about 2 dozen. | Prep: 30m | Ready in: 01h05m

Ingredients
- 3 cups all-purpose flour
- 2 cups sugar

- 1 cup baking cocoa
- 1/2 tsp. baking powder
- 1/2 tsp. baking soda
- 1/2 tsp. salt
- 2 eggs
- 1 cup butter, melted
- 3 tsps. vanilla extract
- 1 can (21 oz.) cherry pie filling
- 1 cup chopped walnuts
- 1/2 cup vanilla or white chips
- 1 tbsp. milk

Direction
1. Whisk together the first 6 ingredients in a big bowl. Beat vanilla, butter and eggs in a separate bowl; pour into dry ingredients. Beat until thoroughly combined (mixture will have thick consistency).
2. For topping, reserve one cup of dough. Grease a 13x9-inch baking dish and press in remaining dough. Layer pie filling evenly on top. Crumble saved dough and sprinkle on top; scatter with walnuts.
3. Bake in 350-degree oven until nuts turn golden brown and the cake's surface is dry, about 35 to 40 minutes. Place on a wire rack until fully cool.
4. Microwave milks and vanilla chip at 70% power until melted; whisk till smooth. Continue to heat in the microwave at extra 10-20 second intervals while stirring until the mixture is smooth. Spread onto the bars.

Nutrition Information
Calories: 285 calories Total Carbohydrate: 40 g Cholesterol: 39 mg Total Fat: 13 g Fiber: 1 g Protein: 4 g Sodium: 175 mg

Chocolate Dipped Bing Cherries
Serving: 24 | Prep: 2h | Ready in: 2h

Ingredients
- 1 cup white sugar
- 1 1/2 tsps. vanilla extract
- 8 oz. semisweet chocolate, chopped
- 24 Bing cherries with stems

Direction
1. In a shallow dish and pour sugar. Form lumps in the sugar by dropping two drops of vanilla at a time into the dish in 24 different places. Put it on one side and let lumps harden.
2. Using a dental tool, carefully pit cherries from the bottom and make sure the stems are still attached.
3. Insert hardened lumps of sugar into the cherries where the pits were. Put on one side. Microwave chocolate and mix in 30-second intervals until melted and smooth.
4. Coat cherries with melted chocolate by dipping cherries while holding by the stem. Leave the top of cherry uncoated. Transfer to waxed paper and let them dry. Keep in refrigerator overnight to allow sugar lumps to melt. Serve.

Nutrition Information
Calories: 85 calories; Total Carbohydrate: 14.8 g Cholesterol: 0 mg Total Fat: 3.1 g Protein: 0.7 g

Sodium: < 1 mg

Chocolate Marshmallow Meltaways

Serving: 3 dozen. | Prep: 20m | Ready in: 30m

Ingredients

- 1/2 cup butter-flavored shortening
- 3/4 cup sugar
- 1 egg
- 1/4 cup 2% milk
- 1 tsp. vanilla extract
- 1-3/4 cups all-purpose flour
- 1/2 cup baking cocoa
- 1/2 tsp. salt
- 1/2 tsp. baking soda
- 18 large marshmallows, halved

FROSTING:

- 3 tbsps. butter, softened
- 3 cups confectioners' sugar
- 3 tbsps. baking cocoa
- 1/8 tsp. salt
- 4 to 6 tbsps. 2% milk

Direction

1. Cream sugar and shortening in a large bowl until fluffy and light. Mix in vanilla, milk and egg. Mix the baking soda, salt, cocoa and flour; gently add to the creamed mixture and combine well.
2. Into ungreased baking sheets, drop by tablespoonfuls 2-inch apart. Place in the oven and bake for 8 minutes at 350°F. Press down a marshmallow half, cut side down, onto each cookie; bake for 2 more minutes. Take out to wire racks to cool.
3. Beat salt, cocoa, confectioner's sugar and butter in a small bowl until smooth. Mix in enough milk to reach a spreading consistency. Then frost cookies.

Nutrition Information

Calories: 261 calories Total Carbohydrate: 46 g Cholesterol: 18 mg Total Fat: 8 g Fiber: 1 g Protein: 3 g Sodium: 147 mg

Chocolate Mint Truffle Tart

Serving: 16 servings. | Prep: 25m | Ready in: 50m

Ingredients

- 2 cups cream-filled chocolate sandwich cookie crumbs
- 3/4 cup softened butter, divided
- 1 package (10 oz.) mint chocolate chips
- 1/2 cup sugar
- 2 tsps. vanilla extract
- 1 cup heavy whipping cream
- 3 eggs, lightly beaten
- Fresh raspberries, optional
- Fresh mint leaves, optional

- Coarsely chopped dark chocolate candy bar, optional

Direction

1. Set oven to 350 degrees and start preheating. Mix together 1/4 cup of butter and cookie crumbs; in an ungreased 9 inches tart pan, press the mixture onto the bottom and up sides. Let it chill for 15 mins.
2. In the meantime, in a food processor, blend vanilla, sugar and chips until chips are chopped. Cook the rest of butter and cream in a small heavy saucepan over medium heat until bubbly around the pan's sides. Blend the chips another time and pour cream mixture on top of chocolate while processing. Mix a little chocolate mixture into eggs then pour all back into the food processor; blend until smooth.
3. Transfer to the crust. Bake for 25 to 30 minutes until set in the middle (mixture will be jiggly). Place on a wire rack to cool entirely. Place chopped dark chocolate, fresh mint leaves and fresh raspberries on top (optional). Let it chill in the refrigerator.

Nutrition Information

Calories: 343 calories Total Carbohydrate: 31 g Cholesterol: 83 mg Total Fat: 24 g Fiber: 2 g Protein: 4 g Sodium: 174 mg

Chocolate Mousse Cake II

Serving: 12

Ingredients
- 1 1/2 cups all-purpose flour
- 1 cup white sugar
- 1/4 cup unsweetened cocoa powder
- 1/4 tsp. salt
- 1 cup hot, brewed coffee
- 1/3 cup vegetable oil
- 1 tbsp. vanilla extract
- 1 egg
- 16 (1 oz.) squares semisweet chocolate
- 1/2 cup unsalted butter
- 1/4 tsp. salt
- 2 tsps. vanilla extract
- 8 egg yolks
- 8 egg whites
- 4 tbsps. white sugar
- 1 1/2 cups heavy whipping cream
- 4 (1 oz.) squares semisweet chocolate
- 1/4 cup heavy whipping cream
- 1/2 cup chopped walnuts

Direction

1. Preheat an oven to 175°C/350°F. Grease then flour/use parchment paper liner on 9-in. springform pan.
2. Mix 1/4 tsp. salt, cocoa, 1 cup sugar and flour in big bowl; create a well in the middle. Add egg, 1 tbsp. vanilla, oil and coffee; beat till combined, the batter will be thin.
3. Put in springform pan; bake for 30-45 minutes at 175°C/350°F till an inserted toothpick in cake

exits clean. Remove from pan when cake is completely cool; use knife to cut top of cake level. Put back in springform pan.
4. Mousse: Melt 1/2 cup butter and 16-oz. chocolate above double boiler; mix 2 tsp. vanilla and 1/4 tsp. salt in. Whisk yolks in. Beat whites till foamy in another bowl; add sugar slowly, beating till stiff. Fold into chocolate mixture. Whisk 1 1/2 cup cream in another bowl; fold into chocolate mixture. Put on leveled cake in the springform pan; set for 1-2 days.
5. Chocolate ganache: Chop 4-oz. semisweet chocolate. Heat 1/4 cup cream and chocolate, occasionally mixing, in top of double boiler till smooth and melted. When cake sets completely, remove from pan; drizzle ganache on top. Press chopped nuts gently into mousse's sides with your hand.

Nutrition Information

Calories: 706 calories; Total Carbohydrate: 62.9 g Cholesterol: 220 mg Total Fat: 48.6 g Protein: 11.6 g Sodium: 161 mg

Chocolate Nut Bark

Serving: 36 | Ready in: 35m

Ingredients

- 2 cups semisweet, bittersweet or milk chocolate chips, melted (see Tip)
- 1½ cups assorted nuts, such as hazelnuts, almonds and cashews, plus more for garnish

Direction

1. Line foil onto a rimmed baking sheet. (Ensure to prevent wrinkles.) In a medium bowl, mix nuts and melted chocolate. Transfer the mixture onto the foil and then spread it to form an approximately 12-by-9-inch rectangle. If desired, sprinkle with more finely chopped nuts. Chill for about 20 minutes until set.
2. Place the bark and foil onto a cutting board. Chop into 1 1/2-inch pieces with a sharp knife.

Nutrition Information

Calories: 74 calories; Total Carbohydrate: 7 g Cholesterol: 0 mg Total Fat: 5 g Fiber: 1 g Protein: 1 g Sodium: 1 mg Sugar: 5 g Saturated Fat: 2 g

Chocolate Rum Fondue

Serving: 1-1/2 cups. | Prep: 5m | Ready in: 10m

Ingredients

- 3 milk chocolate Toblerone candy bars (3.52 oz. each), coarsely chopped
- 2/3 cup heavy whipping cream
- 4 tsps. rum or 1/2 tsp. rum extract
- Pear slices, cubed cake, large marshmallows and/or macaroon cookies

Direction

1. Combine the cream and candy bars in a small, hefty cooking pan. Cook on medium-low heat, stirring until it has blended. Turn off the heat then add the rum, stirring it in.
2. Pour the sauce in a small fondue pot and keep it warm. This can be served and partnered with any of your preferred dippers.

Nutrition Information

Calories: 358 calories Total Carbohydrate: 33 g Cholesterol: 46 mg Total Fat: 23 g Fiber: 1 g Protein: 4 g Sodium: 35 mg

Chocolate Velvet Pudding

Serving: 4 | Ready in: 20m

Ingredients

- 1 large egg
- ⅓ cup nonfat sweetened condensed milk
- ¼ cup unsweetened cocoa powder
- 2 tbsps. cornstarch
- ⅛ tsp. salt
- 2 cups low-fat milk
- 1 oz. bittersweet or semisweet (not unsweetened) chocolate, chopped
- 2 tsps. vanilla extract

Direction

1. In a heavy saucepan, whisk together salt, cornstarch, cocoa, condensed milk and egg until smooth. Whisk in milk gradually, then bring to a boil on moderately low heat for 7-9 minutes while whisking continuously, until thicken.
2. Take away from the heat, then put in vanilla and chocolate while whisking until chocolate melts. Remove to a bowl, then put plastic wrap right on the surface to keep a skin from forming. Serve warm or chill until serving.

Nutrition Information

Calories: 192 calories; Total Carbohydrate: 30 g Cholesterol: 56 mg Total Fat: 5 g Fiber: 3 g Protein: 9 g Sodium: 172 mg Sugar: 26 g Saturated Fat: 3 g

Chocolate-cherry Sandwich Cookies

Serving: 3-1/2 dozen. | Prep: 35m | Ready in: 35m

Ingredients

- 4 oz. cream cheese, softened
- 1/2 cup confectioners' sugar
- 1/2 cup finely chopped maraschino cherries, drained
- 1/4 tsp. almond extract
- 1 package (12 oz.) vanilla wafers
- 18 oz. milk chocolate candy coating, melted
- Red nonpareils or red colored sugar

Direction

1. Beat confectioners' sugar and cream cheese until it becomes smooth in a small bowl. Mix in extract and cherries. Spread a tsp. of cream cheese mixture on half of the wafers' bottoms. Use leftover wafers to cover. Put in the refrigerator until filling is firm or for an hour.
2. Immerse the sandwiches in the candy coating. Let the excess drip off the sandwich. Put on waxed paper and use nonpareils to sprinkle. Let rest until set. Keep in the refrigerator in an airtight container.

Cranberry-kissed Chocolate Silk

Serving: 6 servings. | Prep: 20m | Ready in: 25m

Ingredients

- 1 cup cranberry juice
- 1/8 tsp. salt
- 4 large eggs, beaten
- 1 cup milk chocolate chips
- 1 cup semisweet chocolate chips
- 1 tsp. vanilla extract
- 1 cup fresh or frozen cranberries, thawed
- 1/3 cup sugar
- 3/4 cup sweetened whipped cream
- 3 tbsps. sliced almonds, toasted

Direction

1. In a small heavy saucepan, add salt and cranberry juice, then bring to just a boil. Take away from the heat. Whisk into eggs gradually with hot juice in a small bowl, then turn all back to the pan. Cook on low heat until a thermometer reaches 170 degrees and the mixture thickens, stirring continuously, about 2 to 3 minutes.
2. In a blender, add vanilla, chocolate chips and egg mixture, then allow to stand about 2 minutes. Place a cover and process mixture until smooth, then transfer into 6 dessert dishes. Chill for a minimum of 4 hours and place a cover once cooled fully.
3. In a small food processor, add cranberries and process until chopped finely. Remove to a small bowl and toss together with sugar. Put almonds, whipped cream and cranberries on top of each serving.

Nutrition Information

Calories: 473 calories Total Carbohydrate: 54 g Cholesterol: 151 mg Total Fat: 27 g Fiber: 4 g Protein: 9 g Sodium: 129 mg

Cream Cheese Bonbons

Serving: 1-1/2 dozen. | Prep: 20m | Ready in: 20m

Ingredients
- 1 package (8 oz.) reduced-fat cream cheese
- Sugar substitute equivalent to 1/3 cup sugar
- 1 tbsp. sugar
- 1/2 tsp. vanilla extract
- 1 cup sweetened shredded coconut
- 1 oz. unsweetened chocolate, grated

Direction

1. Beat together vanilla, sugar, sugar substitute and cream cheese in a small bowl until smooth. Stir in coconut and chill until easy to handle, about half an hour.
2. Form into 1-in. balls and roll them into grated chocolate. Chill for a minimum of an hour, then keep in a tightly sealed container in the fridge.

Nutrition Information

Calories: 73 calories Total Carbohydrate: 5 g Cholesterol: 10 mg Total Fat: 6 g Fiber: 0 g Protein: 2 g Sodium: 64 mg

Creamy Soft Caramels

Serving: 2-1/2 lbs.. | Prep: 20m | Ready in: 45m

Ingredients

- 1 tsp. plus 1 cup butter, divided
- 1-1/4 cups packed brown sugar
- 1 cup sugar
- Dash salt
- 1 cup light corn syrup
- 1 can (14 oz.) sweetened condensed milk
- 1 tsp. vanilla extract

Direction

1. Line foil on a pan of 9 inches square; use a tsp. butter to grease the foil; put aside. Mix together remaining butter, salt and sugars in a big saucepan. Put over medium heat and boil while stirring continuously. Whisk in corn syrup and boil again. Take away from the heat; gradually whisk in milk. Put on medium-low heat, cook while stirring until the mixture achieves soft-ball stage, 238 degrees on a candy thermometer. Take away from the heat and mix in vanilla. Transfer to the prepped pan. Allow to cool. Take the candy out by lifting the foil; slice into squares of an inch. Use waxed paper to wrap each piece separately.

Nutrition Information

Calories: 70 calories Total Carbohydrate: 12 g Cholesterol: 8 mg Total Fat: 3 g Fiber: 0 g Protein: 0 g Sodium: 28 mg

Double Chocolate Chipotle Cookies

Serving: 1-1/2 dozen. | Prep: 25m | Ready in: 35m

Ingredients

- 2/3 cup butter, softened
- 1/2 cup sugar
- 1/2 cup packed brown sugar
- 1 egg
- 1 tsp. vanilla extract
- 1/2 tsp. minced chipotle pepper in adobo sauce
- 1 cup plus 2 tbsps. all-purpose flour
- 1/3 cup baking cocoa
- 1 tsp. ground cinnamon
- 1/2 tsp. salt
- 1/2 tsp. baking soda
- 1/4 tsp. cayenne pepper
- 3 milk chocolate candy bars (1.55 oz. each), chopped
- Confectioners' sugar

Direction

1. Cream sugars and butter till fluffy and light in big bowl; beat chipotle pepper, vanilla and egg in. Mix cayenne, baking soda, salt, cinnamon, cocoa and flour; add to creamed mixture slowly. Stir well; mix chopped candy in. Chill till easy to handle, 1 hour.
2. Preheat an oven to 350°; roll to 1 1/2-in. balls. Put on ungreased baking sheets, 4-in. apart. Bake till set, about 10-12 minutes; cool for 4 minutes. Transfer from pans onto wire racks; dust confectioners' sugar over.

Nutrition Information
Calories: 179 calories Total Carbohydrate: 23 g Cholesterol: 31 mg Total Fat: 9 g Fiber: 1 g Protein: 2 g
Sodium: 161 mg

Drop Sugar Cookies

Serving: about 3-1/2 dozen. | Prep: 15m | Ready in: 25m

Ingredients
- 2 eggs
- 3/4 cup sugar
- 2/3 cup vegetable oil
- 2 tsps. vanilla extract
- 1 tsp. grated lemon peel
- 2 cups all-purpose flour
- 2 tsps. baking powder
- 1/2 tsp. salt
- Additional sugar or colored sugar

Direction
1. Whisk together eggs, lemon peel, vanilla, oil and sugar in a large mixing bowl until incorporated. Mix salt, baking powder, and flour together; slowly mix into egg mixture.
2. Drop batter onto greased baking sheets by rounded teaspoonfuls, separating them 2 inches apart. Press down cookies using a glass dipped in sugar. Bake cookies for 8 to 10 minutes at 350° until edges turn brown lightly. Allow to cool on the baking sheets for 1 to 2 minutes before transferring to wire racks to cool entirely.

Nutrition Information
Calories: 140 calories Total Carbohydrate: 16 g Cholesterol: 20 mg Total Fat: 8 g Fiber: 0 g Protein: 2 g
Sodium: 101 mg

Elegant White Chocolate Mousse

Serving: 8 servings. | Prep: 15m | Ready in: 20m

Ingredients
- 12 oz. white baking chocolate, coarsely chopped
- 2 cups heavy whipping cream, divided
- 1 tbsp. confectioners' sugar
- 1 tsp. vanilla extract

Direction
1. Mix and cook 2/3 cup cream and chocolate in small heavy saucepan on medium low heat till smooth. Put in big bowl; cool down to room temperature.
2. Beat leftover cream till it starts to thicken in small bowl. Add vanilla and confectioners' sugar; beat till soft peaks form. Fold 1/4 cup whipped cream into chocolate mixture; fold leftover whipped cream in.
3. Put in dessert dishes; refrigerate for 2 hours minimum, covered.

Nutrition Information
Calories: 230 calories Total Carbohydrate: 5 g Cholesterol: 82 mg Total Fat: 23 g Fiber: 0 g Protein: 1 g
Sodium: 26 mg

Emily's Famous Tiramisu

Serving: 12 | Prep: 45m | Ready in: 5h

Ingredients
LADYFINGERS
* 5 eggs, separated
* 3/4 cup white sugar, divided
* 1 cup all-purpose flour
* 1 tsp. vanilla extract
* 3/4 cup confectioners' sugar for dusting

SYRUP
* 1 cup white sugar
* 1 cup boiling water
* 1/2 cup strong brewed coffee
* 1/4 cup rum

FILLING
* 1 (8 oz.) container mascarpone cheese
* 2 cups confectioners' sugar
* 1/4 cup dark rum
* 1 tsp. vanilla extract
* 2 cups heavy cream

TOPPING
* 2 (1 oz.) squares semisweet chocolate, grated
* 1/8 cup confectioners' sugar for dusting

Direction
1. Oven should be preheated to 350° F (175° C) and line the baking sheets with parchment paper.
2. Using an electric mixer, beat the egg yolks and 1/4 cup of sugar in medium bowl until it becomes thick and pale. Beat the egg whites using clean beaters in a separate bowl until it forms soft peaks. Sprinkle the remaining 1/2 cup sugar portion by portion while beating continuously. Once medium stiff peaks form, fold into the egg whites the egg yolk mixture. Fold in the flour and 1 tsp. of vanilla gradually. The batter needs to be pale yellow and thick.
3. Using a cake pan as a guide, trace two 9-inch circles on the parchment paper. Pipe the batter or spread it to fill the inside lines of the circles completely. The batter should be 1/2 inch thick or tall.
4. Fill up a pastry bag fitted with a half inch tip or hole with the remaining batter. Using another parchment paper, draw parallel lines onto it which are 3 inches apart. Pipe the batter just between the lines, back and forth in a tight S motion, until you have no more batter left. This part is for the outside of the cake where it would be wrapped around. (It's helpful for it to be in one piece but if you choose to, you can also pipe individual fingers by using the guidelines that was drawn on the parchment paper). There might be some extra.
5. Bake for 10 to 15 minutes in the preheated oven until it's just firm, not browned. Take it out of the oven and drizzle with confectioner's sugar generously. Leave it to cool.
6. For the syrup, mix and stir 1 cup sugar, coffee, 1/4 cup rum and boiling water until the sugar has completely dissolved then set it aside.
7. To make the filling, put together in a large bowl the mascarpone, dark rum, 1 tsp. vanilla, and 2 cups confectioners' sugar. Beat the mixture until it's completely smooth. Scrape the bottom of the bowl to

make sure any lumps are removed. Mix in the heavy cream portion by portion. Beat using an electric mixer until it forms soft peaks. When the mixture is showing the first sign of graininess, stop beating.

8. To put everything together, use a waxed or parchment paper and line the sides of a 9-inch springform pan with it. In the bottom of the pan, put one of the lady finger rounds and brush it with syrup generously, making sure not to soak it. To completely cover the sides, place around the inside edge of the pan the 3-inch high strips of ladyfingers and brush it generously with syrup.

9. Cover the first lady finger round in the pan with half of the filling mixture by spreading it over. On top of the filling, put the remaining round of ladyfinger. Completely soak with syrup the ladyfinger round until it can't take any more of it. Use the remaining filling and spread it over that. Smoothen the top and drizzle with grated chocolate. Keep it refrigerated for at least 4 hours.

10. Once ready to serve, take out the sides of the pan and gently peel off the waxed or parchment paper from the outside of the cake. Sprinkle with confectioners' sugar and serve!

Nutrition Information
Calories: 558 calories; Total Carbohydrate: 70.2 g Cholesterol: 155 mg Total Fat: 27 g Protein: 6.2 g Sodium: 56 mg

Homemade Valentine's Chocolates
Serving: 32 | Prep: 15m | Ready in: 50m

Ingredients
- 1/2 lb. high-quality dark chocolate, chopped
- 1/8 tsp. ground dried chipotle pepper
- 1 pinch salt
- 1/2 cup heavy whipping cream
- 3 tbsps. unsweetened cocoa powder, or as needed

Direction
1. Put chocolate in bowl; add salt and chipotle pepper.
2. Heat cream in small saucepan on medium low heat till it reaches a boil. Put cream on chocolate; let stand for 3 minutes.
3. Gently mix till chocolate mixture is fully smooth. Put chocolate mixture out on plastic wrap sheet on work surface. Pick up a plastic edge; roll chocolate to a rough log shape. Keep rolling and wrapping chocolate in plastic. Refrigerate for 30-60 minutes till firm and chilled.
4. Put cocoa in small bowl. Unwrap chocolate; cut in half crosswise. Lengthwise, slice each half to halves. Cut candy to 1/2-in. square "stones" roughly. Put chocolate pieces in cocoa; gently toss to coat.

Nutrition Information
Calories: 48 calories; Total Carbohydrate: 4.9 g Cholesterol: 5 mg Total Fat: 3.6 g Protein: 0.5 g Sodium: 2 mg

Little French Fudge Cakes
Serving: 6 | Prep: 15m | Ready in: 40m

Ingredients
- 1 (4 oz.) bittersweet chocolate bar, chopped
- 1 1/2 (1 oz.) squares unsweetened chocolate, chopped
- 5 tbsps. unsalted butter

- 1 tsp. ground cinnamon
- 1 1/2 tsps. vanilla extract
- 2 eggs
- 1 egg yolk
- 3/4 cup white sugar
- 1/8 tsp. salt
- 3 tbsps. organic all-purpose flour
- 1/2 (4 oz.) bittersweet chocolate bar, broken into 1/2-inch pieces

Direction

1. Preheat the oven to 190 degrees C (375 degrees F). Grease 6 cupcake cups in the dark-colored metal pan for better result.
2. Put butter, unsweetened chocolate and 1 chopped bar of the bittersweet chocolate into the microwave-safe bowl; put the bowl into the microwave and cook on the low power for 2-3 minutes or till chocolate softens and butter melts. Check and whisk frequently to prevent chocolate from burning. Whisk till smooth.
3. In the mixing bowl, stir the salt, sugar, egg yolk, eggs, vanilla extract, and cinnamon till combined thoroughly, and whisk in flour just till blended. Stir in chocolate mixture, whisk batter several times till smooth, and gently stir in half bar of the bittersweet chocolate broken into half-an-in. pieces. Scoop the batter to prepped cupcake cups, filling them to roughly three-fourth full.
4. Bake in preheated oven for roughly 18 minutes or till the knife inserted in the middle of the cake runs out with the streaks of the thick batter. Cakes' tops should be nearly firmed. Let cool down in pan on the rack for 5-10 minutes to serve while warm, or for 20 minutes to serve at the room temperature.

Nutrition Information

Calories: 427 calories; Total Carbohydrate: 47 g Cholesterol: 123 mg Total Fat: 25.3 g Protein: 5.9 g Sodium: 78 mg

Maple Creme Brulee

Serving: 3 servings. | Prep: 20m | Ready in: 02h20m

Ingredients

- 1-1/3 cups heavy whipping cream
- 3 large egg yolks
- 1/2 cup packed brown sugar
- 1/4 tsp. ground cinnamon
- 1/2 tsp. maple flavoring

TOPPING:

- 1-1/2 tsps. sugar
- 1-1/2 tsps. brown sugar

Direction

1. Heat cream in a small saucepan until bubbles appear around sides of pan. Beat the cinnamon, brown sugar and egg yolks in a small bowl. Take off cream from the heat; mix a bit of hot cream into egg mixture. Put all back to the pan, mixing continuously. Mix in maple flavoring.
2. Distribute to three 6-oz. custard cups or ramekins. Put in a 6-quart slow cooker; pour 1 in. of boiling water to slow cooker. Cook on high, covered, for 2 to 2-1/2 hours or until centers are just firm (mixture will be jiggly). Take out ramekins from slow cooker carefully; let cool for 10 minutes.

Chill, covered, for no less than 4 hours.

3. To make topping, mix sugars and dust over ramekins. Keep a kitchen torch about 2 in. above custard surface; spin slowly until sugar is caramelized evenly. Serve right away.
4. Preheat broiler and put ramekins on a baking tray if broiling the custard; let sit for 15 mins at room temperature. Broil 8 inches from heat for 3 to 5 mins until sugar caramelized. Chill for 1-2 hours until set.

Nutrition Information

Calories: 578 calories Total Carbohydrate: 44 g Cholesterol: 350 mg Total Fat: 44 g Fiber: 0 g Protein: 5 g Sodium: 63 mg

Maraschino Party Cake

Serving: 12 servings. | Prep: 20m | Ready in: 50m

Ingredients
- 1/2 cup shortening
- 1-1/3 cups sugar
- 4 large egg whites
- 1/4 cup maraschino cherry juice
- 2-1/4 cups all-purpose flour
- 3 tsps. baking powder
- 1 tsp. salt
- 1/2 cup whole milk
- 16 maraschino cherries, chopped
- 1/2 cup chopped nuts

FROSTING:
- 1-1/2 cups sugar
- 2 large egg whites
- 1/3 cup water
- 1/3 cup corn syrup
- 1/4 tsp. cream of tartar
- 1 tsp. vanilla extract
- Additional maraschino cherries, optional

Direction

1. Cream sugar and shortening in a big bowl until fluffy and light. Beat in cherry juice and egg whites. Mix together salt, baking powder and flour, then put into the creamed mixture alternating with milk, while beating well between additions. Stir in nuts and cherries.
2. Put batter into 2 9-inch round baking pans coated with grease and flour. Bake at 350 degrees until a toothpick exits clean after being inserted into the center, about 30 to 35 minutes. Allow to cool about 10 minutes prior to transferring from pans to wire racks to cool through.
3. To make frosting, mix together in a heavy saucepan on low heat or a double boiler set over simmering water with cream of tartar, corn syrup, water, egg whites and sugar. Beat the mixture using a portable mixer on low speed for a minute. Keep on beating at low speed on low heat for 8 to 10 minutes, until frosting achieves 160 degrees.
4. Transfer into the bowl of a heavy-duty stand mixer, then put in vanilla. Beat on high speed for 7 minutes, until stiff peaks create. Spread between layers and over top and sides of cake. Use cherries to decorate if wanted.

Nutrition Information

Calories: 431 calories Total Carbohydrate: 78 g Cholesterol: 1 mg Total Fat: 12 g Fiber: 1 g Protein: 6 g Sodium: 342 mg

Marbled Chocolate-covered Strawberries

Serving: 24 | Prep: 20m | Ready in: 37m

Ingredients

- 12 oz. pink candy melts (such as Wilton)
- 6 oz. white candy melts (such as Wilton)
- 6 oz. orange candy melts (such as Wilton)
- 24 fresh strawberries

Direction

1. Line a baking sheet with waxed paper.
2. In separate microwave-safe bowls, add orange, white, and pink candy melts. Microwave for 1 minute at 50% power. Stir completely. Continue microwaving and stirring in 30-second intervals until thoroughly melted and smooth.
3. Use a whisk or spoon to drizzle a few tbsps. of orange and white onto the pink base color, but don't stir.
4. Dip 1 strawberry completely into the pink base, turn and twist when lifting them up to make a marbled pattern. Let the excess candy coating drip off. Place strawberry on the lined baking sheet. Drizzle more orange and white on the pink base. Repeat with the rest of the strawberries. Place dipped strawberries into the refrigerator until they harden, for no less than 15 minutes.

Nutrition Information

Calories: 157 calories; Total Carbohydrate: 18 g Cholesterol: 6 mg Total Fat: 9 g Protein: 1.8 g Sodium: 25 mg

Orange Chocolate Mousse Mirror Cake

Serving: 16 servings. | Prep: 45m | Ready in: 45m

Ingredients

- 2 cups crushed Oreo cookies (about 20 cookies)
- 1 tsp. grated orange zest
- 1/4 cup butter, melted

FILLING:

- 1 envelope unflavored gelatin
- 6 tbsps. orange juice
- 8 oz. semisweet chocolate, chopped
- 2-1/2 cups heavy whipping cream, divided
- 3 packages (8 oz. each) cream cheese, softened
- 3/4 cup sugar
- 1/4 cup dark baking cocoa
- 1 tbsp. grated orange zest

GLAZE:

- 1 envelope unflavored gelatin
- 1/2 cup plus 1 tsp. water, divided

- 3/4 cup sugar
- 1/3 cup sweetened condensed milk
- 1 cup white baking chips
- Orange paste food coloring

Direction

1. Mix butter, orange zest and crushed cookies; press on bottom of 9-in. greased springform pan. Put aside.
2. Sprinkle gelatin on orange juice in small saucepan; stand for a minute. Mix on low heat till gelatin melts; put aside.
3. Filling: Melt 1/2 cup cream and chocolate in microwave; mix till smooth. Slightly cool; mix melted gelatin in. Beat cocoa, sugar and cream cheese till smooth in big bowl. Add orange zest and chocolate mixture slowly; stir well. Beat leftover cream till stiff peaks form in another bowl; fold into cream cheese mixture gently. Put on crust with spoon; refrigerate for 4 hours till set, covered. Freeze overnight, covered.
4. Glaze: In small bowl, sprinkle gelatin on 1/4 cup water; put aside. It will solidify. Meanwhile, simmer leftover water, milk and sugar, occasionally mixing, in small saucepan on medium heat. Take off heat; mix gelatin mixture in till melted. Add baking chips; use whisk to mix till melted. Mix food coloring in; stir well. Cool glaze, occasionally mixing, for 40 minutes till it reaches 90°.
5. Put cake on 9-in. inverted pie plate in 15x10x1-in. foil-lined pan. Remove springform's sides; put cooled glaze on frozen cake. Let excess drip off. Set glaze for 15 minutes; remove drips from cake's bottom edge. Before serving, refrigerate for 2 hours.

Nutrition Information

Calories: 610 calories Total Carbohydrate: 47 g Cholesterol: 97 mg Total Fat: 43 g Fiber: 1 g Protein: 7 g Sodium: 244 mg

Pecan Toffee Fudge

Serving: 2-1/2 lbs.. | Prep: 20m | Ready in: 20m

Ingredients

- 1 tsp. butter
- 1 package (8 oz.) cream cheese, softened
- 3-3/4 cups confectioners' sugar
- 6 oz. unsweetened chocolate, melted and cooled
- 1/4 tsp. almond extract
- Dash salt
- 1/4 cup coarsely chopped pecans
- 1/4 cup English toffee bits

Direction

1. Line a 9-in. square pan using foil and butter the foil; put aside. Whip cream cheese in a big bowl until fluffy. Whip in confectioners' sugar slowly. Whip in the salt, extract and melted chocolate until smooth. Mix in toffee bits and pecans.
2. Lather over lined and greased pan. Cover and chill overnight or until set. Lift fudge out of pan with foil. Carefully peel off foil; slice fudge into 1-inch squares. Put in an airtight container to store in the fridge.

Nutrition Information

Calories: 49 calories Total Carbohydrate: 7 g Cholesterol: 3 mg Total Fat: 3 g Fiber: 0 g Protein: 1 g Sodium: 15 mg

Pistachio Chocolate Macarons

Serving: about 1-1/2 dozen. | Prep: 35m | Ready in: 45m

Ingredients

- 3 large egg whites
- 1-1/4 cups confectioners' sugar
- 3/4 cup pistachios
- Dash salt
- 1/4 cup granulated sugar

CHOCOLATE FILLING:

- 4 oz. bittersweet chocolate, chopped
- 1/2 cup heavy whipping cream
- 2 tsps. corn syrup
- 1 tbsp. butter

Direction

1. Allow egg whites to rest for 30 minutes at room temperature. In a food processor, pulse pistachios and confectioners' sugar until powdery.
2. Heat the oven beforehand to 350 degrees. Put salt in the egg whites then beat until get soft peaks formed on medium speed. Put sugar in gradually, 1 tbsp. at a time. Stir on high until stiff peaks formed; fold in pistachio mixture.
3. Slice a mall hole in a corner of a food-safe plastic bag or in the tip of a pastry bag then insert a star tip. Put pistachio mixture in the bag then pipe 1-inch- diameter cookies on baking sheets lined with parchment paper, leaving 1-inch space apart. Bake for 10 to 12 minutes until firm to the touch and lightly browned. Allow to cool completely on pans on wire racks.
4. Put the chocolate in a small bowl. Let corn syrup and cream boil in a small saucepan then pour on chocolate. Whisk till smooth. Whisk in butter then allow to cool at room temperature, occasionally stirring, or for about 45 minutes until filling reaches a spreading consistency. Pour over the bottoms of half of the cookies then cover using the leftover cookies.

Nutrition Information

Calories: 160 calories Total Carbohydrate: 16 g Cholesterol: 10 mg Total Fat: 9 g Fiber: 1 g Protein: 3 g Sodium: 135 mg

Pumpkin Pudding Desserts

Serving: 2 servings. | Prep: 10m | Ready in: 10m

Ingredients

- 3/4 cup canned pumpkin
- 1/2 tsp. ground cinnamon
- 1/4 tsp. ground ginger
- 3/4 cup cold 2% milk
- 1 package (3.3 oz.) instant white chocolate pudding mix
- 1/4 cup whipped topping

Direction

1. Beat ginger, cinnamon, and pumpkin together in a small bowl. Add pudding mix and milk, beat for 2

minute (the mixture should be thick).

2. Remove into separate serving plates. Chill until eating. Use whipped topping to garnish each serving.

Nutrition Information

Calories: 279 calories Total Carbohydrate: 57 g Cholesterol: 7 mg Total Fat: 4 g Fiber: 4 g Protein: 5 g Sodium: 724 mg

Red Wine Chocolate Lava Cakes

Serving: 6 | Prep: 15m | Ready in: 30m

Ingredients

- 4 oz. bittersweet chocolate, coarsely chopped, divided
- 5 tbsps. unsalted butter, divided
- 2 tbsps. red wine, divided
- 2 large eggs
- 1 egg yolk
- 1 tsp. vanilla extract
- ¼ tsp. salt
- 6 tbsps. confectioners' sugar
- 5 tbsps. all-purpose flour
- 1 tbsp. unsweetened Dutch-process cocoa powder

Direction

1. Set the oven to 350 degrees F to preheat. Use cooking spray to coat six cups of a muffin tin.
2. In a big microwavable bowl, add 4 tbsp. of butter and 3 oz. of chocolate, then heat in the microwave on high setting for a minute. Stir and keep on microwaving if necessary, until fully melted while stirring after each 15 seconds. Allow to cool a little bit, then whisk in salt, vanilla, egg yolk, eggs and 1 tbsp. of wine. Sift together cocoa, flour and confectioners' sugar over the batter, whisking until smooth. Split the batter equally between 6 prepped muffin cups with approximately 1/4 cup batter for each.
3. Bake the cakes about 8-10 minutes, until centers still appear gooey and soft while edges are puffed and appear dry. Allow to cool on a wire rack for 2 minutes, until firm. Top pan with a cutting board and invert cakes out on it. If cakes stick, trace a knife around and under them to release.
4. In the meantime, heat in a small microwavable bowl with leftover 1 tbsp. of butter and 1 oz. of chocolate. Microwave on high setting for a minute, then stir and keep on microwaving until melted fully, if necessary, stirring after each 15 seconds. Stir in leftover 1 tbsp. of wine, then remove cakes to serving plates with a thin spatula. Use 1 tsp. of chocolate sauce to drizzle over each cake, then serve warm.

Nutrition Information

Calories: 280 calories; Total Carbohydrate: 23 g Cholesterol: 118 mg Total Fat: 20 g Fiber: 2 g Protein: 5 g Sodium: 124 mg
Sugar: 16 g
Saturated Fat: 11 g

Russian Creme

Serving: 10-12 servings. | Prep: 20m | Ready in: 20m

Ingredients

CREME:

- 1 cup sugar
- 2-1/4 cups water
- 2 envelopes unflavored gelatin
- 1-1/2 cups sour cream
- 1-1/2 tsps. vanilla extract
- 1-1/2 cups heavy whipping cream, whipped

TOPPING:

- 1 package (10 oz.) frozen raspberries
- 1 package (4-3/4 oz.) raspberry-flavored Danish Dessert

Direction

1. Dissolve gelatin and sugar in water on low heat. Take away from the stove; stir in the vanilla and sour cream until it gets smooth. Allow the mixture to chill until lightly thickened (like unbeaten egg whites). Using wire whisk, fold in whipped cream until well combined. Pour into 6-cup ring mold coated with grease; let them chill until set. For topping, strain raspberries, keeping the juice. Following package instructions for pudding, prepare dessert mix, using reserved raspberry juice as part of liquid. Allow the topping to chill; fold in the raspberries. Transfer the molded cream onto the glass serving plate to serve (with minimum of 1 in. bigger than mold). In a small bowl, put the raspberry topping in middle of mold. Guests can serve themselves with a slice of crème pudding and put topping over it using spoon.

Nutrition Information

Calories: 238 calories Total Carbohydrate: 31 g Cholesterol: 40 mg Total Fat: 11 g Fiber: 1 g Protein: 3 g Sodium: 23 mg

Shamrock Toffee Fudge

Serving: about 2-1/4 lbs.. | Prep: 30m | Ready in: 30m

Ingredients

- 1 can (14 oz.) sweetened condensed milk
- 2 cups vanilla or white chips
- 1 cup milk chocolate chips
- 1 tbsp. butter
- Dash salt
- 3/4 cup chocolate-covered English toffee bits
- 1/8 tsp. rum extract
- 1 cup vanilla frosting
- Green food coloring

Direction

1. Using foil, line a 9-in. square pan and grease the foil; put aside. Mix the chips and milk in a big saucepan. Cook and mix on low heat until chips are melted. Put in the salt and butter; mix until smoothened. Take off from the heat; mix in extract and toffee bits. Put into lined and greased pan. Chill for 2 hours, covered, until set.
2. Take fudge out of pan with foil; tear off foil gently. Slice fudge into 1-inch squares. Put the frosting in a small resealable plastic bag; dye with food coloring. Snip a small hole in a corner of bag; pipe a shamrock over each square.

Silky Chocolate Pie

Serving: 8 servings. | Prep: 25m | Ready in: 40m

Ingredients

- Pastry for single-crust pie (9 inches), see below
- 1/3 cup sugar
- 1/4 cup cornstarch
- 2-1/2 cups half-and-half cream
- 4 large egg yolks
- 6 oz. semisweet chocolate, finely chopped
- 3 tbsps. Cognac or brandy
- 1 tsp. vanilla extract

TOPPING:
- 1 cup heavy whipping cream
- 1 tbsp. Cognac or brandy
- 1 tsp. confectioners' sugar
- Baking cocoa

Direction

1. Shape pastry dough to a 1/8-in.-thick flat round on a lightly floured surface; put to a 9-inch pie dish. Cut pastry to 1/2 inch beyond edge of plate; flute edge. Line unpricked pastry with a double thickness of foil. Put in uncooked rice, dried beans or pie weights.
2. Bake for 20 minutes at 400°. Discard foil and weights; bake for 10-12 minutes more or until golden brown. Let cool on a wire rack.
3. Combine cornstarch and sugar in a heavy saucepan. Beat in cream. Cook and mix over medium heat until bubbly and thickened. Take it off the heat. Mix a bit of hot mixture into egg yolks in a small bowl; put all back to the pan, mixing continuously. Cook and mix over low heat for a minute longer. Take it off the heat; mix in the vanilla, chocolate and Cognac until chocolate has melted.
4. Add to a clean bowl; push plastic wrap onto the surface of filling. Let filling cool to room temperature. Scoop into crust. Cover and chill for about 4 hours until cold.
5. To make the topping, whip cream in a small bowl until it starts to thicken. Put in confectioners' sugar and Cognac; whip until soft peaks form. Put evenly on top of pie. Lightly sprinkle with cocoa.

Nutrition Information

Calories: 579 calories Total Carbohydrate: 44 g Cholesterol: 211 mg Total Fat: 39 g Fiber: 2 g Protein: 8 g Sodium: 171 mg

Southern Red Velvet Cake

Serving: 16 | Prep: 20m | Ready in: 2h45m

Ingredients

- 1/2 cup shortening
- 1 1/2 cups white sugar
- 2 eggs
- 1 tsp. vanilla extract
- 1 tsp. butter flavored extract
- 3 tbsps. cocoa powder
- 1/2 oz. red food coloring

- 2 1/2 cups all-purpose flour
- 1 cup buttermilk
- 1 tsp. salt
- 1 tsp. baking soda
- 1 tbsp. distilled white vinegar
- 3 tbsps. all-purpose flour
- 1/2 tsp. salt
- 1 cup milk
- 1/2 cup butter
- 1 cup white sugar
- 1/2 cup shortening
- 2 tsps. vanilla extract
- 2 tsps. butter flavored extract

Direction

1. Start preheating the oven at 350°F (175°C). Grease and dust three 10-inch round pans with flour.
2. Whisk 1 tsp. of butter flavored extract, 1 tsp. of vanilla extract, eggs, 1 1/2 cups of white sugar, and 1/2 cup of shortening in a large bowl. In a small bowl, create a food coloring and cocoa paste and pour into the shortening mixture. Add 2 1/2 cups of flour alternately with the buttermilk, blending until barely combined. Combine vinegar, baking soda, and 1 tsp. of salt in a small bowl, and while bubbling, fold into the batter; blending barely enough to combine evenly. Transfer the batter into the prepared pan.
3. Bake in the prepared oven for 20 to 25 minutes until a toothpick comes out clean when inserted into the center. Let cool in the pans for 10 minutes before transferring to cool fully on a wire rack.
4. For the frosting: Cook milk, 1/2 tsp. of salt, and 3 tbsps. of flour in a skillet on low heat, stirring continually, until thicken. Let cool fully. Beat 1/2 cup of shortening, 1 cup of sugar, and butter in a different bowl. Mix in 2 tsps. each of butter flavored extract, and vanilla extract, and then pour the flour mixture into the bowl and beat together. Frost the cooled cake.

Nutrition Information

Calories: 390 calories; Total Carbohydrate: 49.4 g Cholesterol: 40 mg Total Fat: 19.9 g Protein: 4.2 g Sodium: 369 mg

Strawberry Bavarian Pie

Serving: 10 | Prep: 20m | Ready in: 2h50m

Ingredients

- 3 cups fresh strawberries, plus more for garnish
- ¼ cup sugar
- 1 (.25 oz.) envelope unflavored gelatin
- 3 large egg whites, lightly beaten
- 1 (3 oz.) package ladyfingers, split
- 2 tbsps. orange juice
- ½ (8 oz.) container frozen light whipped dessert topping, thawed (about 1- ⅔ cups), plus more for garnish

Direction

1. Process/blend strawberries, covered, till smooth in a food processor/blender; you should get 1 3/4 cups.

2. Mix gelatin and sugar in a medium saucepan; mix in blended strawberries. Mix and cook on medium heat till gelatin dissolves and it bubbles.

3. Mix 1/2 gelatin mixture into egg whites slowly; put all of it into saucepan. Cook, constantly mixing, on low heat till slightly thick for 2-3 minutes. Don't boil. Put into mixing bowl; chill for 30 minutes, mixing occasionally, for 30 minutes till mixture just mounds when dropped from spoon.

4. Meanwhile, crosswise halve 1/2 of split ladyfingers; stand them on end around outside edge of 9-in. springform pan or 9-9 1/2-in. tart pan with removable bottom. Put leftover split ladyfingers on bottom of pan. Drizzle orange juice on ladyfingers slowly.

5. Into strawberry mixture, fold whipped topping; put into ladyfinger-lined pan. Cover; chill till set for 2 hours in the fridge. Garnish with strawberries and extra whipped topping if desired.

Nutrition Information

Calories: 79 calories; Total Carbohydrate: 12 g Cholesterol: 31 mg Total Fat: 2 g Fiber: 1 g Protein: 3 g Sodium: 31 mg Sugar: 6 g Saturated Fat: 2 g

Strawberry Cheesecake Cupcakes

Serving: 24 servings | Prep: 15m | Ready in: 4h15m

Ingredients

- 2 cups graham cracker crumbs
- 1 cup sugar , divided
- 6 Tbsp. butter , melted
- 2 cups fresh strawberries , divided
- 2 Tbsp. strawberry jam
- 3 pkg. (8 oz. each) PHILADELPHIA Cream Cheese , softened
- 1 pkg. (3 oz.) JELL-O Lemon Flavor Gelatin
- 1 tub (8 oz.) COOL WHIP Whipped Topping , thawed
- 1 Tbsp. lemon zest

Direction

1. Combine together in a bowl the butter, 1/4 cup sugar and graham crumbs and mix well; place onto a 24 paper-lined muffin cups and compress onto bottoms. Place inside the refrigerator until prepared.

2. Slice strawberries enough to measure 1-1/2 cups; put in a medium bowl. Add in jam; lightly stir. Set aside left berries for garnishing later.

3. Whip in a bowl together the left sugar and cream cheese until well combined. Mix in gelatin mix; combine well. Mix in COOL WHIP. Scoop about 1 tbsp. cream cheese mixture on top of every crust. Put chopped strawberry mixture and left cream cheese mixture on top.

4. Place inside the refrigerator for 4 hours or until solid. Use set aside lemon zest and berries to garnish.

Nutrition Information

Calories: 240 Total Carbohydrate: 24 g Cholesterol: 45 mg Total Fat: 15 g Fiber: 1 g Protein: 3 g Sodium: 200 mg Sugar: 18 g Saturated Fat: 9 g

Strawberry Napoleon

Serving: 12 servings. | Prep: 15m | Ready in: 45m

Ingredients

- 1 package (17-1/4 oz.) frozen puff pastry sheets, thawed
- 3/4 cup sugar
- 2 tbsps. cornstarch

- 1/4 tsp. salt
- 1-1/2 cups milk
- 3 egg yolks, beaten
- 1 tbsp. butter
- 3 tsps. vanilla extract

TOPPING:
- 2 cups heavy whipping cream
- 1/2 cup confectioners' sugar
- 1 tsp. vanilla extract
- 3 pints fresh strawberries, sliced
- Additional confectioners' sugar

Direction

1. Roll out each sheet of pastry to a 9" square on a surface slightly dusted with flour. Arrange onto unoiled baking sheets. Bake at 350 degrees until golden brown, or for 30 minutes.
2. In the meantime, mix salt, cornstarch and sugar together in a saucepan. Slowly stir in milk until smooth. Cook, stirring, on medium-high heat until thick and bubbles appear on top. Lower the heat; cook, stirring, for another 2 minutes. Take off the heat. Whisk a small amount of hot filling into egg yolks; bring all back into the pan and stir continuously. Gently boil; cook, stirring, for an additional 2 minutes. Take off the heat. Gently mix in vanilla and butter. Transfer to a bowl; use plastic wrap to cover the surface. Leave in the fridge until chilled without disturbing.
3. In a chilled large bowl, beat cream until it begins to thick to make topping. Put in vanilla and sugar; beat until it forms soft peaks.
4. Bring 1 pastry square onto a serving platter. Add custard, strawberries sweetened whipped cream and the second pastry on top. Dust on top with confectioners' sugar. Leave the rest in the fridge.

Nutrition Information

Calories: 475 calories Total Carbohydrate: 49 g Cholesterol: 114 mg Total Fat: 29 g Fiber: 5 g Protein: 6 g Sodium: 226 mg

Tangerine-chocolate Tart

Serving: 8 | Ready in: 2h30m

Ingredients

Crust
- ½ cup whole-wheat pastry flour
- ½ cup all-purpose flour
- 2 tbsps. sugar
- ¼ tsp. salt
- 3 tbsps. butter
- 2 tbsps. canola oil
- 2 tbsps. ice water, plus more as needed
- 1 large egg yolk, (save egg white for the filling)
- 1 tsp. lemon juice

Filling
- ½ cup slivered almonds, (2 oz.)
- ⅓ cup sugar
- 2 large eggs

- 1 large egg white
- ½ cup tangerine juice, (about 3 tangerines) or orange juice
- 2 tbsps. lemon juice
- 4 tsps. freshly grated orange zest, (2 oranges)
- 3 oz. bittersweet chocolate, coarsely chopped, divided

Direction

1. For the crust: In a medium-sized bowl, combine salt, sugar, all-purpose flour, and whole-wheat flour. Use your fingers or a pastry blender to cut in butter until the mixture looks like coarse crumbs with several big chunks. Pour in oil and use a fork to whisk to mix. In a measuring cup, combine lemon juice, egg yolk, and 2 tbsps. ice water. Form a well in the middle of the dry ingredients. Add just a sufficient amount of the liquid, use a fork to whisk, until the dough holds together. (If the dough appears too dry, add a small amount of water). Invert the dough out onto a surface lightly scattered with flour and knead for a few times. Shape the dough into a ball, and then flatten into a disc. Use plastic wrap to wrap and chill for a minimum of 30 minutes.
2. Spray cooking spray over a 9 1/2-in. tart pan with a removable bottom to coat. On a surface lightly scattered with flour, roll the dough into a rough 12-in. circle, a bit under 1/4-in. thick. Drape over the rolling pin with the dough and remove to the prepared pan. Fit by pressing. Run over the pan's top with the rolling pin to trim the edges, remove the trimmings. Use plastic wrap to wrap the crust and put in the freezer to chill for 15 minutes, or in the fridge for a maximum of 2 days.
3. Turn the oven to 375°F to preheat. Cut a foil or parchment paper into a circle, spray cooking spray over 1 side to coat and put on the cold crust to cover. Use pie weights (or rice or dry beans) to weight. On a cookie sheet, put the pan. Bake the crust, about 8 minutes. Discard the pie weights and paper and keep baking for another 4 minutes until set without turning brown. Put the cookie sheet with the pan aside.
4. For the filling: As the crust bakes, in a small baking pan, spread almonds and put in the oven to toast for 3-5 minutes until turning light golden and aromatic. Remove to a dish to cool.
5. In a food processor, put sugar and almonds, process to grind the almonds. Add orange zest, lemon juice, tangerine juice (or orange juice), egg white, and eggs; process until combined. Scatter over the crust with approximately 2-oz. of the chocolate. Pour into the baked crust with the tangerine filling.
6. Bake the tart at 375° for 25-35 minutes until the filling set. Loosen the edges and release the sides of the pan. Put on a wire rack to fully cool. In a small bowl, put the leftover 1-oz. chocolate and fit it in a small frying pan over lightly simmering water to melt. (Or you can microwave the chocolate to melt). Drizzle decoratively over the tart with the chocolate to garnish (see Tip).
7. Variation: You can use lemon zest instead of orange zest and for Lemon-Almond Tart, substitute lemon juice for tangerine juice. Leave out the chocolate. Use blackberries or raspberries to garnish.

Nutrition Information

Calories: 248 calories; Total Carbohydrate: 31 g Cholesterol: 28 mg Total Fat: 14 g Fiber: 3 g Protein: 4 g Sodium: 67 mg Sugar: 18 g Saturated Fat: 5 g

Valentine Sugar Cookies

Serving: 3-1/2 dozen. | Prep: 10m | Ready in: 20m

Ingredients
- 1 cup butter, softened
- 1-1/2 cups confectioners' sugar
- 1 egg, lightly beaten

- 1 tsp. vanilla extract
- 1 tsp. almond extract
- 2-1/2 cups all-purpose flour
- Red decorator's sugar, optional

Direction

1. Cream the sugar and butter in a bowl. Put extracts and egg; mix in flour. Stir well then put in the refrigerator for several hours. Make 1/4-inch thickness dough by rolling on lightly floured surface. Slice the dough using a 2 1/2 or 3-inch heart-shaped cookie cutter then put on baking sheets without grease. If desired, sprinkle sugar. Bake until lightly browned or for 8 to 10 minutes at 375 degrees.

Nutrition Information

Calories: 169 calories Total Carbohydrate: 20 g Cholesterol: 33 mg Total Fat: 9 g Fiber: 0 g Protein: 2 g Sodium: 91 mg

White Chocolate Creme Brulee

Serving: 2 servings. | Prep: 15m | Ready in: 01h05m

Ingredients

- 3 large egg yolks
- 6 tbsps. sugar, divided
- 1 cup heavy whipping cream
- 2 oz. white baking chocolate, finely chopped
- 1/4 tsp. vanilla extract

Direction

2. Whisk 2 tbsp. sugar and egg yolks in a small bowl; put aside. Heat 2 tbsp. sugar, chocolate and cream in a small saucepan on medium low heat, constantly mixing, till it is smooth and chocolate is melted.
3. Take off heat; mix in vanilla. Mix in small hot filling amount into egg yolk mixture; put all back into pan, constantly mixing.
4. Put into 2 10-oz. ramekins; put into baking pan. To pan, add 1-in. boiling water. Bake at 325°, uncovered, till center is set for 50-55 minutes. Take out of water bath and cool for 10 minutes. Refrigerate for a minimum of 4 hours.
5. Sprinkle leftover sugar if using crème brulee torch; heat sugar with torch till caramelized. Immediately serve.
6. Put ramekins onto baking sheet if broiling custards; stand for 15 minutes at room temperature. Sprinkle leftover sugar; broil 8-in. from heat till sugar is caramelized for 4-7 minutes. Refrigerate till firm for 1-2 hours.

Nutrition Information

Calories: 854 calories Total Carbohydrate: 70 g Cholesterol: 488 mg Total Fat: 62 g Fiber: 0 g Protein: 9 g Sodium: 86 mg

Champagne Julep

Serving: 1 | Prep: 10m | Ready in: 10m

Ingredients

- 10 fresh mint leaves
- 1 tsp. white sugar

- 1 tbsp. warm water
- 1/2 cup crushed ice, or as needed
- 2 fluid oz. cognac
- 2 fluid oz. chilled dry sparkling wine, or as needed

Direction

1. In a tall cocktail glass, place the mint leaves, add warm water and sugar, then muddle gently. Pour in the cognac after adding crushed ice, then stir. Pour sparkling wine on top of the mixture.

Nutrition Information

Calories: 271 calories; Total Carbohydrate: 5.8 g Cholesterol: 0 mg Total Fat: 0 g Protein: 0.1 g Sodium: 6 mg

Asparagus Wraps
Serving: 2 dozen. | Prep: 20m | Ready in: 35m

Ingredients

- 3 tbsps. butter, softened
- 1 tbsp. Mrs. Dash Onion & Herb seasoning blend
- 1/4 tsp. garlic salt
- 1 package (17.3 oz.) frozen puff pastry, thawed
- 1 cup crumbled feta cheese
- 3 oz. thinly sliced prosciutto or deli ham
- 24 thick fresh asparagus spears, trimmed

Direction

1. Preheat oven to 425°F. Combine garlic salt, butter and seasoning blend. Roll out puff pastry on a lightly floured work area. Cover it with 1 1/2 tbsps. butter mixture and scatter 1/2 cup cheese on top. Place prosciutto over cheese, pressing a bit to stick.
2. Cut each sheet into 12 1/2-inch strips using a sharp knife or pizza cutter. Wrap each asparagus spear with a strip of pastry, filling side in. Transfer to baking sheets lined with parchment paper.
3. Bake for about 15 minutes or until golden brown. Serve while still warm.

Nutrition Information

Calories: 139 calories Total Carbohydrate: 12 g Cholesterol: 11 mg Total Fat: 8 g Fiber: 2 g Protein: 4 g Sodium: 248 mg

Avocado Corn Salsa
Serving: 32 | Prep: 30m | Ready in: 8h30m

Ingredients

- 1 (16 oz.) package frozen corn kernels, thawed
- 2 (2.25 oz.) cans sliced ripe olives, drained
- 1 red bell pepper, chopped
- 1 small onion, chopped
- 5 cloves garlic, minced
- 1/3 cup olive oil
- 1/4 cup lemon juice
- 3 tbsps. cider vinegar
- 1 tsp. dried oregano

- 1/2 tsp. salt
- 1/2 tsp. ground black pepper
- 4 avocados - peeled, pitted and diced

Direction

1. Combine in a large bowl the onion, red bell pepper, olives, and corn.
2. Combine in a small bowl the pepper, salt, oregano, cider vinegar, lemon juice, olive oil and garlic. Put into the corn mixture and toss to coat. Then place in the refrigerator, covered, to chill for 8 hours or overnight.
3. Mix avocados into the mixture prior to serving.

Nutrition Information

Calories: 81 calories; Total Carbohydrate: 6.1 g Cholesterol: 0 mg Total Fat: 6.5 g Protein: 1.1 g Sodium: 73 mg

Bacon-chocolate Bruschetta

Serving: 9 | Prep: 20m | Ready in: 35m

Ingredients

- 4 slices bacon
- 9 thin slices of sourdough baguette
- olive oil, or as needed
- 3 oz. miniature chocolate chips

Direction

1. Cook bacon in a big pan over medium heat; turn periodically for 10-14 minutes until evenly brown and crisp. Drain on paper towels then crush once cool.
2. Let the oven broiler heat with the rack 6in. from the source of heat.
3. Put the baguette slices on baking sheet and smear the tops with olive oil. For a minute, bake the slices under the broiler; carefully watch to prevent from burning. Take away toasted baguette slices, then put aside on baking sheet.
4. Let the oven heat to 175°C (350°F).
5. In a bowl, mix together the crushed bacon and chocolate chips then sprinkle a small amount of mixture on each baguette slice. Bake for 5 minutes in the preheated oven until the chocolate chips are soft but still have their shape.

Nutrition Information

Calories: 179 calories; Total Carbohydrate: 20.1 g Cholesterol: 4 mg Total Fat: 9.5 g Protein: 4.8 g Sodium: 256 mg

Berry Bruschetta

Serving: 32 appetizers. | Prep: 15m | Ready in: 20m

Ingredients

- 1 French bread baguette (1 lb.)
- 2 tbsps. olive oil
- 1-1/2 cups chopped fresh strawberries
- 3/4 cup chopped peeled fresh peaches
- 1-1/2 tsps. minced fresh mint
- 1/2 cup Mascarpone cheese

Direction

1. Slice the baguette into 32 pieces with a thickness of 1/2 inch. Transfer the slices onto a baking sheet with no grease. Brush oil over the slices. Broil until slightly toasted for 1 to 2 minutes, 6 to 8 inches away from the heat source.
2. Combine the mint, peaches, and strawberries in a small bowl. Spread a layer of cheese on each slice of toast. Top toast with the fruit mixture. Broil until cheese is a little melted, about 1 to 2 minutes. Serve.

Nutrition Information

Calories: 154 calories Total Carbohydrate: 17 g Cholesterol: 18 mg Total Fat: 8 g Fiber: 1 g Protein: 4 g Sodium: 188 mg

Black Widow Dip

Serving: 1-3/4 cups. | Prep: 10m | Ready in: 10m

Ingredients

- 1 package (8 oz.) cream cheese, cubed
- 1 cup chopped roasted sweet red peppers
- 2 tbsps. minced fresh basil or 2 tsps. dried basil
- 2 tbsps. minced fresh parsley
- 1 to 2 tbsps. lime juice
- 1 garlic clove, chopped
- 1/2 tsp. salt
- 1/4 tsp. white pepper
- Pita chips or assorted vegetables

Direction

1. Mix the first 8 ingredients together in a food processor, then place a cover and process until combined. Serve together with vegetables or pita chips.

Nutrition Information

Calories: 63 calories Total Carbohydrate: 1 g Cholesterol: 18 mg Total Fat: 6 g Fiber: 0 g Protein: 1 g Sodium: 196 mg

Cheese Puffs (gougeres)

Serving: 12 | Prep: 45m | Ready in: 1h25m

Ingredients

- 1 cup all-purpose flour
- 1/2 tsp. salt
- 1/2 tsp. fresh ground black pepper
- 1/2 tsp. dried thyme
- 1/2 tsp. chili powder
- 1 pinch cayenne pepper
- 1 cup whole milk
- 1 stick butter (cut into 1/2 inch cubes)
- 6 large eggs (at room temperature)
- 1/2 cup grated Parmesan or Romano cheese
- 3/4 cup grated Gruyere cheese

- 1 oz. pepperoni, diced (optional)
- 2 tbsps. milk
- 2 tbsps. grated Parmesan cheese

Direction

2. Start preheating the oven to 425°F (220°C).
3. In a big bowl, mix flour with cayenne pepper, chili powder, thyme, black pepper, and salt.
4. In a large saucepan, put butter and milk and boil it. When the butter melts, set the heat to low. Add all the seasoned flour at once. Use a wooden spoon to mix strongly until the dough shapes into a ball. Take away from heat.
5. From 1 egg, separate the yolk and the white, saving the yolk to make the glazing.
6. In a big mixer bowl, place the dough. Whisk for 1 minute at medium speed, and then whisk in 1 egg and the extra egg white. Whisk until fully absorbed into the dough. Then add the rest 4 eggs, 1 egg each time, waiting each time until the dough has fully absorbed the previous egg. Once the dough has fully absorbed all 5 eggs (include the 1 egg white), it should be satiny and smooth.
7. Add Gruyere cheeses and Parmesan, and pepperoni if it's available. Incorporate completely into the dough.
8. On 2 ungreased cookie sheets, pipe the dough with a pastry bag. Using a tsp. to drop the dough works great as well. The mounds should be 1/2 inch in diameter for tiny puffs, 1 inch in diameter for small appetizers, and 1 1/2 inches in diameter for puffs large enough for filling. Make sure the size of the puffs even so that they bake properly. Keep the puffs 1 inch apart from each other.
9. To make a glaze, whisk the rest egg yolk with 2 tbsps. of milk. Gently brush glaze on the puff tops before baking. Use Parmesan cheese to drizzle the top.
10. Put in the preheated oven and bake for 10 minutes (for tiny puffs, bake for 5 minutes). Lower the heat to 300°F (150°C). Bake until the puffs turn golden brown, about another 10 minutes for tiny puffs and another 15-20 minutes for medium-sized or large-sized puffs. You can test by taking a puff out of the oven and crack it open. Inside the puff should be heated through. Bake for an addition of 5 minutes if it's still damp or doughy.
11. Take the pan out of the oven and keep the puffs on the pan to let it cool down enough to eat.

Nutrition Information

Calories: 219 calories; Total Carbohydrate: 9.5 g Cholesterol: 131 mg Total Fat: 15.9 g Protein: 9.7 g Sodium: 327 mg

Chocolate Sea Salt Crostini

Serving: 12 | Prep: 5m | Ready in: 11m

Ingredients

- 1 French baguette, cut into diagonal 1/2 inch slices
- extra virgin olive oil
- 4 oz. high-quality dark chocolate, broken into 1-inch pieces
- 1 tbsp. flaked sea salt

Direction

1. Turn on the oven's broiler and start preheating. Place the oven rack about 6 inches from the heat source. Line parchment paper or a silicon baking mat on a baking sheet.
2. Place baguette slices on the baking sheet in a single layer. Put under broiler and broil for 2 minutes until turning golden. Flip each slice over and broil for an additional 2 minutes. Turn off broiler.
3. Flip each of bread slices over again; sprinkle olive oil on top of each slice. Push a chocolate piece

into the center of each slice and return to oven for another 2 minutes. Remove from oven and lightly sprinkle sea salt on top of each chocolate piece.

Nutrition Information
Calories: 176 calories; Total Carbohydrate: 21.3 g Cholesterol: < 1 mg Total Fat: 8.3 g Protein: 4 g Sodium: 625 mg

Cilantro Shrimp Cups

Serving: 3 dozen. | Prep: 25m | Ready in: 40m

Ingredients
- 36 wonton wrappers
- Cooking spray
- 1-1/4 lbs. peeled and deveined cooked small shrimp, divided
- 1/2 cup chopped pecans
- 1/3 cup shredded carrot
- 1/3 cup finely chopped celery
- 1/4 cup minced fresh cilantro
- 3 tbsps. lime juice
- 3 tbsps. oyster sauce
- 1-1/2 tsps. reduced-sodium soy sauce

Direction
1. Use cooking spray to spray on each side of wonton wrappers, then press into miniature muffin cups gently. Bake at 350 degrees until golden brown, about 11 to 13 minutes. Transfer to wire racks to cool.
2. In the meantime, set aside thirty-six shrimp for decoration, then chop the leftover shrimp. Mix together soy sauce, oyster sauce, lime juice, cilantro, celery, carrot, pecans and chopped shrimp in a small bowl. Scoop into wonton cups and use a reserved shrimp to decorate each.

Nutrition Information
Calories: 55 calories Total Carbohydrate: 6 g Cholesterol: 25 mg Total Fat: 2 g Fiber: 0 g Protein: 4 g Sodium: 135 mg

Cinnamon Heart Popcorn

Serving: 16 | Prep: 5m | Ready in: 40m

Ingredients
- 1 cup butter
- 1/2 cup light corn syrup
- 1 1/2 cups cinnamon red hot candies
- 8 cups popped popcorn

Direction
1. Set the oven to 120°C or 250°F to preheat and use parchment paper to line baking sheets.
2. In a pot, mix together cinnamon candies, corn syrup and butter on medium heat. Bring the mixture to a boil and cook about 5 minutes. Pour over a big, heatproof bowl of popcorn with the syrup, stirring to cover popcorn as evenly as you can. On the prepared baking sheets, spread out the coated popcorn.
3. In the preheated oven, bake for a half hour, until the candy coating is set.

Nutrition Information
Calories: 242 calories; Total Carbohydrate: 30.1 g Cholesterol: 31 mg Total Fat: 13.9 g Protein: 0.5 g
Sodium: 154 mg

Crab And Lobster Stuffed Mushrooms

Serving: 8 | Prep: 10m | Ready in: 20m

Ingredients

- 3/4 cup melted butter, divided
- 1 lb. fresh mushrooms, stems removed
- 1 cup crushed seasoned croutons
- 1 cup shredded mozzarella cheese
- 1 (6 oz.) can crabmeat, drained
- 1 lb. lobster tail, cleaned and chopped
- 3 tbsps. minced garlic
- 1/4 cup shredded mozzarella cheese (optional)

Direction

1. Preheat an oven to 190 degrees C (375 degrees F). Use about 1/4 cup of melted butter to rub a large baking sheet. Spread a single layer of mushroom caps on the baking sheet.
2. Combine crushed croutons, garlic, remaining 1/2 cup of butter, lobster, crabmeat, and shredded cheese in a medium bowl. Place a spoonful of mixture into mushroom caps where stems were in place.
3. Bake in the preheated oven for about 10 to 12 minutes or until browned lightly on top. If desired, drizzle with more cheese and then serve while still hot!

Nutrition Information
Calories: 310 calories; Total Carbohydrate: 6.9 g Cholesterol: 130 mg Total Fat: 22 g Protein: 21.9 g
Sodium: 535 mg

Crab-stuffed Baby Portobellos

Serving: 3 dozen. | Prep: 45m | Ready in: 01h10m

Ingredients

- 1 lb. baby portobello mushrooms
- 3/4 cup butter, divided
- 2 garlic cloves, minced
- 2 cans (6 oz. each) crabmeat, drained, flaked and cartilage removed
- 1/4 cup grated Romano cheese
- 1 tbsp. minced fresh parsley
- 3 tsps. garlic powder
- 1-1/2 tsps. onion powder
- 1/4 cup grated Parmesan cheese
- 1 tsp. garlic salt
- 1/2 cup shredded part-skim mozzarella cheese

Direction

1. Cut off stems from mushrooms and put caps aside. Chop the stems finely.
2. Sauté chopped mushrooms in a big skillet with 1/4 cup of butter just until soft, about 5 minutes. Put

in garlic and sauté until garlic turn golden, about 1 to 2 minutes more. Take away from the heat and stir in onion powder, garlic powder, parsley, Romano and crab.
3. Melt leftover butter and pour into a 13-inch x9-inch baking dish. Stuff crab mixture into mushroom caps, then arrange in the baking dish. Use garlic salt and Parmesan to sprinkle over top.
4. Bake at 350 degrees without a cover until mushrooms soften, about 20 to 25 minutes. Sprinkle mozzarella over, then bake until cheese melts, about 2 to 4 minutes more. Serve warm.

Nutrition Information
Calories: 57 calories Total Carbohydrate: 1 g Cholesterol: 21 mg Total Fat: 5 g Fiber: 0 g Protein: 3 g Sodium: 139 mg

Cranberry Hot Wings
Serving: about 2-1/2 dozen. | Prep: 50m | Ready in: 02h50m

Ingredients
- 1 can (14 oz.) jellied cranberry sauce, cubed
- 2 tbsps. ground mustard
- 2 tbsps. hot pepper sauce
- 2 tbsps. reduced-sodium soy sauce
- 2 tbsps. honey
- 1 tbsp. cider vinegar
- 2 tsps. garlic powder
- 1 tsp. grated orange zest
- 3 lbs. chicken wings
- Blue cheese salad dressing and celery sticks

Direction
1. Combine the first 8 ingredients in a 5-qt. slow cooker. Cover and cook on low until the cranberry sauce is melted, about 45 minutes.
2. In the meantime, chop the wings into 3 parts; remove the wing tip parts. On a greased broiler pan, arrange the wings. Next, broil 4-6 in. from the heat until lightly browned, turning infrequently, about 15-20 minutes.
3. Transfer the wings to the slow cooker; toss to coat well. Cook on high, covered, until softened, about 2-3 hours. Enjoy with celery and dressing.

Cranberry-chili Cheese Spread
Serving: 14 servings. | Prep: 10m | Ready in: 10m

Ingredients
- 2 packages (8 oz. each) cream cheese, softened
- 1 can (14 oz.) whole-berry cranberry sauce
- 1 can (4 oz.) chopped green chilies, drained
- 1 green onion, sliced
- 1 tbsp. lime juice
- 1/2 tsp. garlic salt
- 1/2 tsp. cayenne pepper
- 1/2 tsp. chili powder
- Assorted crackers

Direction

1. On a serving plate, put in the cream cheese. Mix the onion, cranberry sauce, spices, green chilies and lime juice together in a small bowl. Drizzle the prepared cranberry mixture on top of the cream cheese and serve it together with crackers.

Nutrition Information

Calories: 157 calories Total Carbohydrate: 12 g Cholesterol: 36 mg Total Fat: 11 g Fiber: 1 g Protein: 3 g Sodium: 200 mg

Creamy Crab Toast Cups

Serving: 12 servings. | Prep: 30m | Ready in: 45m

Ingredients

- 12 slices white bread, crusts removed
- 1/2 cup butter, melted

FILLING:

- 3 tbsps. butter
- 2 tbsps. all-purpose flour
- 1-1/4 cups 2% milk
- 1 cup shredded cheddar cheese
- 2 tsps. lemon juice
- 1 tsp. ground mustard
- 1 tsp. Worcestershire sauce
- 1/2 tsp. salt
- 1/8 tsp. hot pepper sauce
- 2 cans (6 oz. each) lump crabmeat, drained
- 2 tbsps. minced fresh parsley
- 1 green onion, thinly sliced

Direction

2. Set the oven for preheating to 350°. Flatten each bread slices using a rolling pin. Brush both sides of bread using the melted butter and press into each muffin cups. Let it bake inside the oven for 12-15 minutes or until it turns golden brown.
3. To make the filling, melt the butter in a big saucepan placed over medium heat. Mix in flour until the consistency turns smooth; whisk in the milk little by little. Let the mixture boil while continuously stirring; cook and stir for 3-5 minutes or until it turns thick.
4. Add the pepper sauce, salt, Worcestershire sauce, mustard, lemon juice and cheese; let it cook while stirring until the cheese has melted. Add in crab; mix until heated completely. Stir in green onion and minced parsley. Scoop into cups.

Creamy Orange Fruit Dip

Serving: 1-1/3 cups. | Prep: 5m | Ready in: 5m

Ingredients

- 1/2 cup mayonnaise
- 1/2 cup sour cream
- 1/3 cup orange marmalade
- 1 tbsp. milk

- 1/2 lb. green grapes
- 1/2 lb. strawberries

Direction
1. Whisk together milk, marmalade, sour cream and mayonnaise in a small bowl until combined. Chill until serving, then serve together with fruit.

Nutrition Information
Calories: 128 calories Total Carbohydrate: 11 g Cholesterol: 10 mg Total Fat: 9 g Fiber: 1 g Protein: 1 g Sodium: 61 mg

Creamy Seafood Dip
Serving: 3 cups. | Prep: 15m | Ready in: 15m

Ingredients
- 2 cups (16 oz.) sour cream
- 1/3 cup mayonnaise
- 1 can (6 oz.) crabmeat, drained, flaked and cartilage removed
- 1 cup (5 oz.) frozen cooked salad shrimp, thawed and chopped
- 2 tbsps. onion soup mix
- 1/8 tsp. garlic powder
- 1/8 tsp. paprika
- Corn chips

Direction
1. Mix mayonnaise and sour cream in a small bowl. Mix in garlic powder, soup mix, shrimp and crab. Refrigerate with a cover overnight.
2. Sprinkle paprika over. Serve with corn ships.

Crispy Shrimp Poppers
Serving: 20 appetizers. | Prep: 40m | Ready in: 45m

Ingredients
- 20 uncooked medium shrimp, peeled and deveined
- 4 oz. cream cheese, softened
- 10 bacon strips
- 1 cup all-purpose flour
- 2 eggs, lightly beaten
- 2 cups panko (Japanese) bread crumbs
- Oil for deep-fat frying

Direction
1. Butterfly the shrimp along the outer curves. Spread about 1 tsp. cream cheese inside each shrimp. Slice bacon strips in half lengthways; enclose 1 piece around each shrimp then secure it using toothpicks.
2. Divide the bread crumbs, eggs and flour in three different shallow bowls. Sprinkle flour over the shrimp to coat; dip into eggs and coat with bread crumbs.
3. Heat oil to 375° in a deep-fat fryer or electric skillet. Fry the shrimp for 3 for 4 minutes, a few at a time, or until golden brown. Drain on paper towels. Prior to serving, remove toothpicks.

Deviled Crab

Serving: 8 | Prep: 25m | Ready in: 50m

Ingredients
- 1 3/4 lbs. crabmeat
- 1/8 tsp. salt
- 3/4 tsp. Worcestershire sauce
- 3/4 tsp. hot pepper sauce
- 1 cup dry bread crumbs
- 4 tbsps. vegetable oil
- 1 tbsp. vegetable oil
- 1 tbsp. butter
- 1 cup all-purpose flour
- 2 cloves garlic, minced
- 2 cups clam juice
- 1/2 cup white wine
- 1/8 tsp. freshly ground black pepper
- 1/8 tsp. crushed red pepper flakes
- 1/2 cup heavy cream
- 1 1/2 tbsps. fresh lemon juice
- 1/4 cup fresh parsley, minced
- 1 1/2 tbsps. fresh basil, minced

Direction
1. Put hot pepper sauce, Worcestershire sauce, salt and crabmeat in mixing bowl. Stir well.
2. Form mixture of crab to cakes; roll into bread crumbs.
3. Heat four tbsps. oil in medium-size skillet on moderate heat. Sauté cakes, for approximately 5 minutes. Flip; let cook till golden brown, or for 5 minutes more.
4. Sauce: Heat a tbsp. each of butter and oil in a 1 1/2-quart saucepan. Put flour into oil slowly, mixing continuously. Cook, about 5 minutes.
5. Put in clam juice slowly, mixing vigorously and continuously. Add black pepper, crushed red pepper flakes and white wine. Let simmer. Put in parsley, basil and cream. Allow to simmer yet do not let boil. Once mixture thickens enough to coat back of spoon evenly, it is done.
6. Top crab cakes with sauce to serve.

Nutrition Information
Calories: 380 calories; Total Carbohydrate: 24.3 g Cholesterol: 103 mg Total Fat: 18 g Protein: 26.3 g Sodium: 675 mg

Elegant Baked Brie

Serving: 8 | Prep: 10m | Ready in: 30m

Ingredients
- 1 (8 oz.) round Brie cheese
- 2 tbsps. pesto sauce
- 1/4 cup toasted pine nuts
- 2 tsps. brown sugar
- 1 (8 oz.) package refrigerated crescent rolls

Direction

1. Preheat an oven to 200 °C or 400 °F.
2. Halve Brie cheese horizontally, forming 2 even circles resembles a layered cake. On cut surface of a half, scatter pesto sauce; scatter brown sugar and pine nuts on top of pesto layer. Over pesto mixture, put the other half of Brie.
3. Part crescent rolls and with crescent roll dough, cover Brie round completely, closing all the openings. On a baking sheet, put the covered Brie.
4. In the prepped oven, bake for 20 minutes till crescent rolls are browned slightly and Brie cheese is softened.

Nutrition Information

Calories: 253 calories; Total Carbohydrate: 13.1 g Cholesterol: 30 mg Total Fat: 17.8 g Protein: 9.6 g Sodium: 429 mg

Greek Party Pitas

Serving: 2 dozen. | Prep: 25m | Ready in: 25m

Ingredients

- 4 whole wheat pita pocket halves
- 1/3 cup Greek vinaigrette
- 1/2 lb. thinly sliced deli turkey
- 1 jar (7-1/2 oz.) roasted sweet red peppers, drained and patted dry
- 2 cups fresh baby spinach
- 24 pitted Greek olives
- 24 frilled toothpicks

Direction

1. Brush vinaigrette insides of pita pockets. Fill with spinach, peppers and turkey. Cut every pita pocket to 6 wedges.
2. On toothpicks, thread olives then use to secure the wedges.

Nutrition Information

Calories: 48 calories Total Carbohydrate: 4 g Cholesterol: 3 mg Total Fat: 3 g Fiber: 0 g Protein: 2 g Sodium: 239 mg

Layered Pesto Cheese Spread

Serving: 2-1/2 cups. | Prep: 20m | Ready in: 20m

Ingredients

- 1 package (8 oz.) cream cheese, softened
- 1/2 cup butter, softened
- 1 jar (3-1/2 oz.) prepared pesto
- 1/4 cup grated Parmesan cheese
- 1/2 cup chopped oil-packed sun-dried tomatoes
- Assorted crackers or baked pita chips

Direction

1. Use plastic wrap to line a 3-cup bowl then set aside.
2. Beat butter and cream cheese in a small bowl until smooth. Mix together Parmesan cheese and pesto in a separate bowl. Layer into the prepared bowl with half of the cream cheese mixture, sun-dried

tomatoes and pesto mixture. Repeat layers, then cover and chill for a minimum of an hour.

3. Unmold onto a serving plate and serve together with crackers.

Nutrition Information

Calories: 116 calories Total Carbohydrate: 1 g Cholesterol: 27 mg Total Fat: 12 g Fiber: 0 g Protein: 2 g Sodium: 129 mg

Li'l Lips

Serving: 8 servings. | Prep: 20m | Ready in: 20m

Ingredients

- 1 medium red apple
- 1 tsp. lemon juice
- 1/4 cup chunky peanut butter
- 2 tbsps. reduced-fat cream cheese
- 1/8 tsp. ground cinnamon
- Miniature marshmallows, optional

Direction

1. Cut apple into 16 wedges, then toss together with lemon juice.
2. Combine cinnamon, cream cheese and peanut butter in a small bowl until mixed; spread on one side of half of the apple slices with 2 tsp. of the mixture. Place a second slice on top of each and press to make lips. Press on the peanut butter with marshmallows to make teeth, if wanted. Chill until ready to serve.

Nutrition Information

Calories: 64 calories Total Carbohydrate: 4 g Cholesterol: 3 mg Total Fat: 5 g Fiber: 1 g Protein: 2 g Sodium: 54 mg

Martini Cheese Dip

Serving: 1-1/4 cups. | Prep: 10m | Ready in: 10m

Ingredients

- 1 package (8 oz.) cream cheese, softened
- 1 tbsp. mayonnaise
- 1/4 cup sliced green olives with pimientos, drained and chopped
- 2 to 3 tbsps. vodka
- 2 tbsps. olive juice
- 1/4 tsp. coarsely ground pepper
- Assorted fresh vegetables

Direction

1. Beat mayonnaise and cream cheese in a large bowl to blend. Stir in pepper, olive juice, vodka and olives. Store for at least 2 hours in the fridge. If desired, transfer into a martini glass. Serve with vegetables.

Nutrition Information

Calories: 106 calories Total Carbohydrate: 1 g Cholesterol: 25 mg Total Fat: 9 g Fiber: 0 g Protein: 2 g Sodium: 140 mg

Meatballs In Cherry Sauce

Serving: about 3-1/2 dozen. | Prep: 30m | Ready in: 45m

Ingredients

- 1 cup seasoned bread crumbs
- 1 small onion, chopped
- 1 egg, lightly beaten
- 3 garlic cloves, minced
- 1 tsp. salt
- 1/2 tsp. pepper
- 1 lb. lean ground beef (90% lean)
- 1 lb. ground pork

SAUCE:

- 1 can (21 oz.) cherry pie filling
- 1/3 cup sherry or chicken broth
- 1/3 cup cider vinegar
- 1/4 cup steak sauce
- 2 tbsps. brown sugar
- 2 tbsps. reduced-sodium soy sauce
- 1 tsp. honey

Direction

1. Set an oven to 400 degrees and start preheating. Blend the first 6 ingredients in a large bowl. Add in pork and beef; combine lightly yet thoroughly. Form into 1-inch balls. In a shallow baking pan, arrange on a greased rack. Bake till cooked completely or for 11-13 minutes. Place on paper towels to drain.
2. Blend the sauce ingredients in a large saucepan. Boil and constantly stir on medium heat. Turn down the heat; remove the cover and bring to a simmer until thick, or for 2-3 minutes. Drop in the meatballs; heat thoroughly and gently stir.

Nutrition Information

Calories: 76 calories Total Carbohydrate: 7 g Cholesterol: 19 mg Total Fat: 3 g Fiber: 0 g Protein: 5 g Sodium: 169 mg

Mini Sweet Potato Samosas

Serving: 4 | Prep: 20m | Ready in: 45m

Ingredients

- 1 sweet potato, peeled and diced
- 1 tsp. butter
- 1 tbsp. milk
- 1 tbsp. dry onion soup mix
- curry powder to taste
- 20 wonton wrappers
- sesame oil for brushing

Direction

1. Let the sweet potatoes simmer with a little water until soft; drain. Add in curry powder, butter, onion soup mix, and milk; mash.
2. Preheat the oven to 190°C or 375°F.

3. In the middle of each wonton wrapper, scoop a tsp. of sweet potato mixture. Slather water on two adjoining edges of wonton and fold into a triangle. Seal by pressing the edges together. Slather sesame oil on each side of the samosas; arrange on a baking dish.
4. Bake in the 375°F or 190°C for 10 minutes. Flip the samosas and bake for another 5 minutes.

Nutrition Information

Calories: 169 calories; Total Carbohydrate: 30.6 g Cholesterol: 7 mg Total Fat: 3 g Protein: 4.7 g Sodium: 332 mg

Mushroom And Bacon Cheesecake

Serving: 16 servings. | Prep: 50m | Ready in: 01h45m

Ingredients

- 1-3/4 cups soft bread crumbs
- 1 cup grated Parmesan cheese
- 6 tbsps. butter, melted

FILLING:

- 1 cup finely chopped onion
- 1 cup finely chopped sweet red pepper
- 1 tbsp. olive oil
- 4 cups assorted chopped fresh mushrooms
- 3 packages (8 oz. each) cream cheese, softened
- 1 tsp. salt
- 1 tsp. pepper
- 1/2 cup sour cream
- 4 eggs, lightly beaten
- 12 bacon strips, cooked and crumbled
- 1 cup (4 oz.) crumbled feta cheese
- 1/2 cup minced fresh parsley
- Roasted sliced mushrooms, fresh parsley and additional cooked bacon strips, optional
- Assorted crackers

Direction

1. Position on a double thickness of heavy-duty foil, approximately 18 inches square, with a 9-inch springform pan coated with grease. Use foil to wrap around pan securely.
2. Mix together butter, Parmesan cheese and bread crumbs in a small bowl, then press on the bottom of a 9-inch springform pan coated with grease. Put pan on a baking sheet and bake at 350 degrees until golden brown, about 10 to 15 minutes. Allow to cool on a wire rack.
3. In the meantime, sauté together red pepper and onion in a big skillet with oil about 2 minutes. Put in mushrooms then cook and stir until liquid evaporates, about 10 minutes. Put aside to cool.
4. Beat together pepper, salt and cream cheese in a big bowl until fluffy and light, then beat in sour cream. Put in eggs while beating on low speed just until blended. Fold in mushroom mixture, parsley, feta cheese and bacon, then transfer into crust. Put in a big baking pan with springform pan and then fill a bigger pan with 1 inch of hot water.
5. Bake at 350 degrees until top looks dull and the center is barely set, about 55 to 65 minutes. Take springform pan out of water bath, then allow to cool on a wire rack about 10 minutes. Run around the edge of pan carefully with a knife to loosen cake, then allow to cool about an hour more. Chill overnight.

6. Take off sides of pan, then put more bacon, if wanted, parsley and mushrooms on top. Serve together with crackers.

Nutrition Information
Calories: 322 calories Total Carbohydrate: 7 g Cholesterol: 131 mg Total Fat: 28 g Fiber: 1 g Protein: 12 g Sodium: 617 mg

Nutty Blue Cheese Spread

Serving: 1-1/2 cups. | Prep: 15m | Ready in: 15m

Ingredients
1 package (8 oz.) reduced-fat cream cheese
1-1/4 tsps. sugar
1/8 tsp. salt
1/4 cup crumbled blue cheese
3 tbsps. finely chopped pecans, toasted
Assorted crackers

Direction
1. Beat together salt, sugar and cream cheese in a big bowl until combined. Stir in blue cheese and chill for a minimum of 1 hour. Right before serving, fold in pecans. Serve together with crackers.

Nutrition Information
Calories: 71 calories Total Carbohydrate: 1 g Cholesterol: 15 mg Total Fat: 6 g Fiber: 0 g Protein: 3 g Sodium: 144 mg

Oysters Rockefeller

Serving: 6 | Prep: 30m | Ready in: 1h

Ingredients
- 2 slices bacon
- 24 unopened, fresh, live medium oysters
- 1 1/2 cups cooked spinach
- 1/3 cup bread crumbs
- 1/4 cup chopped green onions
- 1 tbsp. chopped fresh parsley
- 1/2 tsp. salt
- 1 dash hot pepper sauce
- 3 tbsps. extra virgin olive oil
- 1 tsp. anise flavored liqueur
- 4 cups kosher salt

Direction
1. For preheating, set the oven at 450 degrees Fahrenheit or 220 degrees Celsius. In a deep, large skillet, place bacon and cook over a medium-high heat until browned evenly. Drain and crumble, then set aside.
2. Clean the oysters and place them in a large stock pot, pouring enough water to cover the oysters. Bring water and oysters to a boil and remove from heat, drain, then cool. When cooled, break off the top shell from each oyster.
3. Chop parsley, green onions, bread crumbs, spinach, and chopped bacon using a food processor.

4. Add anise-flavored liqueur, olive oil, hot sauce, and salt, processing for 10 seconds until chopped finely but not pureed.
5. On a pan with kosher salt, arrange oysters in their half shells, and spoon a bit of the spinach mixture onto each of the oysters. Bake for 10 minutes until the oysters are cooked through. Change the oven settings to broil and broil until tops are brown and serve hot.

Nutrition Information

Calories: 148 calories; Total Carbohydrate: 7.7 g Cholesterol: 19 mg Total Fat: 8.9 g Protein: 9.3 g Sodium: 61097 mg

Pear Mushroom Strudels

Serving: 2 strudels (12 slices each). | Prep: 45m | Ready in: 01h05m

Ingredients

- 1 cup finely chopped mushrooms
- 1 small onion, finely chopped
- 1/2 cup butter, divided
- 2 small pears, peeled and thinly sliced
- 3/4 cup shredded Gruyere or Swiss cheese
- 1/3 cup sliced almonds
- 1 tbsp. stone-ground mustard
- 1/2 tsp. salt
- 1/4 tsp. pepper
- 10 sheets phyllo dough (14 inches x 9 inches)
- 1/3 cup grated Parmesan cheese

Direction

1. Cook onion and mushrooms with 2 tbsp. butter in a big skillet until softened. Stir in pears and cook for 3 more minutes. Take away from the heat and stir in pepper, salt, mustard, almonds and Gruyere, then allow to cool to room temperature.
2. Melt the leftover butter. On a working surface, place one sheet of phyllo dough, then use butter to coat evenly. Sprinkle over with 1 1/2 tsp. Parmesan cheese. Layer with 4 additional sheets of phyllo, then brush butter to each sheet and sprinkle with cheese. (Prevent the remaining phyllo dough from drying out by covering it with plastic wrap and a wet towel.) Spread in a 2-in.-wide strip along a short side of dough with half of the pear mixture. Roll up jelly-roll style, beginning with the pear side, then pinch seams to seal. Brush with butter and turn to a 15"x10"x1" baking pan lined with parchment paper.
3. Repeat the process with the leftover phyllo, pear mixture, Parmesan cheese and butter.
4. Bake for 16-20 minutes at 375°, until golden brown then allow to cool for 5 minutes. Cut each strudel into 12 slices.

Nutrition Information

Calories: 83 calories Total Carbohydrate: 5 g Cholesterol: 15 mg Total Fat: 6 g Fiber: 1 g Protein: 2 g Sodium: 134 mg

Pesto-pepper Cheese Spread

Serving: 3 cups. | Prep: 25m | Ready in: 25m

Ingredients

- 2 packages (8 oz. each) cream cheese, softened

- 2 cups crumbled goat cheese
- 2 tbsps. olive oil
- 1 tsp. dried thyme
- 2 garlic cloves, minced
- 3 tbsps. prepared pesto
- 1/3 cup chopped roasted sweet red peppers
- Assorted crackers or sliced French bread baguette

Direction

1. Mix thyme, goat cheese, oil, garlic and cream cheese in a large bowl.
2. Line a 1-qt. bowl with plastic wrap. Place a third of the cheese blend in a bowl; top with peppers, half of the remaining cheese blend, pesto and the remaining cheese mixture. Cover and put in the refrigerator for a minimum of 3 hours.
3. Invert cheese mixture on a serving plate; discard plastic wrap. Enjoy with crackers.

Nutrition Information

Calories: 243 calories Total Carbohydrate: 2 g Cholesterol: 58 mg Total Fat: 23 g Fiber: 0 g Protein: 8 g Sodium: 264 mg

Phyllo Crab Cups

Serving: 2-1/2 dozen. | Prep: 15m | Ready in: 35m

Ingredients

- 1 package (8 oz.) cream cheese, softened
- 2 to 3 tbsps. horseradish sauce
- 3/4 cup chopped imitation crabmeat
- 1 tbsp. chopped green onion
- 2 packages (1.9 oz. each) frozen miniature phyllo tart shells
- Paprika

Direction

1. Beat horseradish and cream cheese together in a small bowl until smooth, then stir in onion and crab. Scoop into each tart shell with 2 to 3 tsp. of cream cheese mixture, then sprinkle paprika over top.
2. Put tart shell on a baking sheet and bake at 350 degrees until tops start to brown, about 16 to 18 minutes.

Nutrition Information

Calories: 45 calories Total Carbohydrate: 2 g Cholesterol: 10 mg Total Fat: 3 g Fiber: 0 g Protein: 1 g Sodium: 55 mg

Pistachio Gorgonzola Cheesecake

Serving: 24 servings. | Prep: 30m | Ready in: 30m

Ingredients

- 2 shallots, quartered
- 1 lb. crumbled Gorgonzola cheese, divided
- 1 cup unsalted butter, cubed
- 1 package (8 oz.) cream cheese, softened and cubed
- 1/4 cup Madeira wine
- 2 tbsps. grated orange zest

- 1 tbsp. heavy whipping cream
- 1/2 tsp. white pepper
- 1/2 tsp. ground mustard
- 1-1/2 cups pistachios, toasted and chopped, divided
- 8 green onions, thinly sliced
- 2 tbsps. minced fresh basil
- 2 tbsps. minced fresh parsley
- 2 tbsps. oil-packed sun-dried tomatoes, drained and chopped
- Assorted crackers

Direction

1. Line parchment paper on bottom of 9-in. springform pan; put aside.
2. Process shallots, covered, till chopped in a food processor. Add mustard, pepper, cream, orange zest, wine, cream cheese, butter and 2 cups gorgonzola; cover. Process till blended; put aside.
3. Mix leftover gorgonzola cheese, tomatoes, parsley, basil, green onions and 1 cup pistachios in a small bowl. In prepped pan, spread 1/2 mixture. Put 1/2 cream cheese mixture over. Repeat layers and pat down. Cover; refrigerate for 8 hours – overnight.
4. Remove pan sides. Unmold onto serving platter carefully. Remove parchment paper. Chop leftover pistachios finely; press onto cheesecake's sides. Serve with crackers.

Nutrition Information

Calories: 225 calories Total Carbohydrate: 5 g Cholesterol: 48 mg Total Fat: 20 g Fiber: 2 g Protein: 7 g Sodium: 321 mg

Pomegranate Pistachio Crostini

Serving: 3 dozen. | Prep: 25m | Ready in: 30m

Ingredients

- 36 slices French bread baguette (1/4 inch thick)
- 1 tbsp. butter, melted
- 4 oz. cream cheese, softened
- 2 tbsps. orange juice
- 1 tbsp. honey
- 1 cup pomegranate seeds
- 1/2 cup finely chopped pistachios
- 2 oz. dark chocolate candy bar, grated

Direction

1. Preheat the oven to 400° F. On an ungreased baking sheet, set the bread slices; brush butter on top. Bake for 4 to 6 minutes till toasted lightly. Take off to a wire rack to cool down.
2. Whisk honey, orange juice and cream cheese till incorporated; scatter over toasts. Atop with the rest of the ingredients.

Nutrition Information

Calories: 44 calories Total Carbohydrate: 5 g Cholesterol: 5 mg Total Fat: 3 g Fiber: 0 g Protein: 1 g Sodium: 46 mg

Prosciutto Phyllo Roll-ups

Serving: 2 dozen (1 cup sauce). | Prep: 30m | Ready in: 40m

Ingredients

- 24 sheets phyllo dough (14 inches x 9 inches)
- 1/4 cup butter, melted
- 8 thin slices prosciutto, cut into 1-inch strips
- 24 fresh asparagus spears, trimmed
- 24 fresh green beans, trimmed

ARTICHOKE SAUCE:

- 1/4 cup sour cream
- 1/2 tsp. lemon juice
- 1 jar (6 oz.) marinated artichoke hearts, drained
- 2 oz. cream cheese, softened
- 1/4 cup chopped roasted sweet red peppers, drained
- 3 tbsps. grated Parmesan cheese
- 2 green onions, chopped
- 1 garlic clove, peeled
- 1/4 tsp. white pepper
- 1/4 tsp. cayenne pepper

Direction

1. Line parchment paper on baking sheets; put aside. Put one phyllo dough sheet on work surface. Keep leftover dough covered in plastic wrap and damp towel to keep them from dying out. Brush butter on. Lengthwise, fold in half. Brush butter on then fold in half, widthwise.
2. Brush butter on. Put prosciutto strip on top. At a diagonal, put a green bean and asparagus spear on bottom right corner then roll up. Repeat with leftover veggies, prosciutto, butter and dough.
3. On prepped baking sheets, put roll-ups. Bake till golden brown for 6-8 minutes at 400°. Meanwhile, process sauce ingredients in a blender, covered, till smooth. Put into small bowl; serve with roll-ups.

Roast Beef And Pear Crostini

Serving: 40 appetizers. | Prep: 20m | Ready in: 30m

Ingredients

- 1 French bread baguette (1 lb.)
- 3 tbsps. olive oil
- 1 garlic clove, minced
- 1 cup blue cheese salad dressing
- 1 medium pear, diced
- 1/4 cup thinly sliced green onions
- 2 cups cubed cooked roast beef
- 1 cup diced seeded tomatoes
- 1/2 tsp. salt
- 1/4 tsp. pepper
- 1/2 cup fresh basil leaves, thinly sliced

Direction

1. Slice baguette into 40 pieces. Put together garlic and oil; brush on one side of every bread slice. Put on a not greased baking sheet. Let bake at 350° F for 6 to 9 minutes till toasted lightly.
2. Put together the onions, pear and salad dressing. Mix the pepper, salt, tomatoes and roast beef.

Scatter dressing mixture on top of toasted bread; atop with basil and beef mixture.

Nutrition Information
Calories: 106 calories Total Carbohydrate: 10 g Cholesterol: 7 mg Total Fat: 6 g Fiber: 1 g Protein: 4 g Sodium: 168 mg

Savory Blt Cheesecake

Serving: 24 servings. | Prep: 35m | Ready in: 01h20m

Ingredients
- 3/4 cup dry bread crumbs
- 1/2 cup grated Parmesan cheese
- 3 tbsps. butter, melted

FILLING:
- 4 packages (8 oz. each) cream cheese, softened
- 1/2 cup heavy whipping cream
- 1-1/2 cups crumbled cooked bacon
- 1 cup oil-packed sun-dried tomatoes, patted dry and chopped
- 1 cup shredded Gruyere or Swiss cheese
- 2 green onions, sliced
- 1 tsp. freshly ground pepper
- 4 large eggs, lightly beaten
- Optional toppings: shredded iceberg lettuce, chopped cherry tomatoes and additional crumbled cooked bacon
- Assorted crackers, optional

Direction
1. Preheat an oven to 325°F. Put 9-in. greased springform pan onto double thickness of 18-in. square heavy-duty foil. Wrap foil around pan securely.
2. Mix butter, parmesan cheese and breadcrumbs in a small bowl; press on bottom of prepped pan. Put pan onto baking sheet; bake for 12 minutes. On wire rack, cool.
3. Beat cream and cream cheese till smooth in a big bowl; beat in pepper, onion, gruyere cheese, bacon and tomatoes. Add eggs; beat till just combined on low speed. Put on crust. Put springform pan into big baking pan; put 1-in. boiling water in bigger pan.
4. Bake till top looks dull and center is just set for 45-55 minutes. Take springform pan from the water bath then remove foil. Cool cheesecake for 10 minutes on wire rack; use knife to loosen edges from pan. Cool for 1 hour. Refrigerate overnight.
5. Remove the rim from pan. If desired, serve cheesecake with crackers and toppings.

Nutrition Information
Calories: 248 calories Total Carbohydrate: 5 g Cholesterol: 99 mg Total Fat: 21 g Fiber: 0 g Protein: 9 g Sodium: 438 mg

Shrimp Salad Lettuce Cups

Serving: about 1-1/2 dozen. | Prep: 20m | Ready in: 20m

Ingredients
- 1/3 cup mayonnaise
- 1/2 tsp. lemon juice

- 1/4 tsp. dill weed
- 1/4 tsp. seafood seasoning
- 1/8 tsp. salt
- 1/8 tsp. pepper
- 1/2 lb. cooked shrimp, chopped
- 1 green onion, sliced
- 2 tbsps. chopped celery
- 1 tbsp. diced pimientos
- 2 heads Belgian endive, separated into leaves

Direction

1. Mix the first six ingredients in a small bowl. Mix in the pimientos, celery, onion, and shrimp. Scoop 1 tablespoonful into each endive leaf; put on a platter and arrange them. Keep in the refrigerator until serving time.

Nutrition Information

Calories: 105 calories Total Carbohydrate: 4 g Cholesterol: 52 mg Total Fat: 7 g Fiber: 4 g Protein: 7 g Sodium: 179 mg

Shrimp With Basil-mango Sauce

Serving: 2 servings. | Prep: 10m | Ready in: 15m

Ingredients

- 1 medium ripe mango or 2 medium peaches, peeled and sliced
- 2 to 4 tbsps. minced fresh basil
- 1 tbsp. lemon juice
- 12 cooked medium shrimp, peeled and deveined
- 1 tbsp. butter
- Basil sprigs, optional

Direction

2. Mix together lemon juice, basil and mango in a food processor or blender, then place a cover and process mixture until combined. Transfer to 2 serving plates and put aside.
3. Skewer on each of six 4- to 6-inch soaked wooden or metal skewers with 2 shrimp, making a heart shape. In a big skillet, cook in butter on moderately high heat until shrimp are pink, turning one time, about 4 to 5 minutes. Put over mango sauce and use basil springs to decorate, if wanted.

Nutrition Information

Calories: 186 calories Total Carbohydrate: 19 g Cholesterol: 109 mg Total Fat: 7 g Fiber: 2 g Protein: 13 g Sodium: 134 mg

Strawberries With Chocolate Cream Filling

Serving: 3 dozen. | Prep: 30m | Ready in: 30m

Ingredients

- 1-1/2 oz. semisweet chocolate, grated, divided
- 1 package (8 oz.) cream cheese, softened
- 1 tsp. vanilla extract
- 1 cup whipped topping
- 18 large fresh strawberries, halved

Direction

1. Set 2 tbsps. of chocolate aside for later. Melt the rest of the chocolate in a microwave; stir chocolate until consistency is smooth. Allow chocolate to cool.
2. Beat vanilla and cream cheese together in a small bowl until consistency is smooth. Add the melted chocolate and continue to beat. Add 1 tbsp. of grated chocolate and whipped toppings; fold. Snip a hole on the edge of a food-safe plastic bag or the tip of a pastry bag. Insert the #21-star pastry tip to the pastry bag. Transfer the cream cheese mixture into the bag.
3. Arrange the strawberries cut side up on a serving platter. Pipe the mixture on the strawberries and sprinkle reserved grated chocolate. Leftovers can be refrigerated.

Strawberry Bruschetta

Serving: 12 | Prep: 10m | Ready in: 15m

Ingredients

- 24 slices French baguette
- 1 tbsp. butter, softened
- 2 cups chopped fresh strawberries
- 1/4 cup white sugar, or as needed

Direction

1. Preheat the oven's broiler. On every slice of bread, scatter a thin layer of butter. On a big baking sheet, set slices of bread in 1 layer.
2. Put bread below the broiler for 1 to 2 minutes, shortly till toasted lightly. Scoop some chopped strawberries onto every piece of toast, then scatter sugar on top of strawberries.
3. Put below the broiler once more for 3 to 5 minutes till sugar has caramelized. Serve right away.

Nutrition Information

Calories: 120 calories; Total Carbohydrate: 23.1 g Cholesterol: 3 mg Total Fat: 1.6 g Protein: 3.7 g Sodium: 202 mg

Swiss Potato Puffs

Serving: about 3 dozen. | Prep: 20m | Ready in: 40m

Ingredients

- 1-1/3 cups water
- 1/4 cup butter, cubed
- 1/2 tsp. salt
- 3/4 cup all-purpose flour
- 1/4 cup mashed potato flakes
- 3 eggs
- 1 cup (4 oz.) shredded Gruyere or Swiss cheese

Direction

1. Bring together salt, butter, water in a big saucepan to a boil, then take away from the heat.
2. Mix together potato flakes and flour, then stir into pan gradually. Cook and stir mixture on moderate heat until it creates turns into a smooth ball. Take away from the heat. Put in 1 egg at a time while beating well between additions. Keep on beating until the mixture is shiny and smooth, then stir in cheese.
3. Drop on baking sheets coated in grease with tablespoonfuls of mixture, spacing 2 inches apart. Bake

at 375 degrees until golden brown, about 18 to 22 minutes.

Nutrition Information

Calories: 37 calories Total Carbohydrate: 2 g Cholesterol: 22 mg Total Fat: 2 g Fiber: 0 g Protein: 2 g Sodium: 53 mg

Swiss Souffle Mushrooms

Serving: 32 appetizers. | Prep: 20m | Ready in: 35m

Ingredients

- 2 eggs
- 32 large fresh mushrooms
- 1/4 cup butter, divided
- 1 cup soft bread crumbs
- 3/4 cup shredded Swiss cheese
- 1/2 cup 2% milk
- 1/4 tsp. salt
- 1/8 tsp. pepper
- 1/8 tsp. ground nutmeg, optional

Direction

1. Split eggs and allow to stand for half an hour at room temperature. Take off steams from mushrooms and chop them finely until it measures 1 cup. Put the mushroom caps aside. Reserve leftover mushroom stems for another use or throw away.
2. Sauté chopped mushrooms in a big skillet with 2 tbsp. of butter until soft, then remove to a big bowl. Put in nutmeg, if wanted, pepper, salt, egg yolks, milk, cheese and bread crumbs.
3. Beat egg whites in a big bowl until stiff peaks form. Stir 1/4 of the egg whites into mushroom mixture using a spatula until all white streaks are gone. Fold in leftover egg whites until blended. Scoop into each mushroom cap with 1 tbsp. of filling, then arrange on baking sheets coated with grease. Melt leftover butter and drizzle over mushrooms.
4. Bake at 400 degrees until tops turn golden brown and mushrooms soften, about 12 to 15 minutes.

Nutrition Information

Calories: 38 calories Total Carbohydrate: 2 g Cholesterol: 20 mg Total Fat: 3 g Fiber: 0 g Protein: 2 g Sodium: 52 mg

Tyrokavteri

Serving: 24 | Prep: 15m | Ready in: 15m

Ingredients

- 1 (8 oz.) package cream cheese, softened
- 1 lb. crumbled feta
- 2 tsps. hot pepper sauce, or to taste
- 1 cup lemon juice
- 1/4 tsp. ground white pepper
- 1/2 cup olive oil
- 1 cup half-and-half (optional)
- 4 roasted red peppers, drained and chopped

Direction

1. Mix together lemon juice, white pepper, hot pepper sauce, feta cheese and cream cheese in the bowl of a stand mixer or a big bowl. Mix until combined on low speed. Blend in the olive oil gradually until it is blended completely. Stir in half-and-half until the mixture is soft and smooth. Stir in roasted red peppers if you want. Cover and store in the fridge until serving.

Nutrition Information

Calories: 144 calories; Total Carbohydrate: 3.3 g Cholesterol: 31 mg Total Fat: 13 g Protein: 4 g Sodium: 319 mg

Warm Seafood Spread

Serving: 4 cups. | Prep: 15m | Ready in: 40m

Ingredients

- 3/4 cup mayonnaise
- 1 tbsp. lemon juice
- 1-1/2 tsps. Worcestershire sauce
- 1 tsp. Dijon mustard
- 1/4 tsp. salt
- 1/8 tsp. pepper
- 2 cans (6 oz. each) crabmeat, drained, flaked and cartilage removed
- 1 can (6 oz.) small shrimp, rinsed and drained
- 2 celery ribs, chopped
- 1 small green pepper, chopped
- 1 small onion, finely chopped
- 1/4 cup dry bread crumbs
- Assorted crackers

Direction

1. Mix together pepper, salt, mustard, Worcestershire sauce, lemon juice and mayonnaise in a big bowl, then stir in onion, green pepper, celery, shrimp and crab.
2. Remove to a shallow 1-quart baking dish coated with grease. Sprinkle bread crumbs over top then bake at 350 degrees without a cover until brown slightly and bubbling, about 25 to 30 minutes. Serve together with crackers.

Nutrition Information

Calories: 116 calories Total Carbohydrate: 2 g Cholesterol: 45 mg Total Fat: 9 g Fiber: 0 g Protein: 7 g Sodium: 319 mg

Zippy Shrimp Skewers

Serving: 6 servings. | Prep: 10m | Ready in: 15m

Ingredients

- 2 tbsps. brown sugar
- 2 tsps. cider vinegar
- 1-1/2 tsps. canola oil
- 1 tsp. chili powder
- 1/2 tsp. salt
- 1/2 tsp. paprika
- 1/4 tsp. hot pepper sauce

- 3/4 lb. uncooked medium shrimp, peeled and deveined

Direction

1. Combine the shrimp with the first seven ingredients in a large re-sealable plastic bag. Seal the bag, turn multiple times to coat, and refrigerate for 2-4 hours. Drain the shrimps, discarding its marinade. Thread the shrimps onto six metal or pre-soaked wooden skewers. Grip an oil-moistened paper towel with long-handled tongs and dab on the grill rack to lightly coat with oil. Cook on an open grill over medium heat, or broil 4 in. from the heat, for 2-3 minutes per side or until shrimp just turns pink.

Nutrition Information

Calories: 57 calories Total Carbohydrate: 2 g Cholesterol: 84 mg Total Fat: 1 g Fiber: 0 g Protein: 9 g Sodium: 199 mg

Baked Dijon Salmon

Serving: 4 | Prep: 20m | Ready in: 35m

Ingredients

- 1/4 cup butter, melted
- 3 tbsps. Dijon mustard
- 1 1/2 tbsps. honey
- 1/4 cup dry bread crumbs
- 1/4 cup finely chopped pecans
- 4 tsps. chopped fresh parsley
- 4 (4 oz.) fillets salmon
- salt and pepper to taste
- 1 lemon, for garnish

Direction

1. Set oven to heat to 400 deg F or200 deg C.
2. Mix together honey, mustard, and butter in a small bowl. Set it aside. Mix together pecans, bread crumbs, and parsley in a different bowl.
3. Lightly coat each salmon fillet with the honey mustard mixture and top the fillets with the bread crumb mixture.
4. For 12 to 15 minutes, bake salmon in heated oven, or until with a fork the salmon easily flakes. Use salt and pepper to season and use a wedge of lemon to garnish.

Nutrition Information

Calories: 422 calories; Total Carbohydrate: 17.6 g Cholesterol: 97 mg Total Fat: 29 g Protein: 24.3 g Sodium: 480 mg

Baked Snapper With Mandarin Oranges, Cashews And Ginger

Serving: 4 | Prep: 20m | Ready in: 35m

Ingredients

- 4 (4 oz.) fillets red snapper
- 2 mandarin oranges, juiced
- 2 tbsps. fresh lime juice
- 1 tbsp. brown sugar
- 2 tbsps. soy sauce

- 1 tsp. sesame oil
- 1 pinch red pepper flakes
- 2 tsps. finely chopped fresh ginger
- 2 mandarin oranges - peeled and chopped
- 1/3 cup unsalted cashews, roughly chopped
- 2 green onions, finely chopped

Direction

1. Preheat oven to 225 degrees C/425 degrees F.
2. In one layer, put snapper fillets at the bottom of a shallow baking dish that's lightly greased. Mix together sesame oil, soy sauce, brown sugar, lime juice and mandarin orange juice in a medium bowl. Mix in chopped mandarin oranges, ginger and red pepper flakes. Pour on snapper in the dish.
3. Bake in preheated oven for 12-15 minutes, uncovered, until fish becomes opaque. Put fillets on serving plates. Spoon sauce on fish. Garnish with green onions and sprinkle of cashews.

Nutrition Information

Calories: 256 calories; Total Carbohydrate: 20.4 g Cholesterol: 41 mg Total Fat: 8.3 g Protein: 26.1 g Sodium: 529 mg

Beef Tenderloin With Ginger-shiitake Brown Butter

Serving: 4 | Prep: 30m | Ready in: 50m

Ingredients

4 (8 oz.) filet mignon steaks
Kosher salt and fresh cracked pepper to taste
2 tbsps. olive oil
3 tbsps. unsalted butter
2 tbsps. finely minced fresh ginger
1 tbsp. finely minced garlic
1/2 cup thinly sliced fresh shiitake mushrooms
1/2 tsp. kosher salt
3 tbsps. sake
2 tbsps. mirin (Japanese sweet wine)
1/2 cup unsalted butter
1 tbsp. finely chopped garlic chives

Direction

1. Preheat an oven to 200°C/400°F.
2. Season filets with pepper and salt to taste. In heavy, ovenproof skillet, heat olive oil on medium-high heat till it starts to smoke. Sear steaks, 3 minutes per side, till golden brown on both sides. Put steaks in preheated oven; cook to desired doneness or for 10 minutes. When steaks are done, put aside to rest in a warm area while finishing sauce.
3. Meanwhile, melt 3 tbsp. butter in saucepan on medium heat. Mix ginger and garlic in; gently cook for 1 1/2 - 2 minutes till translucent and fragrant. Add 1/2 tsp. salt and shiitake mushrooms; cook for 3-4 minutes till soft. Put mirin and sake in; reduce by half.
4. Mix leftover 1/2 cup butter in; lower heat to medium-low when melted. Cook for 6-8 minutes till butter is dark golden brown. Season with pepper and salt to taste. Mix chives in. Put sauce on steaks. Serve.

Nutrition Information

Calories: 816 calories; Total Carbohydrate: 5.2 g Cholesterol: 261 mg Total Fat: 56 g Protein: 64.9 g Sodium: 481 mg

Braised Pheasant

Serving: 8 | Prep: 20m | Ready in: 1h20m

Ingredients

- 3 large pheasants, cleaned and rinsed
- 1/4 cup safflower oil
- 3 cups peeled and thinly sliced green apples
- 1 cup thinly sliced onions
- 1/2 cup apple jack
- 1 tsp. nutmeg
- 1/2 cup half-and-half cream
- 1/2 tsp. salt-free seasoning blend
- ground black pepper to taste

Direction

1. Prepare the oven by preheating to 350°F (175°C). Set a big Dutch oven on medium heat, add safflower oil then put in the pheasants and brown on all sides. Insert the onions and sliced apples surrounding the pheasants. Place the applejack on everything then light on fire. Shake the pan until flames stop. Sprinkle tops of pheasants with nutmeg.
2. Place in the preheated oven and bake for approximately 1 hour, covered, or until the juices run clear once a knife is pricked into the thigh. Take the Pheasants, onions, and apples to a platter then leave it warm in the oven.
3. Place the juices to a saucepan then make it simmer on medium heat. Mix in the half-and-half and allow it to simmer for 5 minutes, whisking frequently. Add ground black pepper and salt-free seasoning blend to season and taste. Put on the pheasants to serve.

Nutrition Information

Calories: 684 calories; Total Carbohydrate: 8 g Cholesterol: 219 mg Total Fat: 36.6 g Protein: 68.9 g Sodium: 127 mg

Chef John's Lobster Mac And Cheese

Serving: 2 | Prep: 30m | Ready in: 1h

Ingredients

- 2 tsps. vegetable oil
- 2 lobster tails, split in half lengthwise and deveined
- 2 tbsps. butter
- 1 1/2 tbsps. all-purpose flour
- 1 1/2 cups cold milk
- 1/4 tsp. paprika
- 1 pinch ground nutmeg
- 1 pinch cayenne pepper, or to taste
- 1/2 tsp. salt, or to taste
- 3 drops Worcestershire sauce, or to taste

- 4 oz. grated sharp white Cheddar cheese
- 1 oz. grated Gruyere cheese
- 1 cup elbow macaroni, or more to taste
- 1/2 tsp. fresh thyme leaves

Crumbs:
- 3 tbsps. panko bread crumbs
- 1 tbsp. melted butter
- 2 tbsps. grated Parmesan cheese

Direction
1. Start preheating the oven to 400°F (200°C). Butter 2 oven-proof plates.
2. In a frying pan, heat oil over high heat. Cook lobster tails in the frying pan for 2 minutes per side until halfway heated through and slightly golden. Move the tails to a dish to sit. Once cool enough to touch, separate the lobster meat from the shell and cut the meat. Store the shell.
3. In the same frying pan, heat 2 tbsps. of butter over medium heat. Mix in flour, stir and cook for 1-2 minutes until the flour is cooked off and forms a paste. Add chilled milk to the flour mixture, beat until completely blended. Simmer it; decrease the heat to low, mix in cayenne pepper, nutmeg, and paprika. Cook, tossing sometimes for 3-4 minutes until firm. Use salt to season.
4. Mix Gruyere cheese and Cheddar cheese into the mixture until the cheese is melted. Take away from heat and mix Worcestershire sauce into the cheese sauce.
5. Boil a big pot of water with a pinch of salt and the stored lobster tails. Add elbow macaroni to the boiling water and cook, tossing sometimes for 8 minutes until heated through but firm to the bite. Take out and dispose of the lobster shell, strain the pasta.
6. Mix macaroni into the cheese sauce with thyme leaves. Split the macaroni mixture onto the 2 prepared oven-proof plates. Put the cut lobster meat on top of the macaroni; use a fork to push the meat into the macaroni mixture.
7. In a bowl, mix together the melted butter and bread crumbs. Add Parmesan cheese and mix. Put the bread crumb mixture on top of each oven-proof plate.
8. Bake in the preheated oven for 15-20 minutes until bubbly and golden.

Nutrition Information
Calories: 975 calories; Total Carbohydrate: 61.8 g Cholesterol: 283 mg Total Fat: 53 g Protein: 63.3 g Sodium: 1767 mg

Chestnut Pappardelle With Cremini Mushrooms, White Wine, And Parmigiano-reggiano

Serving: 6 | Prep: 1h | Ready in: 2h25m

Ingredients
Pasta:
- 14 oz. all-purpose flour
- 3 1/2 oz. chestnut flour
- 1 pinch salt
- 3 tbsps. extra-virgin olive oil
- 4 eggs
- 4 egg yolks

Sauce:

- 2 tbsps. butter
- 2 large leeks - washed, trimmed, and thinly sliced
- 2 tbsps. minced shallot
- 2 cloves garlic, chopped
- 1 tbsp. olive oil
- 2 lbs. mixed varieties of fresh mushrooms
- 1 cup dry white wine
- 1 bunch fresh parsley, minced
- 2 tbsps. shredded Parmigiano-Reggiano cheese, or to taste

Direction
1. In a bowl, whisk together salt, chestnut flour and flour, then stir in egg yolks, eggs and 3 tbsp. of olive oil to make a smooth dough. Shape dough into a ball and wrap in a cloth towel, then allow to rest about an hour.
2. Roll pasta on a work surface coated with flour into thin sheets, 5-inch x12-inch in size, then cut sheets into 1-inch x12-inch ribbons. Allow pappardelle pasta to dry on a kitchen towel dusted with flour while you finish remaining steps.
3. In a big skillet, melt butter on moderate heat, then cook and stir garlic, shallot and leeks until white part of leeks become translucent, for 5 minutes. Heat in a separate skillet with 1 tbsp. of olive oil on moderate heat, then in hot olive oil, cook and stir mushrooms for 10-15 minutes, until liquid evaporates and mushrooms turn golden brown. Stir mushrooms to mixture of leek.
4. Stir into mushroom-leek mixture with white wine then scrape up and dissolve any browned bits of food stuck on the bottom of skillet. Bring to a boil then turn heat to low and simmer mixture for 5 minutes, until the mushrooms soften.
5. Bring lightly salted water in a big pot to a boil, then cook pappardelle pasta at a boil for 5 minutes, until pasta floats to top of the water and tender. Drain pasta and remove to a serving bowl, then toss gently together with parsley and mushroom-leek mixture. Put Parmigiano-Reggiano cheese on top.

Nutrition Information
Calories: 607 calories; Total Carbohydrate: 77.8 g Cholesterol: 272 mg Total Fat: 21.5 g Protein: 20.3 g Sodium: 136 mg

Chicken With Sun-dried Tomato And Roasted Pepper Cream Sauce

Serving: 4 | Prep: 15m | Ready in: 40m

Ingredients
- 3 tbsps. olive oil
- 2 cloves garlic, minced
- 4 skinless, boneless chicken breast halves
- 2 cups chicken broth
- 1/2 cup red wine
- 2 tbsps. Italian seasoning
- 1 (6 oz.) jar sun-dried tomatoes packed in oil, drained and chopped
- 1 (16 oz.) jar roasted red peppers, drained and chopped
- 1/2 cup heavy cream
- 8 oz. uncooked spinach fettuccine

- 2 tbsps. all-purpose flour

Direction

1. Heat olive oil in big skillet on medium heat; cook garlic for 2 minutes till soft. Lay chicken breasts in skillet, then cook for 5 minutes per side till lightly browned. Add sun-dried tomatoes, Italian seasoning, red wine and chicken broth. Lower heat to low. Simmer for 15-20 minutes till sauce reduces and chicken isn't pink inside anymore.
2. Put big pot of lightly salted water on rolling boil on high heat. Mix spinach fettucine in when water boils. Boil again. Cook pasta for 8 minutest till cooked through yet still firm to bite, occasionally mixing, uncovered. Drain in colander set in sink well; put fettuccine on serving platter.
3. Mix cream and roasted red peppers into skillet. Bring just to a simmer and let simmer for 5 minutes. Take out chicken breasts, putting on fettuccine. Whisk flour into sauce; simmer for 3 minutes longer, constantly whisking, till thick. Put sauce on pasta and chicken.

Nutrition Information

Calories: 692 calories; Total Carbohydrate: 61.9 g Cholesterol: 108 mg Total Fat: 32.2 g Protein: 37.3 g Sodium: 611 mg

Citrus Scallops II

Serving: 4 | Prep: 15m | Ready in: 30m

Ingredients

- 2 1/2 tbsps. olive oil
- 1 lb. bay scallops
- 2 tbsps. all-purpose flour
- 1 cup white wine
- 1 tbsp. chopped onion
- 1 tbsp. chopped green bell pepper
- 1 1/2 tbsps. chopped fresh dill
- 4 cherry tomatoes, quartered
- 2 tbsps. lemon juice
- 1 tbsp. lemon zest
- 2 tbsps. butter

Direction

1. In a skillet, heat olive oil over medium heat. Flour the scallops lightly, then cook until lightly browned, 1-2 minutes per side. Take the scallops out from the skillet, then drain off the excess oil. Mix in white wine, loosening browned bits from the bottom of the skillet.
2. Combine dill, green bell pepper, and onion into the skillet. Stir and cook for 2 minutes. Stir in lemon zest, lemon juice, and tomatoes. Carry on cooking for a minute and stir in the butter until it melts. Stir and cook until the liquid reduces by the amount you desire. Place the scallops back into the skillet and cook until they are just heated through.

Nutrition Information

Calories: 347 calories; Total Carbohydrate: 12 g Cholesterol: 84 mg Total Fat: 15.4 g Protein: 29.3 g Sodium: 374 mg

Cognac Shrimp

Serving: 4 | Prep: 15m | Ready in: 35m

Ingredients

- 1 tbsp. butter
- 1 tbsp. olive oil
- 2 cloves garlic, minced
- 1/2 cup thinly sliced shallots
- 1 lb. shrimp, peeled and deveined
- salt and pepper to taste
- 1 dash dried red pepper flakes (optional)
- 1/4 cup oil-packed sun-dried tomatoes, drained and diced
- 1/2 cup cognac
- 1/2 cup fat free half-and-half

Direction

1. In a skillet, heat butter and olive oil over medium-high heat, then sauté garlic and shallots till lightly browned. Add shrimp in and stir, use red pepper, pepper, and salt for seasoning. Add sun-dried tomatoes in then mix well. Cook and stir till shrimp gets opaque and lightly browned or for 5 minutes.
2. In the skillet, pour cognac, and loosen browned bits from bottom by stirring. Lower heat to low, then stir in half-and-half. Allow to simmer till slightly thickened, or for 5 minutes.

Nutrition Information

Calories: 276 calories; Total Carbohydrate: 8.3 g Cholesterol: 182 mg Total Fat: 8.7 g Protein: 20.3 g Sodium: 284 mg

Creamy Cajun Chicken Pasta

Serving: 2 | Prep: 15m | Ready in: 30m

Ingredients

- 4 oz. linguine pasta
- 2 boneless, skinless chicken breast halves, sliced into thin strips
- 2 tsps. Cajun seasoning
- 2 tbsps. butter
- 1 green bell pepper, chopped
- 1/2 red bell pepper, chopped
- 4 fresh mushrooms, sliced
- 1 green onion, minced
- 1 1/2 cups heavy cream
- 1/4 tsp. dried basil
- 1/4 tsp. lemon pepper
- 1/4 tsp. salt
- 1/8 tsp. garlic powder
- 1/8 tsp. ground black pepper
- 2 tbsps. grated Parmesan cheese

Direction

1. Use a big pot and fill it slightly salted water and boil. Place the linguini into the boiling water and cook for about eight to ten minutes. Drain water once the pasta is cooked.
2. In a mixing bowl, place in the Cajun seasoning and chicken. Toss so it coats.

3. Heat a big frying pan on medium-heat and sauté the chicken with pieces of butter until it is thoroughly cooked for five to seven minutes. Then, mix in the red and green bell peppers, green onions and sliced mushrooms. Let it cook for another two to three minutes. Turn down the heat then mix in heavy cream. Season sauce with lemon pepper, salt, basil, garlic powder and ground black pepper. Heat well.
4. Transfer the pasta into a big bowl with the sauce. Drizzle with parmesan cheese before serving.

Nutrition Information
Calories: 1109 calories; Total Carbohydrate: 53.7 g Cholesterol: 348 mg Total Fat: 82.2 g Protein: 42.7 g Sodium: 1134 mg

Duck Confit
Serving: 2

Ingredients
- 2 uncooked Peking duck legs
- 1 tbsp. kosher salt
- 1 lemon, zested and thinly sliced
- 3 cloves garlic, crushed
- 1 tbsp. whole allspice berries
- 1 tbsp. juniper berries
- 2 sprigs fresh thyme
- 2 cups rendered duck fat

Direction
1. Massage both sides of the duck legs with kosher salt. Put them inside a big resealable bag. Add lemon slices and zest, allspice berries, garlic, fresh thyme, and juniper berries. Seal the bag. Massage the meat through the bag, making sure the marinade evenly coats the duck. Store inside the fridge for 24 hours to marinate.
2. Preheat the oven to 200°F (93°C).
3. Take the duck legs out of the bag. Wash them off and pat dry. Save the rest of the bag's contents in the base of an oven-safe dish that could accommodate the legs in one layer. Use a glass or enameled cast iron dish if possible. Place the legs so they're skin side down. Place the duck fat in a saucepan and cook over low heat, until it has turned to liquid. Pour this over the legs until they're entirely submerged. Use olive oil if there isn't enough to cover the duck legs. While the legs are cooking, more fat will be rendered from skin. Place a lid on the dish.
4. Let it bake in the oven for 6 to 7 hours. The meat should be easy to pull from the bone. Transfer the legs out of the fat into a sealable container. Remove and discard the duck bones. Be sure that there's ample space at the top of the container. Remove all the solids from the rest of the fat rendered, and discard them. Pour the fat into the container, over the duck. Make sure the duck is completely covered. Seal the container and let it rest to room temperature. When it has cooled down, place it in the fridge and have the meat cure for 2 months. You can keep any of the leftover duck for later use.

Nutrition Information
Calories: 2500 calories; Total Carbohydrate: 9.5 g Cholesterol: 330 mg Total Fat: 270 g Protein: 20.1 g Sodium: 2989 mg

Duck With Honey, Soy, And Ginger
Serving: 2 | Prep: 10m | Ready in: 40m

Ingredients

- 2 duck breast halves
- 1 pinch salt
- 1 pinch cayenne pepper
- 1 pinch ground black pepper
- 1/2 cup chicken stock
- 2 tbsps. honey
- 2 tbsps. soy sauce
- 2 tbsps. rice wine
- 1 tbsp. grated fresh ginger
- 1 tbsp. tomato sauce
- 1 pinch chili powder
- 1 tsp. lime juice

Direction

1. Preheat the oven to 400°F (200°C).
2. Score the duck breasts with a sharp knife, 4 times through fat and skin but just barely reaching the meat. Massage the duck skin with salt, black pepper, and cayenne.
3. Preheat an oven-proof pan over medium-high heat. Place the breasts in the pan skin-side down. Fry for 5 minutes, until the skin is crisp and brown. Remove any excess fat from the bottom of the pan using a spoon. Flip the breasts and cook for 1 more minute.
4. Put the pan in the oven and roast the duck. Cook until an instant-read thermometer placed in the thickest part of the breasts reads 160°F (71°C) for a well-done cook. Adjust the required temperature depending on preferred doneness.
5. Take the duck out of the pan and cover with foil. Let it rest. Remove excess fat from the pan. Put honey, stock, soy sauce, ginger, rice wine, chili powder, tomato sauce, and lime juice in the pan.
6. Whisk the sauce until it thickens over high heat. Let it boil for 2 minutes. Slice the breasts thinly and serve on plates. Pour sauce on top.

Nutrition Information

Calories: 260 calories; Total Carbohydrate: 21.3 g Cholesterol: 106 mg Total Fat: 8.8 g Protein: 20.6 g Sodium: 1186 mg

Easy White Chicken Enchiladas

Serving: 6 | Prep: 10m | Ready in: 40m

Ingredients

- 4 oz. cream cheese, softened
- 1/2 cup sour cream
- 1/2 cup green salsa
- 2 (6 oz.) packages seasoned cooked chicken cubes
- 1 cup shredded Mexican-style cheese blend
- 1 1/2 cups white cheese sauce, or queso dip
- 6 (8 inch) flour tortillas

Direction

1. Set the oven to 190°C or 375°F to preheat. Use cooking spray to coat an 8"x8" glass baking dish lightly.

2. Stir together salsa, sour cream and softened cream cheese until combined, then fold in shredded cheese and chicken. Spread onto the bottom of the baking dish with a small amount of white cheese sauce. Split the filling among tortillas evenly and roll them into firm cylinders. Put into prepped baking dish and use leftover sauce to cover.
3. In the preheated oven, bake for half an hour until bubbly and turn golden, and then let rest for 5 minutes prior to serving.

Nutrition Information
Calories: 625 calories; Total Carbohydrate: 36.7 g Cholesterol: 138 mg Total Fat: 37.4 g Protein: 33.7 g Sodium: 1588 mg

Elegant Stuffed Chicken And Asparagus Bundles
Serving: 2 | Prep: 40m | Ready in: 1h35m

Ingredients
- 2 tbsps. vegetable oil
- 1/2 red onion, chopped
- 1 tbsp. finely minced garlic
- 4 ribs celery, minced
- 1/2 cup grated carrot
- 6 large mushrooms, chopped
- 1 cup cubed corn bread
- 1/2 cup freshly grated Parmesan cheese
- Salt and pepper to taste
- 2 (8 oz.) skinless, boneless chicken breast halves
- 12 asparagus spears, trimmed
- 2 slices thick sliced bacon

Direction
1. Start preheating the oven to 350°F (175°C). Spray cooking spray over a small baking dish, then put aside.
2. In a skillet, heat vegetable oil over medium heat. Stir in garlic and onions; cook about one minute. Put in mushrooms, carrot and the celery, then cook until vegetables have softened. Mix in Parmesan cheese and cornbread. Add in pepper and salt to taste, put aside.
3. On the work surface, lay chicken breasts flat. Create a horizontal cut down one side with the paring knife to make a pocket in each breast; avoid cutting all the way through. Stuff enough cornbread mixture into the breasts to make them quite plump. Season with pepper and salt. Put into prepared baking dish.
4. Bake for 45 mins in prepared oven, until a thermometer reads 160°F (70°C) when inserted into the middle of stuffing.
5. During cooking the chicken, separate asparagus spears into 2, 6-piece portions. Wrap a slice of bacon over each bundle. Put them into the shallow baking dish, bake along with chicken during the last 20 mins. When done, the bacon should be crisp and the asparagus soft.
6. Cut breasts on the diagonal into slices, about 1/4-inch to serve. Fan slices out into the half-moon shape on 1 side of a plate, then arrange on the other an asparagus bundle.

Nutrition Information
Calories: 786 calories; Total Carbohydrate: 35.6 g Cholesterol: 184 mg Total Fat: 38.9 g Protein: 73 g Sodium: 1095 mg

Garithes Yiouvetsi

Serving: 8 | Prep: 30m | Ready in: 45m

Ingredients

- 4 tbsps. extra virgin olive oil
- 1 medium onion, finely chopped
- 3/4 cup chopped green onion
- 2 cloves garlic, crushed
- 2 cups chopped, peeled tomatoes
- 1/2 cup dry white wine
- 1/4 cup chopped fresh parsley
- 1 tbsp. chopped fresh oregano
- salt and pepper to taste
- 2 lbs. large uncooked shrimp, peeled
- 4 oz. crumbled feta cheese

Direction

1. In a skillet, heat the oil over medium heat. In the oil, sauté the onion until it turns transparent. Stir in garlic and green onions; cook and stir often for 2 minutes more. Stir in pepper and salt to taste, oregano, most of the parsley, wine, and tomatoes. Put on a cover and gently simmer for half an hour.
2. Set an oven to 260°C (500°F) and start preheating.
3. On the bottom of a large oven dish, place 1/2 of the sauce. Evenly spread the shrimp on the sauce and top with the rest of the sauce. Dust with the feta cheese.
4. In the prepared oven, cook until the feta is browned lightly and melted and the shrimp turns pink, about 10-15 minutes. Dust with the rest of the parsley and serve right away.

Nutrition Information

Calories: 218 calories; Total Carbohydrate: 5.2 g Cholesterol: 185 mg Total Fat: 10.9 g Protein: 21.4 g Sodium: 436 mg

Garlic Salmon

Serving: 6 | Prep: 15m | Ready in: 40m

Ingredients

- 1 1/2 lbs. salmon fillet
- salt and pepper to taste
- 3 cloves garlic, minced
- 1 sprig fresh dill, chopped
- 5 slices lemon
- 5 sprigs fresh dill weed
- 2 green onions, chopped

Direction

1. Preheat an oven to 230 degrees C (450 degrees F). Use cooking spray to spritz 2 large pieces of aluminum foil.
2. Put the salmon fillet onto one piece of foil. Drizzle the salmon using chopped dill, garlic, salt, and pepper. Spread slices of lemon slices over the fillet and then put a sprig of dill onto each lemon slice. Drizzle chopped scallions onto the fillet.

3. Use a second piece of foil to cover the salmon and then seal tightly by pinching the foil together. Transfer to a big baking dish or to baking sheet.
4. Bake for 20 to 25 minutes in the oven until the salmon is flaked easily.

Nutrition Information
Calories: 169 calories; Total Carbohydrate: 2.1 g Cholesterol: 50 mg Total Fat: 6.7 g Protein: 24.5 g Sodium: 48 mg

Heather's Rosemary Citrus Cornish Hens
Serving: 8 | Prep: 20m | Ready in: 5h20m

Ingredients
- 4 1/2 cups vegetable broth
- 4 1/2 cups water
- 1 tbsp. whole allspice berries
- 1 tbsp. whole black peppercorns
- 1 cup kosher salt
- 4 Cornish game hens
- 1 grapefruit, cut into quarters
- 1 juicy orange, cut into quarters
- 1 lemon, cut into quarters
- 1 lime, cut into quarters
- 1 sprig fresh rosemary, or to taste, chopped
- 1 sprig fresh thyme, or to taste, chopped
- 1/4 cup water
- 1/4 cup olive oil
- salt and ground black pepper to taste

Direction
1. Place together in a large pot the kosher salt, black peppercorns, the allspice berries, 4 1/2 cup cups of water and vegetable broth and make it boil, stir to make the salt dissolve. Get the pot away from heat, and put aside to cool. Once cool enough, put the Cornish hens into the brine and place inside the refrigerator for 2 to 3 hours.
2. Prepare the oven by preheating to 350 degrees F (175 degrees C). Get the game hens from the brine then pat dry. Get rid of brine.
3. In a microwave-safe bowl, put together the thyme, rosemary, lime, lemon, orange and cut-up grapefruit, and place inside the microwave for 2 minutes on high temperature; use tongs to stuff the herbs and fruits into the cavities of the Cornish hens. Brush each hen with olive oil, and drizzle with black pepper and salt. Get a roasting dish and put the hens in it while breast sides up.
4. Place inside the preheated oven for about 1 hour and 45 minutes until pink color at the bone faded and juices dried out. Use an instant-read thermometer to insert into thickest part of the thigh, close to the bone and should read 180 degrees F (82 degrees C). Turn the oven heat up to 400 degrees F (205 degrees C) for extra-crispy skin during the last 15 minutes of cooking. Let the hens rest for 10 minutes and serve.

Lamb Chops With Balsamic Reduction
Serving: 4 | Prep: 10m | Ready in: 40m

Ingredients

3/4 tsp. dried rosemary
1/4 tsp. dried basil
1/2 tsp. dried thyme
salt and pepper to taste
4 lamb chops (3/4 inch thick)
1 tbsp. olive oil
1/4 cup minced shallots
1/3 cup aged balsamic vinegar
3/4 cup chicken broth
1 tbsp. butter

Direction

1. Combine pepper, salt, thyme, basil, and rosemary in a cup or a small bowl. Rub on both sides of the lamb with the mixture. On a dish, put the lamb, put a cover on and put aside for the flavors to soak in, about 15 minutes.
2. In a big frying pan, heat olive oil over medium-high heat. In the frying pan, put the lamb chops, and cook for 3 1/2 minutes each side for medium-rare, or keep cooking until reaching your wanted doneness. Take out of the frying pan, and put on a serving dish to keep warm.
3. Add shallots to the frying pan, and cook until barely browned, about several minutes. Mix in vinegar, scraping any lamb bits from the bottom of the frying pan, and then mix in chicken broth. Keep stirring and cooking over medium-high heat until the sauce has decreased by 1/2, about 5 minutes. Otherwise, the sauce won't be good and be runny. Take away from heat, and mix in butter. Spread over the lamb chops, and enjoy.

Nutrition Information

Calories: 255 calories; Total Carbohydrate: 5 g Cholesterol: 64 mg Total Fat: 19.3 g Protein: 14.6 g Sodium: 70 mg

Lamb For Lovers

Serving: 4 | Prep: 30m | Ready in: 9h

Ingredients

* 2 tbsps. olive oil
* 2 (7 bone) racks of lamb, trimmed, fat reserved
* salt and pepper to taste
* 4 cloves garlic, minced
* 1 large onion, diced
* 4 carrots, diced
* 1 cup celery tops
* 1 cup port wine
* 1 cup red wine
* 1 (14.5 oz.) can low-sodium chicken broth
* 5 sprigs fresh spearmint
* 3 sprigs fresh rosemary
* 1 cup mint apple jelly
* 2 tbsps. olive oil
* salt and pepper to taste
* 1 tbsp. garlic, minced

- 1/4 cup panko bread crumbs
- 2 tbsps. olive oil
- 4 sprigs fresh mint

Direction

1. Making Demi-Glace: In a medium skillet, heat two tbsps. of olive oil on medium heat and then place in trimmings from the lamb. Season with pepper and salt, then brown the fat, lower the heat and add chicken broth, red wine, port, celery leaves, carrots, onion and 4 cloves minced garlic. Place mixture into a slow cooker and let it simmer for 8 hours or overnight on Low.
2. Over medium-low heat, strain the mixture from slow cooker into saucepan. Stir in mint jelly, rosemary and spearmint. Simmer while adding extra broth, wine or port as needed, until the mixture leaves behind a coating like that of a syrup on the back of a spoon, then strain again and keep it warm as the lamb roasts.
3. Roasting the Lamb: Put an oven-proof skillet or a cast iron in an oven and then preheat to 230 degrees C (450 degrees F). Rub the lamb with garlic, pepper, salt and two tbsps. of olive oil, then coat with the panko bread crumbs.
4. Gently take out the heated skillet from oven. Heat two tbsps. of olive oil in skillet and then sear the lamb on each side. Place skillet containing the lamb back into the oven and continue to cook for 5 to 10 minutes, until the internal temperature is 63 degrees C (145 degrees F).
5. Place a little amount of demi-glace onto a platter and then arrange the lamb crisscrossed. Drizzle with additional demi-glace and stud with fresh mint. Serve.

Nutrition Information

Calories: 1246 calories; Total Carbohydrate: 68.4 g Cholesterol: 192 mg Total Fat: 79.4 g Protein: 45.3 g Sodium: 422 mg

Lemon-pepper Salmon
Serving: 4 | Prep: 10m | Ready in: 30m

Ingredients

- 2 tbsps. butter
- 2 tbsps. olive oil
- 4 (4 oz.) salmon steaks
- 1 tsp. minced garlic
- 1 tbsp. lemon pepper
- 1 tsp. salt
- 1/4 cup water
- 1 cup chopped fresh tomatoes
- 1 cup chopped fresh cilantro
- 2 cups boiling water
- 1 cup uncooked couscous

Direction

1. Put olive oil and butter in a large skillet and heat it over medium heat. Add the salmon into the skillet and season it with lemon pepper, salt, and garlic. Pour around salmon with 1/4 cup of water. Add the cilantro and tomatoes. Cover the skillet and cook for 15 minutes until the fish flakes with a fork easily.
2. Boil 2 cups of water in a pot. Remove it from the heat. Stir in couscous. Cover the pot and let it sit for 5 minutes. Place the cooked salmon over the couscous. Drizzle it with the sauce from the skillet;

serve.

Nutrition Information

Calories: 498 calories; Total Carbohydrate: 36.2 g Cholesterol: 89 mg Total Fat: 23.5 g Protein: 31.6 g Sodium: 1039 mg

Lobster Fricassee

Serving: 4 | Prep: 15m | Ready in: 40m

Ingredients

- 1/2 cup finely chopped carrot
- 1/2 cup chopped celery
- 1/2 cup chopped onion
- 2 cups dry white wine
- 2 (1 1/2 lb.) whole lobsters
- 2 tbsps. brandy
- 1/2 cup heavy cream
- 2 tbsps. unsalted butter

Direction

1. Mix white wine, onion, celery, and carrot together in a big frying pan. Boil it. Put lobsters, put a cover on, and cook for 8 minutes until the lobsters are shiny red. Take the lobsters out from the sauce and let it cool down.
2. Once the lobsters are cool enough to touch, slice each one in two lengthwise. Separate the meat from the claws and shell, save it and do not break the shell.
3. Dispose the tomalley if you want. Cut each tail into 4 medallions and put aside.
4. Keep simmering the vegetables and wine in the frying pan for 10 minutes until there is half of the liquid left. Put the shell back to the sauce and mix in the brandy. Simmer for 5 minutes. Use a mesh strainer or a sieve to filter the stock through into a saucepan. Mix in the heavy cream and cook on medium heat for 10 minutes until firm. Mix in the butter just until melted. Put lobster meat in the sauce and cook over low heat until cooked through.

Nutrition Information

Calories: 602 calories; Total Carbohydrate: 9.7 g Cholesterol: 379 mg Total Fat: 19.9 g Protein: 65.3 g Sodium: 1051 mg

Lobster Mac And Cheese

Serving: 8 | Prep: 30m | Ready in: 1h30m

Ingredients

- 1 (16 oz.) package elbow macaroni
- 1 (2 lb.) lobster, split
- 2 tbsps. butter
- 1 small onion, diced
- 1 clove garlic, minced
- 1 shallot, chopped
- 10 black peppercorns
- 2 cups milk
- 5 tbsps. butter

- 5 tbsps. all-purpose flour
- 1 lb. shredded Gruyere cheese
- 3 cups shredded Cheddar cheese
- 1 cup grated Romano cheese
- kosher salt and pepper to taste
- 3 tbsps. panko bread crumbs

Direction

1. Boil light-salted water to rolling boil in a large pot over high heat. When the water gets boiled, mix in the macaroni and keep boiling. Cook the pasta uncovered, stir sporadically for about 8 minutes until the pasta is cooked through but firm enough to bite. Save about 2 cups of the pasta water, use a colander set in the sink to take the pasta out of water and rinse with cold water to cool. Set aside.
2. Take the pasta water to a big pot, put the lobster halves in with cut-side up. Boil up the water, lower to medium-low heat, cover and steam the lobster for about 3 minutes until the meat gets high opacity and firmness. Take the lobster out and let cool for a few minutes, then take out the meat and divide into bite-sized chunks. Save the shells
3. In a saucepan, melt 2 tbsps. of butter over medium heat. Mix in the onion and cook for about 5 minutes until the onion gets softened and translucent, take the onion to a small bowl and set aside. Add milk, peppercorns, shallots, garlic and the saved lobster shells into the saucepan. Let them simmer gently over medium heat, cook for 20 minutes.
4. Set the oven at 175°C (350°F) and start preheating.
5. In a saucepan, melt 5 tbsps. butter over medium-low heat. Mix in the flour, whisk until the mixture reaches the paste texture and light golden brown color, about 10 minutes. Filter the milk with a mesh sieve. Stir the milk into the flour mixture little by little and let it simmer over medium heat. Stir and cook for 10 to 15 minutes until the mixture is smooth and thick.
6. Combine the thickened milk mixture with the Romano, Cheddar and Gruyere cheese, whisk until the cheese is melted and smooth. Use pepper and salt to taste, then mix in the macaroni, onions and reserved lobster. Load a 4-quart casserole with the macaroni and smooth the top. Dredge the panko crumbs on top evenly.
7. Put in the preheated oven and start baking for 8 to 12 minutes until the sauce is bubbly, and the top gets golden brown color.

Nutrition Information

Calories: 913 calories; Total Carbohydrate: 55.4 g Cholesterol: 218 mg Total Fat: 49.2 g Protein: 60.9 g Sodium: 1113 mg

Lobster Ravioli In Tomato Cream Sauce With Shrimp

Serving: 4 | Prep: 30m | Ready in: 2h

Ingredients

For the Shrimp Stock:
- 1/2 lb. unpeeled large shrimp
- 1 yellow onion, quartered
- 2 stalks celery with leaves, cut into pieces
- 1 lemon, halved
- 1 tbsp. dried basil
- 1 tbsp. dried oregano
- 1 tbsp. dried thyme

- 2 tbsps. whole black peppercorns
- 1/2 cup chopped fresh flat-leaf parsley
- 3 cups water

For the Sauce:
- 1 tbsp. unsalted butter
- 1 shallot, minced
- 2 cloves garlic, minced
- 2 tsps. lemon zest
- 1 tsp. kosher salt
- 1/4 tsp. freshly ground black pepper
- 1 cup white wine
- 1 cup canned petite diced tomatoes
- 1/2 cup heavy cream
- salt and freshly ground black pepper to taste
- 16 lobster ravioli

For Garnish:
- 1 tbsp. chopped fresh flat-leaf parsley
- 1 tsp. lemon zest

Direction
1. Remove shell and devein the shrimp, setting aside the heads and shells. Into bite-size pieces, slice the shrimp.
2. For the shrimp stock, in a big pot, put together the shrimp heads and shells, celery, and onion. Into the pot, squeeze out lemon juice, and include the lemon halves too. Put the 3 cups of water, 1/2 cup parsley, peppercorns, thyme, oregano and dried basil. Put pot cover and boil. Lower heat and allow to simmer without cover for an hour, removing any impurities or foam that floats to the surface. Filter the shrimp stock and reserve.
3. In a big skillet, heat the butter over medium heat. Allow the shrimp pieces to cook till it turns pink and nearly cooked through for 1 to 2 minutes. Take off and reserve. To the pan, put the shallots; cook and mix till the shallots have softened and becomes translucent, for about 5 minutes.
4. Mix in the ground pepper, salt, lemon zest and garlic. Cook for half minute, then, put the white wine. Boil and allow to cook for about 5 minutes till white wine is reduced by half. To the pan, put the shrimp stock, boil, and allow to simmer for about 15 minutes till the sauce is reduce by half.
5. Meantime, with heavily salted water, fill a big pot and bring to a rolling boil over high heat. When boiling, mix in ravioli, and bring back to a boil. Allow to cook without cover for 3 to 4 minutes, mixing from time to time till the ravioli rise to the top and the filling is hot. Drain thoroughly, setting aside a bit pasta-cooking water to thin the sauce, if needed.
6. Into the shrimp sauce, mix the cream and diced tomatoes and heat through. Put the shrimp back to the pan, taste the sauce, and season with pepper and salt to taste. Fold ravioli into the sauce.
7. Put 4 ravioli onto each and every 4 warmed pasta plates or bowls and atop with sauce. Jazz up the pasta with lemon zest and chopped parsley.

Nutrition Information
Calories: 606 calories; Total Carbohydrate: 68.7 g Cholesterol: 174 mg Total Fat: 20 g Protein: 28.7 g Sodium: 911 mg

Meat And Spinach Ravioli Filling

Serving: 15 | Prep: 15m | Ready in: 40m

Ingredients

- 1 lb. ground beef
- 1 1/2 cups fresh spinach
- 5 tbsps. grated Parmesan cheese
- 1 1/4 tbsps. dried parsley
- 1/4 cup bread crumbs
- 1/4 cup olive oil
- 1 large egg
- 1/2 tsp. garlic salt
- 1 pinch black pepper

Direction

1. Place a large skillet on the stove and turn to medium-high heat then put in the ground beef. Stir and cook until the beef is equally brown, no longer pink and crumbly. Strain and get rid of extra grease. Mix in the spinach and cook for about 1 to 2 minutes until wilted. Take skillet off heat and let it cool for 10 minutes. Put the beef mixture in a bowl. Add in the pepper, garlic salt, egg, olive oil, bread crumbs, parsley and Parmesan and combine well. Put the filling through a grinder until turns smooth (or use a food processor to puree until becomes smooth).
2. Store the filling inside the refrigerator for up to 4 days or up to 3 months in the freezer.

Nutrition Information

Calories: 107 calories; Total Carbohydrate: 1.6 g Cholesterol: 33 mg Total Fat: 8.2 g Protein: 6.5 g Sodium: 124 mg

Mediterranean Salmon

Serving: 4 | Prep: 10m | Ready in: 25m

Ingredients

- 1/2 cup olive oil
- 1/4 cup balsamic vinegar
- 4 cloves garlic, pressed
- 4 (3 oz.) fillets salmon
- 1 tbsp. chopped fresh cilantro
- 1 tbsp. chopped fresh basil
- 1 1/2 tsps. garlic salt

Direction

1. In a small bowl, combine together the balsamic vinegar and olive oil. Spread salmon fillets onto a shallow baking dish. Brush garlic over the fillets, and then spread the oil and vinegar on top of them flipping once to coat. Season with garlic salt, basil, and cilantro. Save to marinate for ten minutes.
2. Preheat the oven's broiler.
3. Put salmon approximately 6 inches away from the heat and broil for about 15 minutes, flipping once, or until fish is browned on each side and flaked easily with a fork. Baste often with sauce from the pan.

Nutrition Information

Calories: 391 calories; Total Carbohydrate: 3.6 g Cholesterol: 42 mg Total Fat: 35.2 g Protein: 15 g Sodium: 725 mg

Mediterranean Seafood Medley

Serving: 6 | Prep: 1h | Ready in: 3h

Ingredients

- 20 baby squid (tubes and tentacles), cleaned
- 3 cups milk
- 2 tbsps. extra-virgin olive oil
- 8 cloves garlic, minced
- 2 small onions, chopped
- 2 large carrots, chopped
- 2 tomatoes, chopped
- 1 small fennel bulb, diced
- 1/2 cup tomato paste
- 1 cup dry white wine
- 3 cups chicken stock
- 1/2 bunch fresh parsley
- 1/2 bunch fresh tarragon
- 1/2 bunch fresh thyme
- 2 bay leaves
- 1 tsp. black peppercorns
- 1 tbsp. loosely packed saffron threads
- 2 tbsps. extra-virgin olive oil
- 6 cloves garlic, minced
- 1/2 cup oil-packed sun-dried tomatoes, drained and cut into strips
- 6 baby fennel bulbs, halved
- 1/2 bunch fresh thyme, chopped
- 10 fresh oysters in shells, well scrubbed
- 20 littleneck clams
- 20 fresh mussels
- 6 (6 oz.) fillets fresh sea bass
- salt and pepper to taste
- 2 tbsps. extra-virgin olive oil
- 6 sprigs parsley, for garnish

Direction

1. In milk, soak squid for 1-5 hours, preferably longer. When squid finishes soaking, drain then discard milk.
2. In a big pot, heat 2 tbsps. olive oil on medium heat. Mix in diced fennel, tomatoes, carrots, onions, and garlic. Sauté for about 10 minutes until veggies soften. Mix in tomato paste then cook for additional 10 minutes. Put in wine, increase heat up to high. When it boils, add saffron, peppercorns, bay leaves, thyme, tarragon, parsley, and chicken stock. Boil again, reduce heat down to medium, then simmer until all liquid reduces to one and a half cups for about 15 minutes. Strain liquid out. Discard solids.
3. In a big pot, heat 2 tbsps. olive oil on medium heat. Mix in garlic, cooking for about 45 seconds until fragrant. Add fennel and sun-dried tomatoes. Cook for about 2 minutes. Pour in strained saffron broth and the chopped thyme. Bring heat up to medium-high and boil. Put oysters on fennel. Cover

then cook for a minute. Set mussels and clams in the pot. Cover and cook for about 4 minutes until shellfish starts to open. Mix in strained squid, cover again, and cook until squid firms for 1 minute.

4. As shellfish cooks, season sea bass fillets with pepper and salt. In a big skillet, heat leftover 2 tbsps. olive oil on medium-high heat. Put fish in a skillet with the skin-side down. Cover then cook until fish's flesh is firm and not translucent and skin is crispy.

5. Pour fennel-seafood mixture on a serving platter. Put sea bass fillets on it. Garnish with parsley sprigs. Serve.

Nutrition Information

Calories: 641 calories; Total Carbohydrate: 35.8 g Cholesterol: 313 mg Total Fat: 25.8 g Protein: 60.2 g Sodium: 897 mg

New York Steaks With A Vanilla And Cherry Sauce

Serving: 2 | Prep: 15m | Ready in: 40m

Ingredients

- 2 (8 oz.) New York strip steaks
- 2 tbsps. Worcestershire sauce
- salt and pepper to taste
- 3/4 cup red wine
- 1 pint fresh cherries, pitted and halved
- 1 tbsp. white sugar
- 1 tbsp. vanilla extract
- 1/2 tsp. cornstarch
- 1/4 cup water

Direction

1. Set an outdoor grill to high heat. Coat the grate lightly with oil. Rub Worcestershire sauce on both sides of the New York steaks, then sprinkle with salt and pepper to taste.

2. Grill the steaks for 6 to 7 minutes on each side until they are starting to firm, and are hot and a bit pink in the center. A thermometer inserted in the center should read 140°F (60°C). Once the steaks are done, put two layers of aluminum foil to cover them and set aside in a warm area to rest for 10 minutes.

3. Prepare the cherry sauce while the steaks are cooking. Pour red wine in a pan and bring it to a boil over medium-high heat; let it boil for 5 minutes. Add in sugar, cherries and vanilla extract. Bring it back to a boil, then turn down the heat to medium and let the sauce simmer for 5 to 7 minutes until the cherries are soft. Combine cornstarch and water and mix until cornstarch dissolves then pour into the simmering cherry sauce; stir. Continue cooking for a couple more minutes until cherry sauce thickens. Pour sauce over the steaks before serving.

Nutrition Information

Calories: 624 calories; Total Carbohydrate: 37.3 g Cholesterol: 106 mg Total Fat: 28 g Protein: 36.2 g Sodium: 256 mg

Pepper-honey Cedar Plank Salmon

Serving: 6 | Prep: 15m | Ready in: 1h45m

Ingredients

- 2 (12 inch) untreated cedar planks
- 1/4 cup pineapple juice

- 1/3 cup soy sauce
- 2 tbsps. white vinegar
- 2 tbsps. lemon juice
- 1 tbsp. olive oil
- 3/4 cup honey
- 1/4 cup packed brown sugar
- 1 tsp. ground black pepper
- 1/2 tsp. cayenne pepper
- 1/2 tsp. paprika
- 1/4 tsp. garlic powder
- 6 (6 oz.) skinless, boneless salmon fillets
- 1 pinch salt and pepper to taste

Direction

1. Soak cedar planks for 1-2 hours in warm water; if desired, add a splash of bourbon into water.
2. Simmer honey, olive oil, lemon juice, vinegar, soy sauce and pineapple juice in a saucepan on medium-high heat; lower heat to medium-low. Mix garlic powder, paprika, cayenne pepper, 1 tsp. black pepper and sugar in; simmer for 15 minutes till sauce reduces to a syrupy consistency, occasionally mixing. Put aside sauce.
3. Preheat outdoor grill to medium heat; put planks on grate. When they crack a little and begin to smoke, they're ready to cook on.
4. Season salmon with a light sprinkling of pepper and salt. Put fillets onto smoking cedar planks; close grill lid. Cook for 10 minutes. Put a small sauce amount on salmon fillets; cook for 5 minutes longer till fish is opaque in middle. Serve with leftover sauce.

Nutrition Information

Calories: 484 calories; Total Carbohydrate: 47.3 g Cholesterol: 114 mg Total Fat: 16.7 g Protein: 37 g Sodium: 893 mg

Peppery Goat Cheese Ravioli With Pineapple Tomato Sauce

Serving: 6 | Prep: 45m | Ready in: 1h35m

Ingredients

- 1 (10 oz.) package goat cheese
- 1 tsp. extra-virgin olive oil
- 1/3 cup fresh, coarsely ground black pepper, or to taste, lightly toasted
- 1/2 tsp. salt
- 1 lb. fresh pasta sheets
- 1/2 cup extra virgin olive oil
- 1/4 cup extra-virgin olive oil
- 1/2 large onion, finely diced
- 1 tsp. salt
- 1 tsp. ground black pepper
- 1 large yellow heirloom tomato, peeled and chopped
- 1 large red heirloom tomato, peeled and chopped
- 3/4 cup fresh pineapple, chopped

- 4 1/2 tsps. herbes de Provence
- 1 1/2 cups tomato sauce
- 1 clove garlic
- 1 pinch salt
- 5 leaves basil, chopped
- 1 cup coarsely chopped baby arugula

Direction

1. Preheat the oven to 200°C or 400°F. In a bowl, mix 1/2 tsp. salt, toasted black pepper, 1 tsp. olive oil and goat cheese till smooth. Reserve.
2. Roll the pasta sheets to 1/16-inch thickness. Cut pasta into 2 1/2-inch rounds, or preferred shape. Put a heaping tsp. of goat cheese filling in the middle of every pasta circle. Wet the edge of the pasta with a bit water, then fold and secure the pasta to form a half moon. Set ravioli on a baking sheet and sprinkle with half a cup of olive oil.
3. In the prepped oven, bake ravioli for 7 to 12 minutes till lightly crisp and golden brown. Take out from oven and reserve.
4. In a skillet over medium heat, heat a quarter cup olive oil. Mix in the 1 tsp. of pepper, 1 tsp. of salt and onion; cook and mix for 5 minutes till onion has become translucent and softened. Raise heat to medium-high, and mix in the herbes de Provence, pineapple and yellow and red tomatoes. Cook and mix for 5 minutes, and mix in the tomato sauce. Crush garlic with a pinch of salt, and put into the sauce. Allow to simmer for half an hour, mixing from time to time. Take off heat and mix in arugula and basil. Gently toss the ravioli with the sauce to coat, serve right away.

Nutrition Information

Calories: 659 calories; Total Carbohydrate: 47.8 g Cholesterol: 40 mg Total Fat: 44.7 g Protein: 19.2 g Sodium: 1164 mg

Pork Tenderloin With Orange Marmalade Glaze

Serving: 4 | Ready in: 1h35m

Ingredients

- 1 tbsp. soy sauce
- 1 (6 oz.) can frozen orange juice concentrate, thawed
- 1/4 cup orange marmalade
- 3 tbsps. honey
- 1 tbsp. balsamic vinegar
- 1 tsp. minced garlic
- 1 (1 lb.) pork tenderloin
- 1 tsp. cornstarch (optional)
- 2 tsps. water (optional)

Direction

1. Mix garlic, balsamic vinegar, honey, orange marmalade, orange juice concentrate, and soy sauce in a small saucepan over medium heat; heat to a simmer and blend until smooth. Take away from the heat and allow to cool to room temperature.
2. Put the pork tenderloin in a resealable plastic bag and add the marinade. Squeeze to discard the air, seal, and shake the bag sometimes to marinate the pork tenderloin. Put in the refrigerator for 1 to 2 hours.
3. Start preheating the oven at 350°F (175°C).

4. Remove the pork loin and marinade into a baking dish; cover with aluminum foil and roast about 20 minutes until an instant-read thermometer shows at least 155°F (70°C) when inserted into the thickest part. Uncover and keep roasting for extra 5 to 10 minutes until the pork is browned.
5. Uncover and let the meat and juices rest for 10 minutes.
6. To serve, cut the meat and sprinkle with pan juices.
7. If you want a thicker sauce, mix cornstarch in water until smooth, stir into the pan drippings, and arrange over medium heat. Simmer for 2 to 3 minutes until thickened.

Nutrition Information

Calories: 316 calories; Total Carbohydrate: 48.3 g Cholesterol: 63 mg Total Fat: 4.4 g Protein: 22.1 g Sodium: 284 mg

Saffron-scented Lobster Paella

Serving: 8 | Prep: 45m | Ready in: 1h35m

Ingredients

* 2 tbsps. olive oil
* 16 head-on medium shrimp
* 1 red onion, diced
* 2 tsps. minced garlic
* 2 cups Arborio rice
* 5 1/2 cups hot fish stock
* 1/4 tsp. saffron threads
* 1 1/2 tsps. smoked paprika
* 1 tsp. lemon or lime zest
* 1 tbsp. chopped fresh oregano
* sea salt to taste
* 16 mussels, scrubbed and debearded
* 1 lb. red snapper fillets, cut into 1 inch pieces
* 1/4 lb. medium shrimp, peeled and deveined
* 1 (10 oz.) cooked lobster tail, cut into 1/2-inch thick slices
* 2 tomatoes, seeded and diced
* 2 lemons, cut into wedges

Direction

1. In a paella pan or a very big skillet, put in the olive oil and heat up over medium-high heat setting. Put in the head-on shrimp and sear per side until the outside turn orange in color and are a little bit browned (at this point, the shrimp shouldn't be cooked inside yet). Take the seared shrimp from the pan and put it aside.
2. Lower the heat to medium setting then put in the garlic and red onion. Sauté the mixture for a couple minutes until the onion is translucent and soft. Add in the Arborio rice and mix everything together until it is well-coated with oil. Put in the fish stock followed by the lemon zest, saffron, oregano and paprika to taste. Let the mixture simmer over medium-high heat setting then season it with sea salt. Lower the heat to medium-low setting and simmer lightly for 15 minutes without cover while stirring the mixture from time to time.
3. Place the seared head-on shrimp and mussels over the rice in decorative pattern, then cover the pan and simmer for 5 minutes. Press the deveined shrimp and red snapper into the rice afterwards then put the cover back on and simmer for 10 more minutes. Lastly, put in the lobster and spread the

diced tomatoes evenly on top. Cover the pan again and simmer for about 5 additional minutes until the rice has softened, the temperature of the lobster is hot and the shells of the mussels have already opened.

4. Garnish the top with lemon wedges and serve it in the paella pan.

Nutrition Information

Calories: 409 calories; Total Carbohydrate: 52.9 g Cholesterol: 103 mg Total Fat: 6.8 g Protein: 33.4 g Sodium: 803 mg

Sailor Clams

Serving: 2 | Prep: 15m | Ready in: 30m

Ingredients

- 2 lbs. fresh cherrystone clams
- 3 tbsps. olive oil
- 1 tbsp. minced garlic
- 1/2 onion, minced
- 1/2 cup dry white wine
- 1 pinch saffron threads
- 1 tsp. crushed red pepper flakes
- 1/4 tsp. vegetable bouillon powder
- salt to taste
- 1 tbsp. all-purpose flour
- 1/2 cup water
- 1 tsp. chopped fresh parsley

Direction

1. Put clams in a saucepan with a tight-fitting cover then pour in enough water to cover the clams. Secure the lid then boil the clams on high heat. Let it steam for 3-5 minutes until the clams open. Drain and keep the clam water.
2. On medium heat, heat oil in a pan. Add onion and garlic and cook and stir for 3 minutes until the onion is see through and soft. Add white wine and turn heat to high. Put in vegetable bouillon, red pepper flakes, and saffron to season. Pour in the reserved clam water and boil.
3. Combine water and flour until dissolved. Pour into the sauce and mix until thick If required, add salt to taste. Put in the clams in their shells and mix until they are covered with sauce. Serve with chopped parsley on top.

Nutrition Information

Calories: 347 calories; Total Carbohydrate: 12.5 g Cholesterol: 36 mg Total Fat: 21.7 g Protein: 14.8 g Sodium: 69 mg

Sausage Bowties With Artichokes

Serving: 4 | Prep: 15m | Ready in: 35m

Ingredients

- 1 bunch broccoli rabe, ends trimmed, cut into 2-inch pieces
- 1 (12 oz.) package bow tie (farfalle) pasta
- 1 lb. bulk hot Italian sausage
- 5 cloves garlic, crushed

- 1 shallot, chopped
- 1 (6 oz.) jar marinated artichoke hearts, drained and quartered
- 2 roasted red peppers, sliced
- 1 cup freshly grated Parmesan cheese

Direction

1. Boil lightly salted water in a big pot and blanch the broccoli rabe for one minute. Remove from the water using tongs, rinse in cold water until cooled. Add the pasta into the boiling water and cook until al dente, about 8-10 minutes, then drain, setting aside 1 cup pasta water.
2. In a broad skillet, brown sausage over a medium-high heat. When sausage is almost cooked through, drain the leftover grease, and stir in the shallots and garlic. Cook for 5 minutes until shallot are translucent and soft. Add the roasted peppers, artichokes, and broccoli rabe, cook until warmed, about 1-2 minutes. Stir in the hot cooked pasta with Parmesan cheese and sufficient amount of the pasta water to moisten.

Nutrition Information

Calories: 765 calories; Total Carbohydrate: 79 g Cholesterol: 67 mg Total Fat: 33.1 g Protein: 40.6 g Sodium: 1712 mg

Seared Sea Scallops

Serving: 4 | Prep: 15m | Ready in: 30m

Ingredients

- 1/2 cup all-purpose flour
- 2 tsps. seasoning salt
- 1/2 tsp. dried oregano
- 1/2 tsp. dried thyme
- 2 tbsps. lemon pepper
- 16 sea scallops, rinsed and drained
- 2 tbsps. olive oil
- 4 tbsps. chopped fresh parsley, divided
- 4 tsps. lemon juice, divided

Direction

1. In a large bowl, combine lemon pepper, thyme, oregano, salt and flour. Roll scallops in the flour mixture until all sides are lightly coated.
2. In a skillet or frying pan, heat olive oil on high heat. Put 4 scallops into the pan and sear on all sides (2 minutes per side). After flipping scallops, put in 1 tsp. of lemon juice and 1 tbsp. of parsley. Take scallops out of the pan and arrange on a plate in the oven to maintain warmth until serving.
3. Keep cooking until the leftover scallops are cooked, combining each batch with lemon juice and parsley.

Nutrition Information

Calories: 179 calories; Total Carbohydrate: 15.4 g Cholesterol: 20 mg Total Fat: 7.5 g Protein: 12 g Sodium: 1251 mg

Sexy Shrimp Scampi

Serving: 2 | Prep: 20m | Ready in: 45m

Ingredients

- 30 medium shrimp - peeled and deveined
- 2 tbsps. olive oil
- 2 tbsps. butter, melted
- 2 cloves garlic, minced
- 1/2 tsp. kosher salt
- 1/4 tsp. ground black pepper

Direction

1. Preheat the oven to 350°F (175°C).
2. Mix shrimps, melted butter, pepper, salt, olive oil and garlic in a bowl then set aside for 10 minutes. In a round casserole dish, place the marinated shrimps in circle pattern.
3. Put in the preheated oven and bake for about 15 minutes until the shrimps are cooked through and are pink in color.

Nutrition Information

Calories: 342 calories; Total Carbohydrate: 1.2 g Cholesterol: 259 mg Total Fat: 26.3 g Protein: 24.8 g Sodium: 825 mg

Sous-vide Bay Scallops On Soy Ginger Espuma With Mushrooms And Spinach

Serving: 2 | Prep: 30m | Ready in: 1h15m

Ingredients

- 3/4 lb. large bay scallops
- salt and ground black pepper to taste
- Vinaigrette:
- 1/4 cup soy sauce
- 1 1/2 tsps. balsamic vinegar
- 1 1/2 tsps. white sugar
- 1 tsp. lime juice
- 1 tsp. wasabi paste
- 1/2 tsp. sesame oil
- 1/4 cup peanut oil
- Soy Ginger Espuma Sauce:
- 1/2 cup dry white wine
- 1/4 cup mirin (Japanese sweet wine)
- 1 tbsp. chopped fresh ginger
- 1 tbsp. minced shallot
- 2 tbsps. heavy whipping cream
- 1/2 cup unsalted butter
- 2 1/2 tsps. soy sauce
- Mushroom and Spinach Side:
- 2 tbsps. extra-virgin olive oil
- 7 oz. sliced chanterelle mushrooms
- 1 bunch spinach leaves
- 2 tbsps. grapeseed oil

Direction

1. In a sous-vide water bath, heat the water to 52°C (125°F).
2. Flavor the scallops with pepper and salt; put scallops, clustered together, into a sealable plastic bag. Seal the bag (if you use a vacuum sealer, seal on low pressure), release as much air as you can but don't smash the scallops. In the prepared water bath, cook for half an hour.
3. In a bowl, beat together sesame oil, wasabi paste, lime juice, white sugar, balsamic vinegar, and soy sauce. Beat in peanut oil slowly until the vinaigrette becomes smooth.
4. In a skillet, arrange shallots, ginger, mirin, and white wine over medium heat; simmer for 4-5 minutes until most liquid is evaporated. Add cream; simmer for 2 more minutes until thickened. Turn down the heat to low; beat in a tbsp. of butter at a time for 3-5 minutes until the sauce is smooth and thickened. Beat in soy sauce.
5. Strain the sauce into a bowl; pour into the whipping siphon and charge. Shake it to blend.
6. In a large skillet, heat the olive oil over medium heat. Add the mushrooms; stir and cook for 5 minutes until tender and soft.
7. In an individual skillet, heat 1/4 cup of vinaigrette to barely boiling. Put in spinach; cook for half a minute just until it is wilted. Take away from the heat.
8. In a large skillet, heat the grapeseed oil over high heat. Take the scallops out of the plastic bag; use a paper towel to pat them dry. Cook for 30-45 seconds on each side until they turn golden brown.
9. Put mushrooms and spinach on the serving platter. Drizzle the serving platter with some sauce; place scallops on top to serve.

Nutrition Information

Calories: 1415 calories; Total Carbohydrate: 40.7 g Cholesterol: 245 mg Total Fat: 109.1 g Protein: 53.2 g Sodium: 2969 mg

Spaghetti Carbonara II

Serving: 8 | Prep: 20m | Ready in: 40m

Ingredients

- 1 lb. spaghetti
- 1 tbsp. olive oil
- 8 slices bacon, diced
- 1 tbsp. olive oil
- 1 onion, chopped
- 1 clove garlic, minced
- 1/4 cup dry white wine (optional)
- 4 eggs
- 1/2 cup grated Parmesan cheese
- 1 pinch salt and black pepper to taste
- 2 tbsps. chopped fresh parsley
- 2 tbsps. grated Parmesan cheese

Direction

1. In a large pot filled with boiling salted water, cook spaghetti pasta till al dente. Well drain. Stir in 1 tbsp. of olive oil, and leave aside.
2. In the meantime, in a large skillet, cook chopped bacon till crisp slightly; take away and place on paper towels for draining. Keep 2 tbsps. of bacon fat for reserving; put in the rest 1 tbsp. olive oil and heat in reused large skillet. Put in chopped onion, and cook over medium heat till onion is translucent. Mix in minced garlic, and cook for an addition of 1 minute. Add wine if you want; cook

for around one minute more.

3. Place cooked bacon back into pan; put in drained and cooked spaghetti. Coat by tossing and heat through (if it seems dry or is sticking together, add more olive oil). Stir in beaten eggs and cook, tossing constantly using large fork or tongs till eggs are set barely. Quickly add a half cup of Parmesan cheese, and toss again. Put in pepper and salt to taste (keep in mind that Parmesan and bacon are very salty).
4. Serve immediately with extra Parmesan cheese and chopped parsley sprinkled on top at table.

Nutrition Information
Calories: 444 calories; Total Carbohydrate: 44.7 g Cholesterol: 118 mg Total Fat: 21.1 g Protein: 16.4 g Sodium: 369 mg

Surf And Turf For Two
Serving: 2 | Prep: 15m | Ready in: 45m

Ingredients
- 1 tbsp. olive oil
- 1 tbsp. butter, melted
- 1 tbsp. finely minced onion
- 1 tbsp. white wine
- 1 tsp. Worcestershire sauce
- 1 tsp. lemon juice
- 1 tsp. dried parsley
- 1 tsp. seafood seasoning (such as Old Bay)
- 1 clove garlic, minced
- 1/8 tsp. freshly ground black pepper
- 12 medium shrimp, peeled and deveined
- 2 (4 oz.) filet mignon steaks
- 2 tsps. olive oil
- 1 tsp. steak seasoning

Direction
1. Whisk black pepper, garlic, seafood seasoning, parsley, lemon juice, Worcestershire sauce, wine, onion, butter and 1 tbsp. olive oil in bowl; add shrimp. Toss to evenly coat. Use plastic wrap to cover bowl; refrigerate for a minimum of 15 minutes to merge flavors.
2. Preheat outdoor grill to medium-high heat; oil grate lightly. Use 2 tsp. olive oil to coat steaks. Sprinkle steak seasoning on.
3. Cook steaks, 5-7 minutes per side, till they start to firm and reach preferred doneness. An inserted instant-read thermometer in the middle should read 60°C/140°F. Put steaks on platter; tent with an aluminum foil piece loosely.
4. Take shrimp out of marinade; grill for 2-3 minutes per side till meat isn't transparent in the middle anymore and bright pink on the outside.

Nutrition Information
Calories: 444 calories; Total Carbohydrate: 2.7 g Cholesterol: 166 mg Total Fat: 35.2 g Protein: 26.9 g Sodium: 926 mg

Tagliatelle With Coriander Pesto
Serving: 4 | Prep: 15m | Ready in: 25m

Ingredients

- 1 bunch chopped fresh cilantro
- 6 tbsps. pine nuts
- 1 tsp. lemon juice, or to taste
- 1/3 cup crumbled feta cheese
- salt and ground black pepper to taste
- 1/2 cup olive oil
- 1 (12 oz.) package dry tagliatelle or wide fettucine pasta
- 1 tsp. extra-virgin olive oil

Direction

1. In a food processor or a work bowl, add black pepper, salt, feta cheese, lemon juice, pine nuts, and cilantro. Pulse a couple of times until the ingredients are minced. While the machine is still running, drizzle 1/2 cup of olive oil. Process until pesto paste is slightly textured.
2. In a large pot over high heat, fill with slightly salted water and bring to a boil. Once boiling, pour in tagliatelle pasta and stir, then return to a boil. Cook pasta without covering for 8 minutes until al dente, or firm to the bite, stirring occasionally. Set a colander in the sink and drain pasta.
3. Transfer cooked pasta to a big serving bowl. Toss with pesto to evenly coat pasta. Drizzle a small amount of extra-virgin olive oil on pasta. Serve while hot.

Nutrition Information

Calories: 663 calories; Total Carbohydrate: 64.8 g Cholesterol: 11 mg Total Fat: 39.4 g Protein: 16.5 g Sodium: 190 mg

Tarragon Lover's Scallops

Serving: 4 | Prep: 10m | Ready in: 25m

Ingredients

- 2 tbsps. olive oil
- 5 tbsps. butter, divided
- 1 1/2 lbs. sea scallops, rinsed and drained
- 1 tsp. salt to taste
- 1/4 tsp. freshly ground black pepper
- 1/2 cup dry white wine
- 1 lemon, zested
- 2 tbsps. chopped fresh tarragon

Direction

1. Heat 1/2 tbsp. butter and 1 tbsp. olive oil in a big skillet on medium heat. Use pepper and salt to season the scallops. Without crowding, put 1/2 scallops in the skillet; cook for 2-3 minutes per side till browned. Put scallops on a plate. Heat 1/2 tbsp. butter and 1 tbsp. olive oil in the skillet; cook leftover scallops. Put on a plate.
2. Wipe the skillet out; put skillet on medium heat. Add wine; boil till reduced to 2 tbsp. for 1-2 minutes. Lower the heat to low; whisk leftover 4 tbsp. butter in to just soften the butter to make a smooth sauce. Mix tarragon, lemon zest and salt in; put sauce on scallops.

Nutrition Information

Calories: 365 calories; Total Carbohydrate: 5.4 g Cholesterol: 94 mg Total Fat: 22.5 g Protein: 28.9 g Sodium: 960 mg

Turducken

Serving: 24 | Prep: 1h | Ready in: 5h

Ingredients

- 1 (3 lb.) whole chicken, boned
- salt and pepper to taste
- Creole seasoning to taste
- 1 (4 lb.) duck, boned
- 1 (16 lb.) turkey, boned
- 3 cups prepared sausage and oyster dressing

Direction

1. Start preheating oven to 375 degrees F or 190 degrees C. With the skin-side down, put the boned chicken on a plate and generously season with Creole seasoning, pepper, and salt. With the skin-side down, put the boned duck on top the chicken and generously season with Creole seasoning, pepper, and salt. Cover; place in refrigerator.
2. Skin-side down, put the boned turkey on a flat surface. Add a layer of chilled Sausage and Oyster Dressing, make sure to push it into the wing and leg cavities so it looks like the bones are still there.
3. Put the duck, skin-side down on top the turkey and add a layer of the chilled dressing. Put the chicken, skin-side down on top the duck and add a layer of the chilled dressing.
4. With someone's help, wrap the turkey skin around and use toothpicks to secure them. Take kitchen string and lace it between the toothpicks to help hold everything in. Gently put the turducken in a big roasting pan breast side up.
5. With the cover on, roast until turducken is golden brown, 4 hours. Remove cover and roast until thermometer poked into thigh reads 180 degrees F and when poked in stuffing says 165 degrees F, 1 hour. Check every few hours to baste and remove any extra liquid. There should be enough cooking juices to make one gallon of gravy. Carve the turducken and enjoy.

Nutrition Information

Calories: 836 calories; Total Carbohydrate: 5.3 g Cholesterol: 262 mg Total Fat: 52.8 g Protein: 78.7 g Sodium: 360 mg

Valentine's Salmon

Serving: 4 | Prep: 20m | Ready in: 1h5m

Ingredients

- 8 green onions
- 1 slice bacon, sliced
- 1 clove garlic
- 1 leek, white and tender green parts only, halved lengthwise and sliced
- salt to taste
- 1/2 tsp. butter
- 1 1/2 cups diced Yukon Gold potatoes
- 3 cups water, or more as needed
- 1 pinch cayenne pepper
- 2 (12 oz.) center-cut salmon fillets
- 1 tsp. tarragon Dijon mustard
- salt and freshly ground black pepper to taste

- 1 tbsp. vegetable oil
- 2 tbsps. Asian chili paste (sambal), or more to taste (optional)
- 1 green onion, chopped

Direction

1. Boil a large pot filled with lightly salted water. Add the eight green onions. Cook for 30 seconds while uncovered until softened slightly. Immerse them immediately in ice water for a few minutes until they are cold enough to cease the cooking process. Once the onions are cold, drain them well and put them aside.
2. In a large skillet, cook the bacon over medium-low heat for 8 minutes until browned. Mix in the salt, garlic, butter, and leek. Cook and stir for 10 minutes until the leek has softened. Add the potatoes. Cover them with enough water, about 3 cups. Season the mixture with cayenne pepper and salt. Bring the mixture to a simmer. Adjust the heat to low. Cook for 15 minutes until the potatoes are tender; put aside.
3. Set the oven to 375°F (190°C) for preheating. Use a parchment paper to line the baking dish. Coat the paper lightly with vegetable oil.
4. Cut off the belly from skin of each salmon fillet, about 1/3 of the fillet's bottom. Slice the remaining 2/3 of the fillet away from the skin and cut it into half. Slice the belly horizontally in half. Spread tarragon mustard onto each piece and top each with a salmon belly slice. Season them with salt and black pepper. Wrap the salmon packet with 2 green onions, wrapping them crisscross like ribbons. Tuck their ends on the underside.
5. Arrange the salmon packets onto the prepared parchment belly-side up. Drizzle each packet with vegetable oil.
6. Let them bake inside the preheated oven for 15 minutes until the insides are no longer translucent and the salmon is firm enough when touched.
7. Heat the potato leek soup. Mix in the chopped green onion. Season the mixture with black pepper and salt. Distribute the mixture among the shallow bowls. Top each soup with 1 salmon packet. Garnish each bowl with chili paste. Serve.

Nutrition Information

Calories: 444 calories; Total Carbohydrate: 20.9 g Cholesterol: 122 mg Total Fat: 21.8 g Protein: 39.3 g Sodium: 265 mg

Aphrodite's Dream

Serving: 6 | Prep: 20m | Ready in: 20m

Ingredients

- 1/3 cup olive oil
- 3 tbsps. white wine vinegar
- salt to taste
- ground black pepper to taste
- 1 pinch dried sage, or to taste
- 1 pinch cayenne pepper, or to taste
- 1 tbsp. orange juice, or to taste
- 1 (10 oz.) package mixed baby salad greens
- 1 pomegranate, peeled and seeds separated
- 1 orange, peeled and cut into bite-size pieces

Direction

1. Mix white wine vinegar, sage, orange juice, black pepper, cayenne pepper, olive oil, and salt in a large salad bowl.
2. In a salad bowl with baby salad greens, pour in the dressing and toss lightly until well-coated.
3. Sprinkle the salad with orange pieces and pomegranate seeds.
4. Toss the salad. Serve.

Nutrition Information

Calories: 146 calories; Total Carbohydrate: 9.5 g Cholesterol: 0 mg Total Fat: 12.2 g Protein: 1.2 g Sodium: 15 mg

Apple Almond Crunch Salad

Serving: 6 | Prep: 10m | Ready in: 10m

Ingredients

- 1 (10 oz.) package mixed salad greens
- 1/2 cup slivered almonds
- 1/2 cup crumbled feta cheese
- 1 cup tart apple, cored and chopped
- 1/4 cup sliced red onion
- 1/4 cup golden raisins
- 1 cup raspberry vinaigrette salad dressing

Direction

1. Combine raisins, red onion, apple, feta cheese, almonds and salad greens in a large salad bowl. Toss till blended. On individual servings, add salad dressing.

Nutrition Information

Calories: 166 calories; Total Carbohydrate: 13.6 g Cholesterol: 19 mg Total Fat: 10.7 g Protein: 6.6 g Sodium: 248 mg

Asparagus And Smoked Salmon Salad

Serving: 8 | Prep: 15m | Ready in: 25m

Ingredients

- 1 lb. fresh asparagus, trimmed and cut into 1 inch pieces
- 1/2 cup pecans, broken into pieces
- 2 heads red leaf lettuce, rinsed and torn
- 1/2 cup frozen green peas, thawed
- 1/4 lb. smoked salmon, cut into 1 inch chunks
- 1/4 cup olive oil
- 2 tbsps. lemon juice
- 1 tsp. Dijon mustard
- 1/2 tsp. salt
- 1/4 tsp. pepper

Direction

1. Boil a pot of water. Stir in asparagus and cook for 5 minutes until tender. Let it drain; set aside.
2. In a skillet, cook the pecans over medium heat for 5 minutes, stirring constantly until lightly toasted.
3. Combine the asparagus, toasted pecans, salmon, peas, and red leaf lettuce and toss in a large bowl.
4. In another bowl, combine lemon juice, pepper, Dijon mustard, salt, and olive oil. You can coat the

salad with the dressing or serve it on its side.

Nutrition Information

Calories: 159 calories; Total Carbohydrate: 7 g Cholesterol: 3 mg Total Fat: 12.9 g Protein: 6 g Sodium: 304 mg

Avocado And Lobster Salad

Serving: 2 | Prep: 20m | Ready in: 25m

Ingredients

- 2 tbsps. butter
- 1 1/2 cups cooked lobster meat, diced
- 1 tsp. seafood seasoning
- 1 tomato, diced
- 1/2 avocado, diced
- 2 cups chopped iceberg lettuce
- 1/4 cup crumbled feta

Direction

1. In a skillet over medium high heat, melt the butter and add lobster. Slowly reheat until hot. Add seafood seasoning to taste then move to a serving dish. Toss with lettuce, avocado and tomato. Drizzle with crumbled feta cheese.

Nutrition Information

Calories: 357 calories; Total Carbohydrate: 10.5 g Cholesterol: 126 mg Total Fat: 23.7 g Protein: 27.1 g Sodium: 968 mg

Chicken, Avocado And Mango Salad

Serving: 8 | Prep: 30m | Ready in: 30m

Ingredients

- 2 tbsps. brown sugar
- 1/4 cup water
- 1/3 cup lime juice
- 1/2 cup chili garlic sauce
- 4 cups shredded, cooked chicken
- 2 medium mangos - peeled, seeded and diced
- 2 avocados - peeled, pitted and diced
- 1 (10 oz.) package spring lettuce mix

Direction

1. In a saucepan, mix together water and brown sugar over medium-high heat. Boil it, and then add to a medium-sized bowl. Mix in lime juice and garlic chili sauce. Put the dressing aside.
2. Mix avocados, mangos, and chicken together in a big bowl. On serving dishes, put the spring salad mix, and then put the chicken mixture on top by several spoonfuls. Pour over the top with the dressing.

Nutrition Information

Calories: 296 calories; Total Carbohydrate: 19.8 g Cholesterol: 55 mg Total Fat: 16.4 g Protein: 19.1 g Sodium: 698 mg

Dennie's Fresh Lobster Salad

Serving: 4 | Prep: 10m | Ready in: 30m

Ingredients

- 1 lb. cooked lobster meat, cut into bite-sized pieces
- 1/4 cup butter, melted
- 1/4 cup mayonnaise
- 1/8 tsp. ground black pepper

Direction

1. In a medium-sized bowl, put lobster pieces, add melted butter. Mix to coat, mix in mayonnaise and use black pepper to season. Put a cover on and refrigerate for 20 minutes until serving.

Nutrition Information

Calories: 303 calories; Total Carbohydrate: 1.1 g Cholesterol: 144 mg Total Fat: 23.4 g Protein: 21.6 g Sodium: 496 mg

Easy Arugula Salad

Serving: 4 | Prep: 15m | Ready in: 15m

Ingredients

- 4 cups young arugula leaves, rinsed and dried
- 1 cup cherry tomatoes, halved
- 1/4 cup pine nuts
- 2 tbsps. grapeseed oil or olive oil
- 1 tbsp. rice vinegar
- salt to taste
- freshly ground black pepper to taste
- 1/4 cup grated Parmesan cheese
- 1 large avocado - peeled, pitted and sliced

Direction

1. Prepare a large plastic bowl that comes with a lid. In the bowl, combine Parmesan cheese, vinegar, oil, pine nuts, cherry tomatoes and arugula. Add salt and pepper to taste. Put the lid on to cover and shake until ingredients are well mixed.
2. Separate salad onto plates, put avocado slices on top and serve

Nutrition Information

Calories: 257 calories; Total Carbohydrate: 10 g Cholesterol: 4 mg Total Fat: 23.2 g Protein: 6.2 g Sodium: 381 mg

I Love My Pear Salad

Serving: 12 | Prep: 10m | Ready in: 4h20m

Ingredients

- 1 (15 oz.) can pear halves
- 1 (3 oz.) package lemon flavored Jell-O
- 1 (8 oz.) package cream cheese
- 1/2 cup chopped pecans
- 2 cups frozen whipped topping, thawed

Direction

1. Drain pears; save 1 cup syrup; add water to measure 1 cup, if necessary.
2. Combine gelatin and syrup in a saucepan over medium-high heat. Heat to a boil; mix until gelatin dissolves. Take away from heat; chill until partly set.
3. Mix pears and cheese together in a big bowl until smooth. Put in whipped topping, pecans, and gelatin mixture; mix until smooth. Keep in bowl or transfer to mold. Keep chilled 3 hours until firm.

Nutrition Information

Calories: 171 calories; Total Carbohydrate: 14.2 g Cholesterol: 21 mg Total Fat: 11.7 g Protein: 2.6 g Sodium: 95 mg

Kumquat Salad

Serving: 4 | Prep: 20m | Ready in: 20m

Ingredients

- 1/3 cup extra virgin olive oil
- 1/3 cup red wine vinegar
- 1 tsp. brown sugar
- 1/4 tsp. freshly ground black pepper
- 5 oz. mixed baby greens
- 2 green onions, chopped
- 1/2 cup chopped celery
- 1 carrot, julienned
- 1/2 cup broccoli florets
- 1/2 cup cauliflower florets
- 1 avocados - peeled, pitted and diced
- 1 tsp. fresh lemon juice
- 2 oz. grated Asiago cheese
- 3 oz. pine nuts, toasted
- 4 oz. kumquats - rinsed, seeded and sliced

Direction

1. To make the dressing, prepare a small container that comes with a lid. Put pepper, brown sugar, red wine vinegar and extra virgin olive oil in the container and shake properly to blend
2. Toss cauliflower, broccoli, carrot, celery, green onions and baby salad greens together in a medium bowl. Drizzle lemon juice on avocado, put in the salad mixture, toss well. Add pine nuts and Asiago cheese on top of the mixture. Add in kumquats, toss well. Pour in olive oil dressing and serve.

Nutrition Information

Calories: 473 calories; Total Carbohydrate: 19.4 g Cholesterol: 13 mg Total Fat: 41.3 g Protein: 11.6 g Sodium: 221 mg

Lisa's Grapefruit And Avocado Salad

Serving: 4 | Prep: 15m | Ready in: 15m

Ingredients

- 2 pink grapefruit, peeled and sectioned
- 1 large ripe avocado - peeled, pitted, and diced
- 1 cup alfalfa sprouts

- 1 lemon, juiced
- 3 tbsps. olive oil
- 1 pinch salt
- 1 pinch ground black pepper

Direction

1. Onto a salad plate, nicely place 1/4 of the diced avocado and 1/4 of the grapefruit sections. Add 1/4 cup of sprouts over it. Repeat this process onto more plates with the leftover grapefruit, the recipe is normally enough for 4 plates.
2. In a small bowl, whisk together black pepper, salt, olive oil, lemon juice and add drizzles of this dressing mixture over the salads.

Nutrition Information

Calories: 277 calories; Total Carbohydrate: 25.1 g Cholesterol: 0 mg Total Fat: 20.7 g Protein: 3.8 g Sodium: 7 mg

My Favorite Beet Salad

Serving: 8 | Prep: 30m | Ready in: 1h30m

Ingredients

- 6 large beets, trimmed
- 1/4 cup extra virgin olive oil
- salt and ground black pepper to taste
- 1 (8 oz.) package baby spinach leaves
- 2 tomatoes, cut into bite-sized pieces
- 2 avocados - peeled, pitted, and cut into bite-sized pieces
- 1/2 red onion, chopped, or to taste
- 1 (4 oz.) container crumbled feta cheese
- 1/2 cup balsamic vinegar
- 1/2 cup extra-virgin olive oil
- 1 tbsp. Dijon mustard, or more to taste

Direction

1. Set the oven to 375°F or 190°C for preheating.
2. In a large bowl, put the beets and drizzle with 1/4 cup of olive oil, black pepper and salt. On a work surface, lay out 2 large squares of aluminum foil. On the center of each sheet, put 3 beets. Fold the aluminum foil into 2 envelopes to seal the beets into the packets. Arrange the packets into the baking dish.
3. Let them bake inside the preheated oven for 1-1 1/2 hours until tender. After an hour, try piercing the beet using a fork to check its tenderness. Open the foil and let the beets cool until you are able to handle them. Peel the beets and slice.
4. Lay out the spinach leaves on an elegant oblong-shaped serving platter. Sprinkle avocado and tomato pieces on top of the spinach leaves. Place the chopped red onion on its top. Arrange sliced warm beets over the salad and sprinkle with crumbled feta cheese.
5. Whisk the Dijon mustard, 1/2 cup of olive oil and balsamic vinegar together until smooth. Drizzle the dressing over the salad. Serve.

Nutrition Information

Calories: 413 calories; Total Carbohydrate: 28.2 g Cholesterol: 13 mg Total Fat: 31.9 g Protein: 7.2 g

Sodium: 400 mg

Pink Valentine Salad

Serving: 4 | Prep: 10m | Ready in: 10m

Ingredients

- 1 (15 oz.) can sliced beets, drained and cut into bite-size pieces
- 1 (15 oz.) can hearts of palm, drained and cut into bite-size pieces
- 1/4 cup sour cream, or more to taste
- 2 tbsps. minced garlic
- 2 tbsps. dried minced onion flakes
- 1/2 tsp. adobo seasoning
- 1 tbsp. chile paste (optional)

Direction

1. In a bowl, mix chile paste, adobo seasoning, onion flakes, garlic, sour cream, hearts of palm and beets. Toss until thoroughly mixed. Chill in refrigerator or serve right away.

Nutrition Information

Calories: 115 calories; Total Carbohydrate: 18.3 g Cholesterol: 6 mg Total Fat: 4.4 g Protein: 4.6 g
Sodium: 701 mg

Red Cabbage Mango Pistachio Salad

Serving: 5 | Prep: 20m | Ready in: 20m

Ingredients

- 1/2 large head red cabbage, shredded
- 1 mango - peeled, seeded, and cut into wedges
- 1/4 cup roasted, shelled pistachios
- 1 tbsp. chopped fresh mint, or to taste (optional)
- 2 tbsps. truffle oil
- 1 tbsp. agave nectar
- 1 tbsp. lime juice
- 1 tbsp. champagne vinegar
- 1/2 tsp. salt
- 1 sprig fresh mint

Direction

1. In a large salad bowl, stir together 1 tbsp. mint, pistachios, mango and red cabbage.
2. In a small bowl, put salt, champagne vinegar, lime juice, agave nectar and truffle oil, whisk well. Pour dressing into salad bowl, toss until well combined. Decorate with 1 sprig fresh mint.

Nutrition Information

Calories: 154 calories; Total Carbohydrate: 18.9 g Cholesterol: 0 mg Total Fat: 8.7 g Protein: 3.1 g
Sodium: 290 mg

Red Cabbage-asparagus Salad With Tahini Dressing

Serving: 4 | Prep: 30m | Ready in: 33m

Ingredients

- 1 bunch asparagus, ends trimmed

- 2 tbsps. tahini
- 1 tbsp. water
- 2 tbsps. lemon juice
- 1 clove minced garlic
- white sugar to taste
- 3/4 lb. thinly sliced red cabbage
- 2 radishes, thinly sliced
- 2 green onions, sliced
- 2 tbsps. crumbled feta
- 1/4 cup toasted pine nuts
- 2 sprigs dill, chopped

Direction

1. Boil salted water in a large pot over high heat. Blanch the asparagus till tender then drain; stop the cooking process by immediately transfer into ice water. Drain the cold asparagus and slice on the diagonal into pieces with 1-in. size.
2. Stir garlic, lemon juice, water and tahini together in a small bowl. Add sugar to taste and stir.
3. In a large bowl, toss dill, pine nuts, feta, green onions, radishes, red cabbage and asparagus together. Mix in tahini dressing till combined.

Nutrition Information

Calories: 161 calories; Total Carbohydrate: 15.5 g Cholesterol: 4 mg Total Fat: 9.6 g Protein: 7.9 g Sodium: 90 mg

Roasted Peppers With Pine Nuts And Parsley

Serving: 10 | Prep: 20m | Ready in: 55m

Ingredients

- 2 red bell peppers
- 2 yellow bell peppers
- 2 oz. pine nuts
- 1/3 cup golden raisins
- 1 clove garlic, minced
- 1/2 cup chopped fresh parsley
- 1/2 cup olive oil
- salt and ground black pepper to taste

Direction

1. Start preheating the oven broiler, put the oven rack at about 6 inches away from the heat source. Use aluminum foil to line a baking sheet. Use a knife to separate peppers in half from top to bottom; remove the ribs, seeds and stem, then on a prepared baking sheets, place the peppers cut sides down. Cook in the oven broiler for about 10 minutes until the peppers skin turn blistered and blackened. In a bowl, place in blackened peppers and cover tightly with plastic wrap. Allow to steam for about 20 minutes while cooling down. When cool, remove and throw away the skin.
2. In a small dry skillet, toast pine nuts over medium-low heat, swirl the pine nuts for 1 to 2 minutes until they have nutty scent and turn to light tan color. Remove from the heat, pour into a small bowl in order to avoid overcooking.
3. Cut the roasted peppers into strips, and on a serving platter, place peppers strips decoratively by alternating yellow and red ones. Sprinkle peppers with parsley, garlic, raisins and toasted pine nuts.

Add in olive oil in a drizzle; put salt and black pepper to season.

Nutrition Information
Calories: 160 calories; Total Carbohydrate: 8.4 g Cholesterol: 0 mg Total Fat: 13.8 g Protein: 2.1 g
Sodium: 4 mg

Romance-in-a-bowl Salad
Serving: 2 | Prep: 10m | Ready in: 10m

Ingredients
- 4 cups baby salad greens
- 1 carrot, peeled and sliced
- 2 green onions, chopped
- 6 strawberries, hulled and sliced
- 12 fresh raspberries
- 1 tsp. minced garlic
- 1/4 cup chopped walnuts
- 1/4 cup seasoned almond slices
- 1/4 cup dried currants
- 1/4 cup crumbled feta cheese
- 1/2 cup seasoned croutons
- 1/2 cup herbed vinaigrette salad dressing, or to taste

Direction
1. Toss feta cheese, currants, almond slices, walnuts, garlic, raspberries, strawberries, green onions, carrot and salad greens together in a big bowl, then split between 2 salad bowls. Put some croutons on top of each bowl and serve together with vinaigrette dressing.

Nutrition Information
Calories: 468 calories; Total Carbohydrate: 55.1 g Cholesterol: 29 mg Total Fat: 23.4 g Protein: 13.5 g
Sodium: 1487 mg

Romantic Valentine's Day Salad
Serving: 2 | Prep: 10m | Ready in: 40m

Ingredients
- 1 large beet
- 2 cups mixed salad greens
- 1 tbsp. extra-virgin olive oil, or to taste
- salt to taste

Direction
1. In a saucepan, add beet and water to cover, then bring to a boil. Lower heat and simmer for half an hour, until beet is cook through. Drain beet and let it cool.
2. Peel beet and cut into slices with the thickness of 1/4 inch. Use a heart-shaped cookie cutter to cut out red hearts.
3. In a bowl, add salad greens, then drizzle olive oil over and use salt to season. Into the salad, put beet hearts and toss, then top salad with a couple of read hearts to serve.

Nutrition Information
Calories: 122 calories; Total Carbohydrate: 13.4 g Cholesterol: 0 mg Total Fat: 7 g Protein: 2.8 g

Sodium: 190 mg

Seared Scallop And Asparagus Salad

Serving: 4 | Prep: 15m | Ready in: 20m

Ingredients
Dressing:
- 3/4 cup olive oil
- 1/4 cup balsamic vinegar
- 1 tsp. chopped garlic
- 1/2 tsp. salt
- 1/2 tsp. ground black pepper

Salad:
- 2 tsps. olive oil, or to taste
- 1/2 lb. bay scallops
- 1 bunch fresh asparagus, trimmed
- 1 (10 oz.) bag fresh spinach

Direction
1. In a bowl, beat salt, pepper, garlic, vinegar and 3/4 cup olive oil until smooth.
2. In a skillet, heat 2 tsps. of olive oil over medium-high heat. Sear asparagus and scallops in hot oil for 2 to 3 minutes per side until caramelizing.
3. In a large mixing bowl, place spinach. Pour dressing over spinach, toss until well coated; add asparagus and scallops on top.

Nutrition Information
Calories: 503 calories; Total Carbohydrate: 12.3 g Cholesterol: 34 mg Total Fat: 43.9 g Protein: 18.9 g Sodium: 517 mg

Shrimp And Avocado Salad

Serving: 4 | Prep: 20m | Ready in: 20m

Ingredients
- 1 cup cooked salad shrimp
- 2 tbsps. chopped fresh chives
- 1/3 cup mayonnaise
- 1 tbsp. Worcestershire sauce
- 2 tbsps. chili sauce
- salt to taste
- 2 avocados, halved lengthwise and pitted
- 1 tbsp. lemon juice
- Bibb lettuce leaves
- 1 tsp. paprika
- sliced pimento peppers, for garnish

Direction
1. Combine in a bowl the chili sauce, Worcestershire sauce, mayonnaise, chives and shrimp. Add salt to taste.
2. Pile the shrimp mixture into avocado halves, and drizzle with lemon juice. Put avocado halves on

Bibb lettuce leaves that have been sprinkled with paprika. Decorate with strips of pimento then serve.

Nutrition Information

Calories: 341 calories; Total Carbohydrate: 12.7 g Cholesterol: 69 mg Total Fat: 29.9 g Protein: 9.8 g Sodium: 268 mg

Spinach Salad With Warm Bacon-mustard Dressing

Serving: 4 | Prep: 15m | Ready in: 20m

Ingredients

- 1 (10 oz.) bag baby spinach leaves
- 4 hard-cooked eggs, peeled and sliced
- 1 cup sliced mushrooms
- 4 strips crisply cooked bacon, crumbled
- 10 oz. Swiss cheese, shredded
- 1/2 cup toasted sliced almonds
- 1 tbsp. olive oil
- 1 large shallot, minced
- 1 tsp. garlic, minced
- 1/3 cup white wine vinegar
- 1/3 cup Dijon mustard
- 1/3 cup honey
- 2 strips crisply cooked bacon, crumbled
- salt and pepper to taste

Direction

1. In a large serving bowl, put spinach, with almonds, Swiss cheese, 4 crumbled strips of bacon, mushrooms and hard cooked eggs.
2. Place a small skillet on medium heat then put olive oil. Mix in garlic and shallots, and cook for about two minutes until translucent and softened. Add in the two crumbled strips of bacon, honey, Dijon mustard and vinegar; use pepper and salt to taste, then cook until warm.
3. Put hot dressing on top of spinach and toss to coat.

Nutrition Information

Calories: 663 calories; Total Carbohydrate: 40.1 g Cholesterol: 293 mg Total Fat: 40.6 g Protein: 36.1 g Sodium: 1123 mg

Stacked Tomato And Burrata Salad

Serving: 1 | Prep: 15m | Ready in: 15m

Ingredients

- 1 vine-ripened tomato, cored and cut into 1/2-inch slices
- flaked sea salt and freshly ground black pepper to taste
- 1/4 cup burrata cheese, or more to taste
- 1 tbsp. torn fresh basil leaves, or to taste
- 1 tbsp. extra-virgin olive oil

Direction

1. In a plate, place bottom of tomato slice, add sea salt and black pepper to season. Scatter burrata

cheese over tomato slice, add torn basil leaves on top. Pour olive oil over tomatoes. Put next tomato slice on top. Repeat the process of layering cheese and tomato with remaining slices. Finish with top tomato slice.

Nutrition Information

Calories: 329 calories; Total Carbohydrate: 5.9 g Cholesterol: 45 mg Total Fat: 27.4 g Protein: 10.4 g Sodium: 486 mg

Strawberry And Feta Salad

Serving: 10 | Prep: 15m | Ready in: 15m

Ingredients

- 1 cup slivered almonds
- 2 cloves garlic, minced
- 1 tsp. honey
- 1 tsp. Dijon mustard
- 1/4 cup raspberry vinegar
- 2 tbsps. balsamic vinegar
- 2 tbsps. brown sugar
- 1 cup vegetable oil
- 1 head romaine lettuce, torn
- 1 pint fresh strawberries, sliced
- 1 cup crumbled feta cheese

Direction

1. Heat a frying pan over medium-high heat, put in almonds and cook, stir frequently until lightly toasted. Take away from heat, place aside.
2. To make the dressing, mix vegetable oil, brown sugar, balsamic vinegar, raspberry vinegar, Dijon mustard, honey, and garlic in a bowl.
3. Mix feta cheese, strawberries, romaine lettuce, and the toasted almonds in a big bowl. Put a cover on the dressing mixture, mix to serve.

Nutrition Information

Calories: 378 calories; Total Carbohydrate: 12.4 g Cholesterol: 22 mg Total Fat: 34.3 g Protein: 7.1 g Sodium: 301 mg

Strawberry Spinach Salad I

Serving: 4 | Prep: 10m | Ready in: 1h10m

Ingredients

- 2 tbsps. sesame seeds
- 1 tbsp. poppy seeds
- 1/2 cup white sugar
- 1/2 cup olive oil
- 1/4 cup distilled white vinegar
- 1/4 tsp. paprika
- 1/4 tsp. Worcestershire sauce
- 1 tbsp. minced onion
- 10 oz. fresh spinach - rinsed, dried and torn into bite-size pieces

- 1 quart strawberries - cleaned, hulled and sliced
- 1/4 cup almonds, blanched and slivered

Direction
1. Mix Worcestershire sauce, onion, paprika, vinegar, olive oil, sugar, poppy seeds, and sesame seeds in a medium bowl. Cover then chill for an hour.
2. Mix almonds, strawberries, and spinach in a big bowl. Pour dressing on salad then toss. Keep in fridge for 10-15 minutes then serve.

Nutrition Information
Calories: 491 calories; Total Carbohydrate: 42.9 g Cholesterol: 0 mg Total Fat: 35.2 g Protein: 6 g Sodium: 63 mg

Tomato And Avocado Salad
Serving: 4 | Prep: 15m | Ready in: 15m

Ingredients
- 1 tsp. Dijon mustard
- 1/4 cup extra-virgin olive oil
- 1/2 cup balsamic vinegar
- 1 pinch ground black pepper
- 1 avocado - peeled, pitted and sliced
- 2 small tomatoes, each cut into 8 wedges

Direction
1. Combine in a small bowl the pepper, balsamic vinegar, olive oil, and mustard. Alternately lay out avocado slices and tomato like the spokes of a wheel on one big serving plate or individual plates. Then drizzle lightly with the dressing and serve right away.

Nutrition Information
Calories: 236 calories; Total Carbohydrate: 11.1 g Cholesterol: 0 mg Total Fat: 21.5 g Protein: 1.5 g Sodium: 45 mg

Valentine's Day Salad
Serving: 12

Ingredients
- 1 (6 oz.) package strawberry flavored Jell-O
- 2 cups boiling water
- 1 (16 oz.) package strawberries, partially frozen
- 2 bananas, peeled and diced
- 1 (20 oz.) can crushed pineapple, drained
- 1 (8 oz.) container frozen whipped topping, thawed (optional)

Direction
1. Bring water in a medium saucepan to a boil on high heat and put in gelatin. Once gelatin is dissolved, put in pineapple, bananas and strawberries, mixing well. Take away from the heat.
2. Scoop mixture into a 13"x9" baking dish or separate heart molds, then refrigerate until firm.
3. Put whipped topping on top of each serving if you want, then serve.

Nutrition Information

Calories: 169 calories; Total Carbohydrate: 31.6 g Cholesterol: 0 mg Total Fat: 4.9 g Protein: 2.1 g
Sodium: 65 mg

Warm Bok Choy, Beet And Feta Salad

Serving: 3 | Prep: 15m | Ready in: 1h5m

Ingredients

- 4 small beets, trimmed, leaving 1 inch of stems attached
- 4 cloves garlic, chopped, divided
- 1 tsp. olive oil
- 3 heads baby bok choy, chopped
- 2 tbsps. peanut oil
- 1 1/2 tsps. butter
- 1/3 cup crumbled feta cheese

Direction

1. Preheat the oven to 425°F (220°C). Get a piece of heavy aluminium foil to place the olive oil, 1/4 of the chopped garlic and beets on then fold the foil around the beets into a sealed packet.
2. Place beets inside of the preheated oven and roast until it can be pierced easily with a fork, about 40-60 minutes. Leave the beets to cool down until they can be handled. Wipe them with a paper towel and remove the skins off then chop them into 1/2-inch cubes and put it aside.
3. In a heavy skillet, heat butter and peanut oil over medium high heat then cook and stir the bok choy in together with the remaining garlic. Cook for 5 minutes until the boy choy softens but is still crunchy. Move it away from the heat then mix the feta and beets in. Serve the dish warm.

Nutrition Information

Calories: 212 calories; Total Carbohydrate: 12.5 g Cholesterol: 20 mg Total Fat: 16.5 g Protein: 5.5 g
Sodium: 334 mg

Wedge Salad With Elegant Blue Cheese Dressing

Serving: 8 | Prep: 30m | Ready in: 1day30m

Ingredients

- 1/2 lb. crumbled blue cheese
- 1/4 cup sour cream
- 1/3 cup buttermilk
- 1/2 cup mayonnaise
- 1/4 cup red wine vinegar
- 1 tbsp. extra-virgin olive oil
- 1 1/2 tbsps. white sugar
- 1 clove garlic, minced
- ground black pepper to taste
- 1 head iceberg lettuce, cut into 8 wedges
- 2 roma tomatoes, diced
- 1 small red onion, thinly sliced
- 1/2 lb. crumbled blue cheese

Direction

1. In a bowl, combine sour cream, a half lb. of blue cheese, mayonnaise, buttermilk, olive oil, vinegar,

pepper, garlic, and sugar; use a hand mixer to blend, chill until serving.

2. Place 1 lettuce wedge on each of 8 plates to build the salad. Sprinkle equal amounts of dressing over each wedge. Top each salad with 1/2 lb. blue cheese, onion, and tomatoes.

Nutrition Information

Calories: 362 calories; Total Carbohydrate: 9.1 g Cholesterol: 51 mg Total Fat: 30.6 g Protein: 13.7 g Sodium: 892 mg

Winter Salad With Baby Greens And Broccolini

Serving: 2 | Prep: 10m | Ready in: 13m

Ingredients

- 1 tsp. salt
- 4 broccolini stalks, bottoms trimmed
- 2 tsps. olive oil
- 1 pinch red pepper flakes
- 1 clove garlic, minced
- 1 1/2 cups baby greens mix (such as spinach, chard, kale, and arugula)
- 2 tsps. lemon vinaigrette, or to taste
- coarse sea salt to taste

Direction

1. Boil water in a pot then add 1 tsp of salt. Lower heat then place in broccolini stalks. Simmer for 1 minute till broccolini is bright green. Place broccolini into a bowl with ice water; once cool, drain the broccolini. Chop into pieces with 1-in. size.
2. Bring the pot back to stove then heat red pepper flakes and olive oil over medium heat. Place in broccolini and cook to warm through. Add garlic, cook and stir for 30-60 seconds till fragrant but not browned. Take the pot away from the heat.
3. Stir sea salt, vinaigrette and baby greens into the broccolini mixture. Toss for 1-2 minutes to warm through but the greens are not wilted.

Nutrition Information

Calories: 71 calories; Total Carbohydrate: 4.1 g Cholesterol: 0 mg Total Fat: 5.7 g Protein: 1.5 g Sodium: 1383 mg

Bethany's Favorite Valentine Cut Out Sugar Cookies

Serving: 12 | Prep: 15m | Ready in: 3h25m

Ingredients

- 1 cup butter, softened
- 1 cup white sugar
- 1 egg, beaten
- 2 tbsps. milk
- 1 tsp. vanilla extract
- 1/2 tsp. almond extract
- 2 1/2 cups flour
- 1 tsp. baking powder

Direction

1. In a large bowl, cream almond extract, vanilla extract, milk, egg, sugar and butter together.

2. Mix in baking powder and flour.
3. Put into the refrigerator with a cover for 2 hours until firm.
4. Turn on the oven to 400°F (200°C) to preheat.
5. Cut the dough into 3 pieces. Roll out each piece on a lightly floured surface until they are 1/4-inch thick.
6. Use a floured cookie cutter to cut cookies.
7. On an ungreased baking sheet, place cookies 1-inch away from each other.
8. Put into the oven to bake for 6-9 minutes until lightly golden.
9. Allow to cool completely on a wire rack.

Nutrition Information

Calories: 304 calories; Total Carbohydrate: 36.8 g Cholesterol: 56 mg Total Fat: 16.1 g Protein: 3.5 g Sodium: 157 mg

Black Bottom Cupcakes II

Serving: 24 | Prep: 10m | Ready in: 30m

Ingredients

- 1 1/2 cups all-purpose flour
- 1 tsp. baking soda
- 1/4 cup unsweetened cocoa powder
- 1/2 tsp. salt
- 1 cup white sugar
- 1/3 cup vegetable oil
- 1 cup water
- 1 tbsp. vinegar
- 1 tsp. vanilla extract
- 1 (8 oz.) package cream cheese, softened
- 1 egg
- 1/3 cup white sugar
- 1/8 tsp. salt
- 1 cup miniature semisweet chocolate chips

Direction

1. Set the oven to 350°F or 175°C for preheating. Use paper liners to line the two 12-cup muffin pans. Sift the salt, cocoa powder, flour, and baking soda. Put the mixture aside.
2. Beat the oil, water, and a cup of sugar in a large bowl till combined. Mix in the vanilla and vinegar. Whisk in flour mixture until well-incorporated. Put the mixture aside.
3. Whisk the cream cheese, salt, egg, and 1/3 cup of sugar in a medium bowl. Mix in the chocolate chips.
4. Distribute the chocolate batter among the muffin cups, filling them 1/3 full. Top the batter with a heaping tbsp. of cream cheese mixture. Let them bake inside the preheated oven for 20-25 minutes until their tops spring back when they are pressed lightly.

Nutrition Information

Calories: 171 calories; Total Carbohydrate: 22.4 g Cholesterol: 18 mg Total Fat: 8.9 g Protein: 2.3 g Sodium: 145 mg

Brownies V

Serving: 32 | Prep: 10m | Ready in: 1h

Ingredients

- 1 cup butter
- 8 (1 oz.) squares unsweetened baking chocolate
- 4 eggs
- 1 1/2 cups packed brown sugar
- 1 1/2 cups white sugar
- 2 tsps. vanilla extract
- 2 tsps. orange zest
- 6 tbsps. brandy-based orange liqueur (such as Grand Marnier)
- 1 1/2 cups all-purpose flour
- 1 cup semisweet chocolate chips
- 1 cup chopped walnuts (optional)

Direction

1. Preheat the oven to 175°C or 350°F. Grease and spread flour onto a 9x13-in. baking dish.
2. Melt butter over medium heat in a medium saucepan. Add in the unsweetened chocolate squares and stir till smooth and melted completely. Take away from the heat and put aside till cool.
3. Beat eggs in a large bowl till fluffy and light then slowly add in white sugar and brown sugar. Keep beating for 3 minutes. Stir in Grand Marnier, orange zest, vanilla and the melted chocolate mixture. Gradually mix in flour on low speed then use your hand to fold in nuts and chocolate chips. Evenly spread the batter in the prepped pan.
4. Bake in the preheated oven for 45 minutes till the top feels firm when touched and the sides are slightly dry. Let the brownies cool then slice into squares. You can store these at room temperature, covered.

Nutrition Information

Calories: 251 calories; Total Carbohydrate: 31.1 g Cholesterol: 39 mg Total Fat: 14.1 g Protein: 3.1 g Sodium: 55 mg

Butter Cookies IV

Serving: 18

Ingredients

- 3 cups all-purpose flour
- 1 1/2 tsps. baking powder
- 1/2 tsp. salt
- 1 cup white sugar
- 1 cup butter
- 1 egg
- 3 tbsps. cream
- 1 tsp. vanilla extract
- 2 1/4 oz. colored candy sprinkles

Direction

1. Sift together sugar, salt, baking powder and flour, then mash in butter until the mixture looks like coarse crumbs. Stir in vanilla extract, cream and egg, then blend well. Use your hands to do this process best.

2. Shape dough into flattened ball, then wrap and chill for a minimum of 24 hours. You can store this mixture for a few days.
3. Set the oven to 205°C or 400°F to preheat.
4. Roll dough out on a board coated with flour to the thickness of 1/4 -1/8 inch. Use a cookie cutter to cut out shapes and use different types of sprinkles to garnish.
5. Bake about 5-8 minutes at 205°C or 400°F.

Nutrition Information

Calories: 239 calories; Total Carbohydrate: 29.8 g Cholesterol: 41 mg Total Fat: 12.3 g Protein: 2.7 g Sodium: 184 mg

Butter Crisps

Serving: 12

Ingredients

- 1 cup butter
- 1/2 (8 oz.) package cream cheese
- 1 cup white sugar
- 1 egg
- 1 tsp. vanilla extract
- 2 1/2 cups all-purpose flour
- 1/2 tsp. baking powder

Direction

1. Cream butter and cream cheese together. Put in egg and sugar gradually, keep on beating until combined.
2. Gradually put baking powder and flour into cream cheese mixture, then refrigerate dough about 1 to 2 hours.
3. On a board coated with flour, roll out the dough and cut in preferred shapes. Bake at 175°C or 350°F until light brown, about 12 minutes. Use desired frosting to frost.

Nutrition Information

Calories: 335 calories; Total Carbohydrate: 36.9 g Cholesterol: 66 mg Total Fat: 19.3 g Protein: 4.1 g Sodium: 163 mg

Cake Pops

Serving: 24 | Prep: 30m | Ready in: 1h40m

Ingredients

- 1 (12 oz.) package colored candy coating melts, divided
- 24 plain doughnut holes
- 24 lollipop sticks
- 1 tbsp. multicolored candy sprinkles (jimmies), as desired

Direction

1. Melt 1/4 cup of candy melts in the microwave for 30 seconds at 40% power. Stir. Continue to heat in 30-second intervals until completely melted and just warm.
2. Insert a lollipop stick halfway through a donut hole. Dip one end of the stick into the melted coating. Stick it back into the hole. This keeps them in place firmly. Stick the donut pops upright into a plastic foam block. Chill for 1 hour to set and firm up.

3. Once firmly attached to the sticks, melt the rest of the candy coating dots in the microwave for 1 minute at 40% power. Stir and melt some more until it's smoothly melted and warm, in 30-second intervals. Dip the doughnut hole and coat it completely. Hold it over a bowl. Garnish with colored candy sprinkles. Let the pops set by returning them into the foam block.

Nutrition Information
Calories: 131 calories; Total Carbohydrate: 14.5 g Cholesterol: 4 mg Total Fat: 7.6 g Protein: 1.7 g Sodium: 57 mg

Caramels
Serving: 60

Ingredients
- 2 cups white sugar
- 1 cup packed brown sugar
- 1 cup corn syrup
- 1 cup evaporated milk
- 1 pint heavy whipping cream
- 1 cup butter
- 1 1/4 tsps. vanilla extract

Direction
1. Coat a 15x12-inch pan with oil.
2. Mix the brown sugar, evaporated milk, sugar, butter, corn syrup and whipping cream together in a medium pot. Use a candy thermometer to keep track of the heat temperature of the mixture as you give it a stir. Remove the pot away from the heat once the candy thermometer indicates 250°F (120°C).
3. Add in the vanilla and mix well. Spread the prepared sugar mixture evenly into the prepared pan and allow the mixture to fully cool down. Slice the caramel mixture into small bite-sized squares once it has fully cooled down and use a wax paper to enwrap each of the caramel squares to store.

Nutrition Information
Calories: 115 calories; Total Carbohydrate: 14.8 g Cholesterol: 20 mg Total Fat: 6.3 g Protein: 0.5 g Sodium: 30 mg

Cardamom Rose Meringues
Serving: 12 | Prep: 15m | Ready in: 1h45m

Ingredients
- 2 egg whites
- 1/4 tsp. cream of tartar
- 2/3 cup white sugar
- 1/4 cup water
- 2 tsps. rose extract
- 1/4 tsp. ground cardamom
- 1/8 tsp. salt
- 1 drop red food coloring (optional)

Direction
1. Set the oven to 120°C or 250°F to preheat. Use parchment paper to line a baking sheet.

2. Use an electric mixer to beat together cream of tartar and egg whites in a mixing bowl on high speed until the mixture holds stiff peaks.
3. In a saucepan, add food coloring, salt, cardamom, rose extract, water and sugar, then bring to a simmer on low heat while stirring until sugar is dissolved. Simmer the mixture about 1-2 minutes while stirring continuously. Pour the syrup in a thin stream very gradually into egg whites while using electric mixer to beat continuously on high speed. Beat until the syrup is blended and meringue becomes shiny as well as stiff.
4. Drop on prepped baking sheet by spoonfuls of meringue or pipe into rosettes with a star tip.
5. In the preheated oven, bake about 1- 1 1/2 hours, until meringues become hard, then turn off the oven and let meringues cool inside oven to complete baking internal parts.

Nutrition Information

Calories: 46 calories; Total Carbohydrate: 11.2 g Cholesterol: 0 mg Total Fat: 0 g Protein: 0.6 g Sodium: 34 mg

Champagne Cupcakes

Serving: 24 | Prep: 15m | Ready in: 1h15m

Ingredients
- cooking spray
- 1 (18.25 oz.) package white cake mix
- 1 1/4 cups Champagne or other sparkling white wine at room temperature
- 1/3 cup vegetable oil
- 3 eggs
- 1/2 cup butter, softened
- 4 cups confectioners' sugar
- 1/4 cup Champagne or other sparkling white wine at room temperature
- 1 tsp. vanilla extract

Direction
1. Preheat the oven to 175°C or 350°Fahrenheit.
2. Use cooking spray to grease 24 muffin cups.
3. In a big mixing bowl, combine 1 1/4 cup champagne and cake mix; mix in eggs and vegetable oil. Beat for 2 minutes on medium speed using an electric mixer.
4. Transfer in greased muffin cups until 3/4 full.
5. Bake for 20 minutes in the preheated oven until an inserted toothpick in the center comes out without residue.
6. Cool for 10 minutes in the pan then remove. Completely cool for another half hour.
7. In a bowl, combine vanilla extract, butter, quarter cup champagne and a cup of confectioners' sugar. Mix in the rest of the confectioners' sugar, a cup at one time, until creamy and smooth; slather over cooled cupcakes.

Nutrition Information

Calories: 255 calories; Total Carbohydrate: 37.9 g Cholesterol: 33 mg Total Fat: 9.9 g Protein: 1.8 g Sodium: 178 mg

Cheesecake Pops

Serving: 24 | Prep: 45m | Ready in: 6h10m

Ingredients

- 3 (8 oz.) packages cream cheese, softened
- 3/4 cup sugar
- 1/3 cup sour cream
- 3 tbsps. all-purpose flour
- 1 tsp. vanilla
- 1/4 tsp. salt
- 3 eggs
- 24 lollipop sticks
- 10 oz. white confectioners' coating
- miniature semisweet chocolate chips
- toasted coconut

Direction

1. Set oven to preheat at 350°F (175°C).
2. Whip sugar and cream cheese in a big bowl until smooth. Stir in sour cream and scrape down sides of the bowl; mix well. Add vanilla, flour and salt. Stir well. Add an egg at a time. Mix well before adding each egg. Avoid overbeating, though. Transfer batter into a 9-inch springform pan.
3. Bake in the oven until the cake edges start to become golden, for 50 minutes. Let it cool for an hour on a wire rack. Chill overnight, or for 3 hours, in the fridge.
4. Scoop out balls of cheesecake with a cookie scoop. Roll to make 1 1/2-inch balls. Arrange on a wax paper-lined cookie sheet. Poke each with a lollipop stick. Put the tray in the freezer for half an hour, until firm.
5. Melt semi-sweet chocolate or white confectioners' coating. Coat the cheesecake pops with the melted coating. Dip them into your topping of choice. Let them set on waxed paper.
6. Chill before serving. Store in the fridge.

Nutrition Information

Calories: 217 calories; Total Carbohydrate: 16.4 g Cholesterol: 58 mg Total Fat: 15.6 g Protein: 3.9 g Sodium: 130 mg

Chocolate Black Tea Cake

Serving: 12 | Prep: 20m | Ready in: 1h20m

Ingredients

- 4 eggs, separated
- 1 cup butter
- 1 2/3 cups white sugar
- 1 cup brewed black tea, cold
- 2 cups all-purpose flour
- 1 1/2 tbsps. baking powder
- 1/3 cup dry bread crumbs
- 1/3 cup unsweetened cocoa powder
- 1 cup chopped hazelnuts

Direction

1. Set the oven at 360°F (180°C) and start preheating. Coat a 9-in. Bundt pan with grease and flour.
2. Cream white sugar, butter and egg yolks together in a large bowl till fluffy and light. Slowly beat in black tea. Toss hazelnuts, cocoa powder, bread crumbs, baking powder and flour together; fold into the tea mixture till just incorporated.

3. Whip egg whites till it forms stiff peaks in a large clean metal bowl or glass bowl. Fold the egg whites into the tea batter. Transfer the batter into the prepared pan.
4. Bake in the preheated oven for 60-70 minutes, or till a toothpick comes out clean when inserted into the center. Allow the cake to cool for at least 20 minutes in the pan; remove and let cool completely on a wire rack.

Nutrition Information

Calories: 421 calories; Total Carbohydrate: 49.3 g Cholesterol: 103 mg Total Fat: 23.5 g Protein: 6.7 g Sodium: 282 mg

Chocolate Pizzelles

Serving: 12

Ingredients

- 4 eggs
- 1/4 cup cocoa powder
- 1 cup white sugar
- 1/2 tsp. ground cinnamon
- 1/4 tsp. salt
- 1 tbsp. baking powder
- 1 cup unsalted butter
- 3/4 cup ground hazelnuts
- 2 cups all-purpose flour

Direction

1. Whisk together salt, sugar and eggs until light. Melt butter and mix in egg mixture.
2. Sift the entire leftover ingredients together excluding hazelnuts, and fold in.
3. Stir hazelnuts in last.
4. Heat Pizzelle iron and put on each imprint with 1 tsp. of batter, then close iron to bake about half a minute.
5. Allow to cool on racks and sprinkle powdered sugar over top.

Nutrition Information

Calories: 358 calories; Total Carbohydrate: 35.5 g Cholesterol: 103 mg Total Fat: 22.6 g Protein: 6 g Sodium: 197 mg

Chocolate Wine Balls

Serving: 48 | Prep: 30m | Ready in: 30m

Ingredients

- 3 1/4 cups crushed vanilla wafers
- 3/4 cup confectioners' sugar
- 1/4 cup unsweetened cocoa powder
- 3 tbsps. corn syrup
- 1/2 cup full-bodied red wine (Cabernet Sauvignon, Cotes du Rhone, Zinfandel, Shiraz or Barolo)
- 1 cup red decorator sugar

Direction

1. Mix red wine, corn syrup, cocoa powder, confectioners' sugar and vanilla wafers in a big bowl. Combine using your hands or a sturdy spoon to form a smooth dough. Form to an-inch balls and turn

into the red decorator sugar. Keep refrigerated in container with cover. Bring to room temperature prior to serving.

Nutrition Information

Calories: 88 calories; Total Carbohydrate: 16.1 g Cholesterol: 0 mg Total Fat: 2.4 g Protein: 0.6 g Sodium: 38 mg

Cinfully Delicious Chocolate Cupcakes

Serving: 24 | Prep: 20m | Ready in: 1h5m

Ingredients

- 1 (18.25 oz.) package chocolate cake mix
- 1 cup milk
- 3 eggs
- 1/2 cup butter, melted
- 1 tsp. ground cinnamon
- 1 tsp. vanilla extract
- 1 tsp. cinnamon sugar, or as needed
- 1/2 cup butter
- 1/2 cup butter-flavored shortening
- 1 pinch sea salt
- 1 tsp. vanilla extract
- 1 tbsp. ground cinnamon
- 1 tbsp. unsweetened cocoa powder
- 3 cups confectioners' sugar
- 1/4 cup milk
- 2 cups confectioners' sugar, or more as needed

Direction

1. Set the oven to 175°C or 350°F to preheat.
2. Use paper liners to line 24 muffin cups.
3. Use an electric mixer to beat 1 tsp. of vanilla extract, 1 tsp. of cinnamon, 1/2 cup of melted butter, eggs, 1 cup of milk, and chocolate cake mix together in a bowl on low speed until moist. Beat on medium speed about 2 minutes longer.
4. Pour batter into each muffin cup until 2/3 full.
5. Sprinkle cinnamon sugar over cupcakes.
6. In the preheated oven, bake for 15 minutes, until a toothpick exits clean after being inserted into the center.
7. Allow to cool in pans about 10 minutes prior to transferring to a wire rack to cool through.
8. In a bowl, cream together shortening and 1/2 cup of butter until smooth.
9. Stir in 3 cups of confectioners' sugar, cocoa powder, 1 tbsp. of cinnamon, 1 tsp. of vanilla extract and sea salt.
10. Stir in milk.
11. Combine in 2 additional cups of confectioners' sugar or as necessary until preferred consistency is attained.
12. Spread cooled cupcakes with frosting.

Nutrition Information

Calories: 320 calories; Total Carbohydrate: 43 g Cholesterol: 45 mg Total Fat: 16.4 g Protein: 2.6 g

Sodium: 260 mg

Classic Butter Cookies II
Serving: 48

Ingredients
- 2 1/2 cups all-purpose flour
- 1 cup butter
- 1/2 cup white sugar
- 1 egg
- 1/2 tsp. almond extract

Direction
1. Cream butter until light. Slowly add in sugar and beat until fluffy and light. Beat in almond extract and egg.
2. Slowly mix in the flour. Cover up and allow to chill for at least 1 hour.
3. Preheat the oven to 350°F (175°C).
4. On a lightly floured surface, roll the dough out to the thickness of 1/8 inch. Cut into shapes as desired with lightly floured cookie cutters. Arrange the cookies on ungreased cookie sheets.
5. Bake at 350°F (175°C) until golden, about 8-12 minutes. Transfer to wire racks for completely cooling. Decorate as desired.

Nutrition Information
Calories: 67 calories; Total Carbohydrate: 7.1 g Cholesterol: 14 mg Total Fat: 4 g Protein: 0.8 g Sodium: 29 mg

Cream Cheese Sugar Cookies
Serving: 72 | Prep: 15m | Ready in: 9h25m

Ingredients
- 1 cup white sugar
- 1 cup butter, softened
- 1 (3 oz.) package cream cheese, softened
- 1/2 tsp. salt
- 1/2 tsp. almond extract
- 1/2 tsp. vanilla extract
- 1 egg yolk
- 2 1/4 cups all-purpose flour

Direction
1. Mix together the butter, sugar, cream cheese, vanilla extracts, almond, egg yolk and salt in a big bowl. Beat the mixture until the consistency turns smooth. Add in flour and stir until completely incorporated. Keep the dough inside the fridge to chill for 8 hours, or up to overnight.
2. Set the oven for preheating to 375°F (190°C).
3. Dust your work surface lightly with flour. Roll out the dough 1/3 at a time to 1/8 inch in thickness, keeping the remaining dough in the fridge until ready to use. Form into preferred shapes using a lightly floured cookie cutters. Arrange the cookies an inch apart on the cookie sheets that's ungreased. Leave them plain for frosting, or brush them up with slightly beaten egg white and decorate with colored sugar or candy sprinkles.
4. Let it bake inside the oven for 7 to 10 minutes, or until the cookies becomes light and golden brown

in color. Allow them to cool through before decorating with frosting.

Nutrition Information
Calories: 53 calories; Total Carbohydrate: 5.8 g Cholesterol: 11 mg Total Fat: 3.1 g Protein: 0.6 g
Sodium: 38 mg

Cupcake Princess' Vanilla Cupcakes
Serving: 12 | Prep: 15m | Ready in: 1h45m

Ingredients
- 1 1/4 cups all-purpose flour
- 3/4 tsp. baking soda
- 1 pinch salt
- 5 tbsps. butter, cut into pieces
- 2/3 cup milk
- 1 cup white sugar
- 2 eggs
- 1 egg yolk
- 1 tsp. vanilla extract

Direction
1. Set oven temperature to 350 degrees F (175 degrees C) and preheat. Use 12 paper cupcake liners to line a conventional muffin tin. Mix salt, flour and baking soda in a bowl leave to one side.
2. Put milk and butter in a small saucepan and heat on low heat setting until the butter complete melts. Mix eggs, vanilla, egg yolk, and sugar in a big bowl by beating with an electric mixer, until the consistency is thicker and it has a lighter color. At low speed setting, introduce the flour mix while beating until evenly mixed. Gradually pour in the heated milk and continue beating until mixed evenly.
3. Separate the batter equally between the cupcake liners. Bake for 20 minutes until an inserted toothpick can be removed without any residue. Allow to cool for 10 minutes on the cupcake pan. Shift cupcakes onto a cooling rack to allow cooling to occur completely.

Nutrition Information
Calories: 178 calories; Total Carbohydrate: 27.4 g Cholesterol: 62 mg Total Fat: 6.4 g Protein: 3.1 g
Sodium: 131 mg

Dark Chocolate Peppermint Fudge
Serving: 16 | Prep: 10m | Ready in: 1h15m

Ingredients
- 3 cups semisweet chocolate chips (such as Hershey's Special Dark)
- 1 (14 oz.) can sweetened condensed milk
- 1/4 cup butter
- 1 1/2 tsps. pure peppermint extract
- 1 pinch salt
- 1/2 cup crushed peppermint candies, or more to taste

Direction
1. In a large microwave-safe bowl, mix together butter, chocolate chips, sweetened condensed milk, peppermint extract, and salt.

2. Place bowl in the microwave and heat for 5 to 6 minutes on medium-high power, or until the chocolate chips are melted; stir every 2 minutes.
3. Pour melted chocolate mixture into an 8 x 8-inch silicone pan; sprinkle with crushed peppermint candies. Using the back of the spoon, lightly press candies into the chocolate mixture. Chill in the refrigerator for 1 hour or until set.

Nutrition Information

Calories: 285 calories; Total Carbohydrate: 40.5 g Cholesterol: 16 mg Total Fat: 14.5 g Protein: 3.3 g Sodium: 58 mg

Egg Paint
Serving: 1

Ingredients
- 1 egg yolk
- 4 drops red food coloring

Direction
1. Mix a small amount of food coloring with the egg yolk in small bowl or cup. Create designs on the cookies with a clean paintbrush before baking them.

Egyptian Rose Leaves
Serving: 36

Ingredients
- 1/3 cup shortening
- 1 cup white sugar
- 2 eggs
- 1 tsp. rosewater
- 2 cups all-purpose flour
- 1/4 tsp. salt

Direction
1. Combine together rose fluid, eggs, sugar and shortening until fluffy. Stir together salt and flour, then blend in butter mixture. The resulting dough will become soft; refrigerate for a few hours to overnight.
2. Set the oven to 175°C or 350°F to preheat. Coat baking sheets lightly with grease or line them with parchment paper.
3. Roll a third of dough at time into balls with the diameter of 3/4 inch while keeping the remaining dough chilled. Arrange dough balls on cookie sheets and use your hand to flatten until about half of the initial thickness. Imagine flattened cookie as a clock. Cut 2 slits in cookie with length of 1/2 inch each, at 10:00 and 2:00. Pinch the bottom to make base of petal, then sprinkle pink or red decorator's sugar over top.
4. Bake at 175°C or 350°F until bottom turns brown slightly, about 8 to 10 minutes. Avoid browning tops of cookies.

Nutrition Information

Calories: 68 calories; Total Carbohydrate: 10.9 g Cholesterol: 10 mg Total Fat: 2.2 g Protein: 1.1 g Sodium: 20 mg

Grownup Chai Chocolate Cupcakes

Serving: 10 | Prep: 15m | Ready in: 45m

Ingredients

- 1/2 cup unsalted butter
- 2 (1 oz.) squares unsweetened chocolate, chopped
- 4 chai tea bags
- 1/2 cup all-purpose flour, sifted
- 3/4 cup white sugar
- 2 eggs
- 1 tsp. vanilla extract

Direction

1. Set the oven to 325°F or 165°C for preheating. Use 10 paper liners to line the muffin tin.
2. In the double boiler's top, melt the chocolate and butter over simmering water for 5-10 minutes, stirring often and scraping the sides down using the rubber spatula to prevent it from scorching until smooth.
3. Open the tea bags and pour the chai mixture into the spice grinder and grind for 5-10 seconds until it is grounded into a fine powder.
4. In a large bowl, mix the chai powder, sugar, and flour. Add the eggs, one at a time and beat well every after addition until the batter is smooth. Mix in the vanilla extract. Drizzle the batter with the chocolate mixture, mixing well until just blended. Distribute the batter among the prepared muffin cups.
5. Bake them inside the preheated oven for 25 minutes until the tops are cracked slightly and glossy and the inserted toothpick into the muffin's center comes out clean. Transfer the muffins from the tin onto the wire rack immediately; cool.

Nutrition Information

Calories: 207 calories; Total Carbohydrate: 21.8 g Cholesterol: 62 mg Total Fat: 13.2 g Protein: 2.7 g Sodium: 17 mg

Cherry Breeze Martini

Serving: 1 | Prep: 5m | Ready in: 5m

Ingredients

- ice
- 1 1/2 fluid oz. cherry vodka
- 1 1/2 fluid oz. cranberry juice
- 1 1/2 fluid oz. pineapple juice

Direction

1. Fill ice in a cocktail shaker. Pour pineapple juice, cranberry juice and vodka over ice. Shake vigorously. Into a chilled martini glass, strain the drink.

Cherry Smash

Serving: 1 | Prep: 5m | Ready in: 5m

Ingredients

- 3 frozen cherries
- 1 dash Angostura bitters
- 1 cup ice, or as needed

- 2 fluid oz. rye whiskey (such as Michter's)
- 1 fluid oz. sweet Italian vermouth
- 1/2 fluid oz. simple syrup
- 1/2 tsp. lemon juice, or to taste

Direction

1. In a low boy glass, place the cherries then splash with bitters. Muddle the cherries till smashed to the consistency you desire.
2. Add ice to fill a cocktail shaker then pour in lemon juice, simple syrup, vermouth and rye. Cover then shake vigorously. Pour over cherries.

Nutrition Information

Calories: 240 calories; Total Carbohydrate: 17.7 g Cholesterol: 0 mg Total Fat: 0.2 g Protein: 0.3 g Sodium: 11 mg

Cherry Vodka Sour

Serving: 1 | Prep: 5m | Ready in: 5m

Ingredients

3 fluid oz. vodka
3 fluid oz. sweet and sour mix
1 tbsp. cherry grenadine syrup

Direction

In an 8-oz. glass, stir grenadine, sweet and sour mix, and vodka together. Add ice.

Chocolate Coffee Kiss

Serving: 1 | Prep: 2m | Ready in: 2m

Ingredients

- 3/4 fluid oz. coffee liqueur
- 3/4 fluid oz. Irish cream liqueur
- 1/2 fluid oz. creme de cacao liqueur
- 1 tsp. brandy-based orange liqueur (such as Grand Marnier)
- 1 cup hot brewed coffee
- 2 tbsps. whipped cream
- 1 1/2 fluid oz. chocolate syrup
- 1 maraschino cherry

Direction

1. Mix Grand Marnier, creme de cacao, Irish cream and coffee liqueur in a coffee mug. Fill hot coffee in the mug. Put a dollop of whipped cream on top. Add chocolate syrup and use a maraschino cherry as garnish.

Chocolate Covered Cherry Shooters

Serving: 2 | Prep: 5m | Ready in: 5m

Ingredients

- 2 (1.5 fluid oz.) jiggers amaretto liqueur
- 1 tsp. grenadine syrup
- 2 tsps. chocolate syrup

- 2 tsps. heavy cream

Direction

1. Put ice in a cocktail shaker until full; add heavy cream, amaretto, chocolate syrup, and grenadine syrup. Shake then filter into shot glasses.

Chocolate Lover's Hot Chocolate

Serving: 3 | Prep: 5m | Ready in: 15m

Ingredients

- 2 1/2 cups milk
- 1/2 tsp. brown sugar
- 1/2 tsp. maple syrup
- 1/2 tsp. vanilla extract
- 1/2 tsp. honey
- 3 1/2 tbsps. unsweetened cocoa powder
- 1/2 cup milk

Direction

1. In a saucepan, heat 2 1/2 cups of milk on moderate heat for 5 minutes until steaming. Stir in vanilla extract, honey, maple syrup and brown sugar, then bring mixture to a boil and stir in cocoa powder. Take away from the heat and put in leftover 1/2 cup of milk. Place the saucepan back on heat and simmer for 2 minutes longer, until heated through. Scoop into cups to serve.

Nutrition Information

Calories: 148 calories; Total Carbohydrate: 17.5 g Cholesterol: 20 mg Total Fat: 5.7 g Protein: 9.3 g Sodium: 102 mg

Chocolate Martini A La Laren

Serving: 2 | Prep: 5m | Ready in: 5m

Ingredients

- 4 fluid oz. chocolate liqueur
- 3 fluid oz. vodka
- 1 (1 oz.) square semisweet chocolate, grated

Direction

1. Mix vodka and chocolate liqueur into a cocktail mixer filled with ice. Shake vigorously. Into 2 chilled martini glasses, strain the drink and use chocolate shavings to garnish.

Chocolate Martini Cocktail

Serving: 1 | Prep: 5m | Ready in: 5m

Ingredients

- 1 1/2 fluid oz. chocolate liqueur
- 1 1/2 fluid oz. creme de cacao
- 1/2 fluid oz. vodka
- 2 1/2 fluid oz. half-and-half
- 1 cup ice

Direction

1. In a cocktail shaker, mix ice, half-and-half, vodka, creme de cacao and chocolate liqueur. Cover and

shake till chilled. Into a chilled cocktail glass, strain in the drink.

Nutrition Information

Calories: 511 calories; Total Carbohydrate: 50.9 g Cholesterol: 28 mg Total Fat: 9 g Protein: 2.2 g Sodium: 46 mg

Chocolate Martinis For Two

Serving: 2 | Prep: 5m | Ready in: 5m

Ingredients

- 2 tbsps. chocolate syrup (such as Hershey's)
- ice
- 1/2 cup vodka (such as Absolut)
- 1 fluid oz. chocolate liqueur (such as Godiva)
- 1 fluid oz. white creme de cacao
- 2 maraschino cherries

Direction

1. Start from 2/3 of the way up 2 martini glass's side, pour in the chocolate syrup. Allow the chocolate to run to the bottom. Put aside.
2. Fill a cocktail shaker with ice. Add in creme de cacao, chocolate liqueur and vodka. Cover and shake till it's frosty on the outside of the shaker. Into the prepped martini glasses, strain the drink. Serve with maraschino cherries as garnish.

Nutrition Information

Calories: 323 calories; Total Carbohydrate: 30.1 g Cholesterol: 0 mg Total Fat: 0.3 g Protein: 0.4 g Sodium: 20 mg

Chocolate-covered Cherry Martini

Serving: 1 | Prep: 10m | Ready in: 10m

Ingredients

- ice
- 2 fluid oz. vanilla-flavored vodka
- 2 fluid oz. chocolate liqueur
- 1 fluid oz. Irish cream liqueur
- 1 maraschino cherry with juice
- 1 tsp. chocolate sauce, or to taste

Direction

1. Fill ice halfway in a cocktail shaker. Pour a splash of maraschino cherry juice, Irish cream, chocolate liqueur and vodka over ice. Cover and shake till chilled.
2. Sprinkle a martini glass's bottom with chocolate sauce. Drop into the glass's bottom maraschino cherry. Strain the shaker's drink into prepped glass.

Nutrition Information

Calories: 528 calories; Total Carbohydrate: 51.6 g Cholesterol: 0 mg Total Fat: 0.4 g Protein: 0.2 g Sodium: 16 mg

Chocomint Toddy

Serving: 1 | Prep: 10m | Ready in: 10m

Ingredients

- 1 fluid oz. coffee flavored liqueur
- 1 fluid oz. peppermint schnapps
- 6 fluid oz. boiling water
- 1 (1 oz.) envelope instant hot chocolate mix
- whipped cream for garnish
- shaved semisweet chocolate, for garnish

Direction

1. Combine peppermint schnapps and coffee flavored liqueur in a large mug. Add in boiling water and hot chocolate mix; stir to blend well. Place chocolate shavings and whipped cream on top.

Church Lady Martini

Serving: 1 | Prep: 5m | Ready in: 5m

Ingredients

- 1 1/2 (1.5 fluid oz.) jiggers vanilla vodka
- 1 1/2 (1.5 fluid oz.) jiggers hazelnut liqueur, such as Frangelico
- 1 1/2 (1.5 fluid oz.) jiggers coffee liqueur, such as Kahlua

Direction

1. Combine coffee liqueur, hazelnut liqueur and vodka together in a cocktail shaker or a big glass filled with ice. Shake for about 20 seconds till it's frosty on the outside of the shaker. Into a chilled martini glass, strain the drink.

Dark Chocolate Hot Cocoa

Serving: 1 | Prep: 5m | Ready in: 15m

Ingredients

- 1 cup whole milk
- 1 1/2 tsps. brown sugar, or to taste
- 2 oz. dark chocolate (such as Moser Roth 85% Dark Chocolate), or to taste
- 1 tbsp. heavy whipping cream, or more to taste
- 1 pinch ground cinnamon, or more to taste

Direction

1. In a saucepan, heat milk on moderate heat about 3-4 minutes, until just prior to boiling. Put in brown sugar and stir for a minute, to dissolve. Mix dark chocolate to milk for 2-3 minutes, until melted. Take saucepan away from the heat and stir into milk mixture with cinnamon and cream.

Nutrition Information

Calories: 493 calories; Total Carbohydrate: 57 g Cholesterol: 45 mg Total Fat: 28.2 g Protein: 11 g Sodium: 120 mg

Ginger Champagne

Serving: 1 | Prep: 2m | Ready in: 2m

Ingredients

- 3 strips pickled ginger
- 1 cup ice cubes
- 1 fluid oz. vodka

- 1/2 cup champagne

Direction
1. Put ginger strips in a shaker. Press to release its flavor, add vodka and ice cubes, then shake and strain mixture into a champagne glass. Top it with champagne.

Ginger Kiss
Serving: 1 | Prep: 5m | Ready in: 5m

Ingredients
- 1 very thin sliver habanero pepper
- 2 slices fresh ginger root
- 1 1/2 fluid oz. gin
- 3/4 fluid oz. lime juice
- 1/2 fluid oz. simple syrup
- 1 cup ice cubes
- 1 thin slice fresh ginger root

Direction
1. In a cocktail shaker, muddle 2 slices of fresh ginger and the habanero pepper slices together. For 20 seconds, muddle it until it pulverized. Put ice, simple syrup, lime juice and gin then cover. Shake it well to make it cool. To strain, use a fine mesh strainer and pour in a cocktail glass.
2. Use a thin slice of ginger on a toothpick to garnish.

Nutrition Information
Calories: 158 calories; Total Carbohydrate: 12.7 g Cholesterol: 0 mg Total Fat: 0.1 g Protein: 0.3 g Sodium: 10 mg

Gourmet Chocolate-covered Cherry Jell-o Shots
Serving: 12 | Prep: 10m | Ready in: 4h10m

Ingredients
- 1 (6 oz.) package cherry-flavored gelatin (such as Jell-O)
- 1 cup boiling water
- 1/2 cup vodka
- 1/2 cup chocolate liqueur (such as Godiva)

Direction
1. On a baking sheet that can fit inside the refrigerator, place twelve 2oz plastic cups.
2. Gently stir water in a bowl with cherry-flavored gelatin until it dissolves. Stir in chocolate liqueur and vodka.
3. Transfer the gelatin mixture in the prepared cups.
4. Place in the refrigerator for at least 4hrs to overnight.

Nutrition Information
Calories: 116 calories; Total Carbohydrate: 17.4 g Cholesterol: 0 mg Total Fat: 0 g Protein: 1.3 g Sodium: 65 mg

Hibiscus Sangria
Serving: 16 | Prep: 20m | Ready in: 9h25m

Ingredients

- 6 cups water
- 3/4 cup dried hibiscus petals
- 1/2 cup honey
- 2 cinnamon sticks
- 1 tsp. ground cardamom
- 2 (750 milliliter) bottles rose wine
- 3/4 cup brandy
- 1/2 cup brown sugar
- 1/2 cup elderflower syrup (optional)
- 1/4 cup triple sec
- 1/2 fresh pineapple - peeled, cored, and cut into chunks
- 2 Granny Smith apples, cut into chunks
- 1 pint strawberries, cut into chunks
- 2 oranges, cut into small chunks
- 1 lemon, cut into small chunks

Direction

1. In a big pot, mix cardamom, cinnamon sticks, honey, hibiscus petals and water together. Bring it to a boil. Turn the heat off. Leave it for an hour to let it steep. Strain it. Put triple sec, elderflower syrup, brown sugar, brandy and wine into the strained hibiscus water. Stir together until sugar is dissolved. Put the lemon, oranges, strawberries, apples and pineapples. Leave it in the fridge for 8 hours or overnight.

Nutrition Information

Calories: 225 calories; Total Carbohydrate: 29.2 g Cholesterol: 0 mg Total Fat: 0.2 g Protein: 0.8 g Sodium: 11 mg

His-n-hers Cocktails

Serving: 2 | Prep: 5m | Ready in: 5m

Ingredients

- His Ingredients:
- 2 fluid oz. vanilla vodka
- 1 fluid oz. hazelnut liqueur
- 1/2 cup ice cubes
- Her Ingredients:
- 1 fluid oz. raspberry vodka
- 1 fluid oz. creme de cacao
- 1 tsp. chocolate syrup
- 1 fluid oz. half-and-half cream
- 2 maraschino cherries

Direction

1. For his cocktail, in a rock glass over ice, pour hazelnut liqueur and vanilla vodka. Pour the mixture into a cocktail shaker, then pour back to the rock glass to combine.
2. For her cocktail, in a cocktail shaker over ice, pour creme de cacao and raspberry vodka. Cover and shake until frost appear on the outside of the shaker. Strain mixture into a martini glass with the rim coated in chocolate syrup, pour in half-and-half, decorate with maraschino berries.

3. Combine the flavors by kissing.

Indiana Martini

Serving: 1 | Prep: 5m | Ready in: 5m

Ingredients
- 3 fluid oz. lemon-lime flavored soda
- 1 1/4 fluid oz. raspberry-flavored vodka (such as Smirnoff)
- 1/4 fluid oz. triple sec
- 1 maraschino cherry

Direction
1. Fill ice into a cocktail shaker. Pour in triple sec, vodka and lemon-lime soda. Place a cover and shake, then strain into martini glass. Use a cherry to decorate.

Nutrition Information
Calories: 151 calories; Total Carbohydrate: 14.9 g Cholesterol: 0 mg Total Fat: 0 g Protein: 0 g Sodium: 11 mg

Jelly Bean Martini

Serving: 2 | Prep: 10m | Ready in: 40m

Ingredients
- 1/4 cup red and white jelly beans
- 3 fluid oz. whipped cream-flavored vodka (such as Pinnacle)
- ice
- 2 fluid oz. orange liqueur
- 1/2 fluid oz. white creme de cacao
- 2 white jelly beans
- 2 red jelly beans
- 2 slices lemon

Direction
1. In a small bowl, put 1/4 cup of jelly beans and pour vodka on top. Use plastic wrap to cover the bowl and leave it in the fridge for at least 30 minutes till chilled.
2. Fill ice in the shaker. Shake bowl with vodka and chilled jelly beans. Strain mixture into shaker through a strainer; remove jelly beans. Stir in creme de cacao and orange liqueur. Into 2 chilled martini glasses, strain vodka mixture. Into each glass's bottom, drop 1 red jelly bean and 1 white jelly bean. On each rim, place 1 lemon slice.

Nutrition Information
Calories: 366 calories; Total Carbohydrate: 54.4 g Cholesterol: 0 mg Total Fat: 0.1 g Protein: 0.2 g Sodium: 24 mg

Kir

Serving: 1 | Prep: 5m | Ready in: 5m

Ingredients
- 3/4 cup white wine
- 4 tsps. creme de cassis liqueur

Direction

1. In a wine glass, add creme de cassis and wine. Stir to serve.

Kir Royale Cocktail

Serving: 1 | Prep: 3m | Ready in: 3m

Ingredients
- 1 tbsp. creme de cassis liqueur
- 6 fluid oz. chilled Champagne

Direction
1. Using a big Champagne flute or white wine glass, pour in creme de cassis and top with Champagne.

Nutrition Information
Calories: 213 calories; Total Carbohydrate: 13.1 g Cholesterol: 0 mg Total Fat: 0.1 g Protein: 0.1 g
Sodium: 10 mg

Kirstin's Favorite Black Cherry Martini

Serving: 1 | Prep: 5m | Ready in: 5m

Ingredients
- 1 tbsp. white sugar
- 1 tbsp. lemon juice
- 1 cup ice cubes, or as needed
- 2 fluid oz. vodka
- 2 fluid oz. black cherry juice
- 1/2 fluid oz. grapefruit juice
- 1 tsp. agave nectar
- 1 maraschino cherry

Direction
1. Spread over a small plate with sugar. Pour lemon juice on a separate small plate. Dip a martini glass's rim in the lemon juice, then coat in the sugar.
2. Fill ice in the cocktail shaker. Add agave nectar, grapefruit juice, black cherry juice and vodka. Put the lid on the shaker and shake vigorously for 10 seconds till chilled. Into prepped martini glass, strain drink and use maraschino cherry to garnish.

Nutrition Information
Calories: 249 calories; Total Carbohydrate: 31.3 g Cholesterol: 0 mg Total Fat: 0 g Protein: 0.1 g
Sodium: 15 mg

Lemony Lemon Drop Martini

Serving: 1 | Prep: 10m | Ready in: 10m

Ingredients
- 1 tbsp. white sugar
- 1 cup ice cubes
- 3 lemons, peel grated and juiced
- 2 large mint leaves
- 2 (1.5 fluid oz.) jiggers vodka
- 2 tbsps. simple syrup

Direction

1. Use water or lemon juice to moisten a martini glass's rim then dip it in sugar. Put aside.
2. Fill ice in a cocktail shaker. Add simple syrup, vodka, mint leaves, lemon juice and lemon peel. Shake till well chilled. Transfer into the prepped martini glass.

Nectar Of The Gods - A Champagne Beverage

Serving: 1 | Prep: 5m | Ready in: 5m

Ingredients

- 1 (1.5 fluid oz.) jigger raspberry-flavored liqueur (such as Chambord)
- 1 1/2 fluid oz. agave nectar
- 4 fluid oz. champagne, or as needed

Direction

1. Stir the agave nectar and raspberry-flavored liqueur together with a spoon in a tall glass with thin sides. Lean the glass at slant and pour in the champagne.

Nutrition Information

Calories: 386 calories; Total Carbohydrate: 57.4 g Cholesterol: 0 mg Total Fat: 0.1 g Protein: 0.1 g Sodium: 9 mg

Original Champagne Cocktail

Serving: 1 | Prep: 3m | Ready in: 3m

Ingredients

- 1 sugar cube
- 2 dashes Angostura bitters
- 6 fluid oz. chilled Champagne
- 1 lemon twist

Direction

1. Place bitters and sugar onto a Champagne flute that has been chilled. Fill the glass with Champagne and add a lemon peel twist.

Nutrition Information

Calories: 158 calories; Total Carbohydrate: 7.6 g Cholesterol: 0 mg Total Fat: 0 g Protein: 0.2 g Sodium: 9 mg

Pink Crush

Serving: 8 | Prep: 5m | Ready in: 5m

Ingredients

- 10 fluid oz. coconut flavored rum
- 6 fluid oz. pineapple juice
- 16 fluid oz. strawberry-flavored soda (such as Crush Strawberry)

Direction

1. Into a cocktail mixing cup, pour pineapple juice and rum, then stir to mix. Pour strawberry soda gently into mixture, pouring down the side of the mixing cup to keep soda from going flat. Tilt the mixing cup back and forth slowly several times to mix, then transfer into cocktail glasses.

Nutrition Information

Calories: 107 calories; Total Carbohydrate: 17.2 g Cholesterol: 0 mg Total Fat: 0 g Protein: 0.1 g

Sodium: 18 mg

Pomegranate Champagne Spritzer

Serving: 1 | Prep: 10m | Ready in: 10m

Ingredients

- 1 cup ice cubes, or as needed
- 2 fluid oz. pomegranate liqueur (such as PAMA)
- 1 fluid oz. orange juice
- 2 fluid oz. dry champagne
- 1 orange wedge
- 1 orange peel strip
- 1 tsp. white sugar, or as needed

Direction

1. Using a cocktail shaker filled with ice, add orange juice and pomegranate liqueur, then cover with a lid and shake. Remove the lid and slowly pour in the champagne. Gently stir the drink until mixed then strain into a champagne flute.
2. Squeeze an orange wedge to extract the juice onto an orange peel. In a small bowl, pour in sugar and roll the orange peel on it until it is covered. Take the sugar-coated peel and float it on the cocktail.

Nutrition Information

Calories: 299 calories; Total Carbohydrate: 37.4 g Cholesterol: 0 mg Total Fat: 0.3 g Protein: 0.4 g
Sodium: 15 mg

Pomosa

Serving: 1 | Prep: 5m | Ready in: 5m

Ingredients

- 1/2 cup brut Champagne
- 2 tbsps. bottled pomegranate juice
- 1 tsp. pomegranate seeds (optional)

Direction

1. Pour Champagne until a flute is 3/4 full. Then, top it with pomegranate juice. Use a few pomegranate seeds as garnish.

Popped Cherry

Serving: 1 | Prep: 5m | Ready in: 5m

Ingredients

- 1 cup ice
- 1 fluid oz. maraschino cherry juice
- 2 fluid oz. vodka
- 4 fluid oz. orange juice
- 3 maraschino cherries

Direction

1. Put ice into a highball glass to fill. Pour in orange juice, vodka, and cherry juice. Stir until mixed well, and decorate with some maraschino cherries. Serve.

Raspberry Lady Martini

Serving: 1 | Prep: 10m | Ready in: 10m

Ingredients

- 1 fluid oz. amaretto liqueur
- 1 fluid oz. coffee-flavored liqueur (such as Kahlua)
- 1 fluid oz. raspberry-flavored liqueur (such as St. George Spirits)
- 2 ice cubes, or as needed
- 3 fresh raspberries, or as needed

Direction

1. In a cocktail shaker, mix together ice cubes, raspberry-flavored liqueur, coffee-flavored liqueur and amaretto, then cover and shake. Transfer into a cocktail glass and use raspberries to decorate.

Nutrition Information

Calories: 329 calories; Total Carbohydrate: 39.5 g Cholesterol: 0 mg Total Fat: 0.3 g Protein: 0.1 g Sodium: 8 mg

Red Rocket

Serving: 1 | Prep: 5m | Ready in: 5m

Ingredients

- 1/2 oz. peach schnapps
- 1/2 oz. watermelon schnapps
- 1/2 oz. orange juice
- 1 oz. vodka
- 1/2 oz. pineapple juice (optional)
- 1 splash grenadine

Direction

1. In a cocktail shaker with ice, decant vodka, orange juice, grenadine, pineapple juice, watermelon schnapps and peach schnapps. Close lid and shake until the outside is frosty. Serve in an ice-cold glass.

Rhubarb Slush

Serving: 20 | Prep: 10m | Ready in: 25m

Ingredients

- 6 cups fresh rhubarb, chopped
- 2 cups white sugar
- 1 (6 oz.) can frozen orange juice concentrate, thawed
- 1 (6 oz.) can frozen lemonade concentrate, thawed
- 1 cup gin (optional)
- 3 cups water
- 1 (2 liter) bottle lemon-lime flavored carbonated beverage, chilled

Direction

1. In a big saucepan, add rhubarb and fill water in to cover. On a medium high heat, bring to a boil and let cook until softened. Drain and use a blender to puree or mash it.
2. Whisk water, gin, lemonade concentrate, orange juice concentrate, sugar and rhubarb puree together,

put in the freezer. Put into serving glasses with scoops of frozen mixture, then fill lemon-lime soda in the rest of the glass.

Nutrition Information

Calories: 193 calories; Total Carbohydrate: 41.7 g Cholesterol: 0 mg Total Fat: 0.1 g Protein: 0.6 g Sodium: 14 mg

Sicilian Sunset

Serving: 4 | Prep: 10m | Ready in: 10m

Ingredients

- 2 cups ice cubes
- 1 cup Prosecco (Italian sparkling wine)
- 1 cup orange juice
- 1 cup cranberry juice
- 2 lemons, zested

Direction

1. In a glass pitcher with ice, pour in cranberry juice, orange juice, and Prosecco then stir. Pour it into Champagne flutes and serve with a sprinkle of lemon zest.

Nutrition Information

Calories: 115 calories; Total Carbohydrate: 17.2 g Cholesterol: 0 mg Total Fat: 0.2 g Protein: 0.5 g Sodium: 9 mg

Snickers Martini

Serving: 1 | Prep: 10m | Ready in: 10m

Ingredients

- 1 fluid oz. coffee-flavored liqueur (such as Kahlua)
- 1 fluid oz. Irish cream liqueur
- 1 fluid oz. amaretto liqueur
- 1 fluid oz. hazelnut liqueur (such as Frangelico)
- 1/2 fluid oz. vodka
- 1 tsp. heavy whipping cream, or to taste

Direction

1. Add ice into a cocktail shaker till full, then add cream, vodka, hazelnut liqueur, amaretto liqueur, Irish cream liqueur and coffee-flavored liqueur. Place a cover and shake, then strain drink into a martini glass.

Nutrition Information

Calories: 484 calories; Total Carbohydrate: 52.3 g Cholesterol: 7 mg Total Fat: 2.2 g Protein: 0.2 g Sodium: 11 mg

Strawberry Bellini

Serving: 3 | Prep: 10m | Ready in: 20m

Ingredients

- 3 cups strawberries, hulled and sliced
- 1/4 cup confectioners' sugar
- 1 tbsp. brandy

- 1 1/2 cups chilled sparkling wine
- 3 large strawberries

Direction

1. Pour 3 cups of strawberries, brandy, and confectioner's sugar in a blender and blend until smooth. Chill strawberry mixture in a refrigerator for about 10 minutes.
2. Pour strawberry mixture equally among 3 champagne flutes, topping each with 1/2 cup sparkling wine, and stir. Garnish champagne glasses with 1 strawberry each.

Nutrition Information

Calories: 298 calories; Total Carbohydrate: 37.5 g Cholesterol: 0 mg Total Fat: 0.5 g Protein: 1.3 g Sodium: 13 mg

Strawberry Cheesecake Jell-o Shots

Serving: 12 | Prep: 20m | Ready in: 1h50m

Ingredients

- 6 graham crackers
- 2 tbsps. melted butter
- 1 tsp. white sugar
- 1 (.25 oz.) package unflavored gelatin
- boiling water
- 1 (12 oz.) container whipped cream cheese
- 1/3 cup confectioners' sugar, or more to taste
- 1/2 tsp. vanilla extract
- 1 1/2 cups vodka, divided
- 1/2 (3 oz.) package strawberry flavored gelatin (such as Jell-O)
- 1/4 cup boiling water
- 3 ice cubes

Direction

1. In a food processor or blender, process the graham crackers until crushed; blend in sugar and melted butter until evenly incorporated. Gently push the graham cracker mix in twelve tall shot glasses.
2. In a bowl, combine a quarter cup of boiling water and unflavored gelatin together until well blended.
3. In a blender, pulse the gelatin mixture, cream cheese, vanilla extract, and confectioners' sugar together for a few times; blend in 1 cup of vodka until smooth. Add more confectioners' sugar according to taste. On top of the graham cracker layer, spread the cream cheese mixture leaving about 1 inch of space on top. Place in the refrigerator for at least 1 hour.
4. In a bowl, combine a quarter cup of boiling water and strawberry gelatin together until well blended; put in ice cubes and the remaining half cup of vodka. Mix until the mixture starts to thicken and the ice is melted; pour on top of the cream cheese layer. Refrigerate shots for at least half an hour.

Nutrition Information

Calories: 225 calories; Total Carbohydrate: 13.6 g Cholesterol: 32 mg Total Fat: 10.6 g Protein: 2.7 g Sodium: 192 mg

Sweet Seduction

Serving: 2 | Prep: 5m | Ready in: 5m

Ingredients

- 1 fluid oz. Malibu rum
- 1 fluid oz. banana liqueur
- 1/2 cup pineapple juice
- ice cubes
- 1 tbsp. grenadine

Direction

1. Measure into a cocktail shaker with pineapple juice, banana liqueur and rum. Put in a liberal scoop of ice, then cover and shake mixture for half a minute, until the outside of shaker frosts. Strain drink into a glass filled with ice and pour on top gently with grenadine. It should float.

Sweet Tart Punch

Serving: 25

Ingredients

- 2 (46 fluid oz.) cans unsweetened pineapple juice
- 2 (2 liter) bottles ginger ale
- 1 gallon lime sherbet
- 2 trays ice cubes

Direction

1. Thoroughly mix ice cubes, pineapple juice, lime sherbet, and ginger ale together in a big punch bowl. Serve right away.

Nutrition Information

Calories: 285 calories; Total Carbohydrate: 65.5 g Cholesterol: 7 mg Total Fat: 2.6 g Protein: 1.8 g Sodium: 80 mg

The Milky Way Martini

Serving: 1 | Prep: 5m | Ready in: 5m

Ingredients

- 1 1/2 cups ice cubes
- 1/4 cup cold water
- 2 fluid oz. vanilla-flavored vodka
- 2 fluid oz. white creme de cacao
- 2 fluid oz. Irish cream liqueur
- 1 tbsp. chocolate syrup

Direction

1. Fill cold water and 1/2 cup of ice into a martini glass to chill.
2. Put a cup of ice cubes in a cocktail shaker. Pour Irish cream liqueur, white creme de cacao and vanilla-flavored vodka over the ice in a shaker. Cover then shake vigorously. Remove water and ice from the martini glass. Use chocolate syrup to drizzle the inside of the glass. Strain the cocktail into the glass. Serve.

Triple Fionn Maccool

Serving: 1 | Prep: 5m | Ready in: 5m

Ingredients

- 2 fluid oz. Irish cream liqueur

- 1 fluid oz. Canadian rye whiskey
- 1/4 cup cold milk
- 1 pinch cinnamon
- 2 cups ice cubes

Direction

1. Shake Canadian rye whiskey and Irish cream liqueur together with a few cubes of ice in a cocktail shaker. Fill a glass with ice cubes and strain the shaken mixture into. Put a dash of cinnamon and milk on top. Stir gently and serve.

Bacon Rose Quiche

Serving: 10 | Prep: 20m | Ready in: 1h30m

Ingredients

- 1 (9 inch) unbaked deep dish pie crust
- 13 slices bacon, divided
- 1 tsp. butter
- 1 tsp. olive oil
- 1 cup cremini mushrooms, sliced
- 1 small onion, diced
- 1/4 tsp. salt
- 1/8 tsp. ground black pepper
- 1 cup shredded Swiss cheese
- 1/2 cup shredded Gruyere cheese
- 3 green onions, thinly sliced
- 6 eggs
- 1 1/2 cups heavy whipping cream
- 3/4 tsp. salt
- 1/2 tsp. garlic powder
- 1/4 tsp. white sugar
- 1/8 tsp. ground nutmeg
- 1/8 tsp. cayenne pepper

Direction

1. Set oven to 450°F (230°C) and preheat.
2. In a big frying pan, place 10 slices bacon and heat over medium-high, turning sporadically for 7 to 10 minutes, until crunchy and evenly browned. Transfer bacon slices onto paper towels to drain and crumble.
3. In a same frying pan, cook butter and olive oil over medium- high heat. Mix in onion and mushrooms. Put in pepper and 1/4 tsp. salt. Cook, mixing sporadically about 8 minutes, until onions and mushrooms are little soft and brown.
4. Scatter green onions, Gruyere cheese, Swiss cheese, crumbled bacon, mushroom-onion mixture into the pie crust.
5. In a bowl, whisk eggs slightly; beat in cream, cayenne pepper, nutmeg, sugar, garlic powder and 3/4 tsp. salt. Transfer egg mixture gently into the pie crust.
6. Pass a toothpick through 1 end of 1 of the remaining bacon slices and shape into a rose by rolling the bacon around the toothpick. Do the same with the remaining slices. On top of the quiche, set the bacon roses up.

7. Bake for 15 minutes in the preheated oven.
8. Decrease oven heat to 300°F (150°C). Keep baking for 30 minutes or more, until a knife inserted in the centre comes out clean. Use aluminum foil to cover if surface becomes too brown. Allow quiche to stand for 10 minutes before cutting.

Nutrition Information
Calories: 404 calories; Total Carbohydrate: 12.6 g Cholesterol: 191 mg Total Fat: 32.8 g Protein: 14.9 g Sodium: 730 mg

Bloody Mary Ceviche
Serving: 8 | Prep: 20m | Ready in: 3h20m

Ingredients
- 1 lb. cooked, peeled, and deveined shrimp
- 1 lb. roma (plum) tomatoes, chopped
- 1/2 red onion, chopped
- 1 cucumber, chopped
- 1 bunch cilantro, chopped
- 3/4 cup bottled Bloody Mary mix
- 2 limes
- hot pepper sauce to taste
- salt and black pepper to taste

Direction
1. In a bowl, gently combine cilantro, cucumber, red onion, tomatoes, and shrimp, then add in the Bloody Mary mix. Squeeze over the mixture with limes; add a dash of hot pepper sauce, and sprinkle pepper and salt over. Stir again, put a cover on the bowl, and chill for 3-4 hours, tossing sometimes.

Nutrition Information
Calories: 74 calories; Total Carbohydrate: 7.3 g Cholesterol: 86 mg Total Fat: 0.7 g Protein: 10.5 g Sodium: 219 mg

Chef John's Butter Puff Biscuit Dough
Serving: 6 | Prep: 30m | Ready in: 1h30m

Ingredients
- 2 cups self-rising flour
- 3/4 cup cold water, or as needed
- 7 tbsps. frozen unsalted butter

Direction
1. In the bowl of a stand mixer, add cold water and self-rising flour. Knead for about 2 minutes with dough hook attachment till forms a dough that is slightly elastic, soft yet not too sticky. Shape dough into a ball and use plastic wrap to wrap it. Chill for minimum of 30 minutes.
2. On a floured surface, lay chilled dough and roll out to a rectangle with 1/2-inch of thickness using just enough flour to prevent dough from sticking. Grate onto the surface of the dough with approximately 4 tbsps. of frozen butter to within approximately 1/2 inch of the edge. Flour a sheet of plastic wrap lightly. Spread the plastic wrap onto the butter with the floured side down and press the butter into the dough gently. Remove the plastic wrap carefully.

3. Fold one-third of the dough over the middle third; then fold the other one-third over the middle to form a tri-fold with two layers of butter. Roll dough into a rectangle again, brush to remove excess flour, and form another tri-fold. Keep rolling again till gets approximately 1-inch thick. Use plastic wrap to wrap dough and let sit for 30 more minutes in the refrigerator.
4. On a floured surface, lay chilled dough again, roll into a rectangle shape, and form another tri-fold. Roll back out again to form a rectangle shape with 1/2-inch of thickness. On the surface of the dough, grate approximately 3 tbsps. of butter. Use floured plastic wrap to cover and press butter into dough. Get plastic wrap out. Make another tri-fold and press together layers. Roll out dough and fold in half. Roll out once more, and fold in half again. Roll out dough once again. Use plastic wrap to wrap and chill till ready to serve.
5. Allow to bake at 200°C (400°F).

Nutrition Information

Calories: 266 calories; Total Carbohydrate: 30.9 g Cholesterol: 36 mg Total Fat: 13.8 g Protein: 4.3 g Sodium: 532 mg

Scandinavian Sweetheart Waffles

Serving: 5 | Prep: 20m | Ready in: 40m

Ingredients

- 2 eggs, separated
- 1/4 cup white sugar
- 1 tsp. vanilla sugar
- 1/4 cup water
- 3 tbsps. butter, melted
- 1 cup buttermilk
- 1 1/2 cups all-purpose flour
- 1/4 tsp. ground cardamom
- 1 pinch salt

Direction

1. In a big mixing bowl, add egg yolks together with sugar and beat until frothy and light. Blend in water and vanilla sugar until mixed evenly, then stir in half of the flour, half of buttermilk and half of the melted butter. Once the mixture is smooth, stir in the rest of each flour, cardamom, salt, buttermilk and butter. Beat the mixture again to make a smooth batter.
2. Use an electric mixer to beat egg whites in a separate bowl until creating stiff peaks, then fold gently into the batter, incorporating as much volume as you can.
3. Following the manufacturer's directions, prepare a waffle iron.
4. Scoop about 1/3 cup of the batter into the preheated waffle iron, then lock the lid and cook for 5 minutes, until waffle turns golden brown. Transfer waffle to a plate. In case you use a heart-shaped iron, break waffle into single hearts to serve. Do the same process with leftover batter.

Nutrition Information

Calories: 288 calories; Total Carbohydrate: 42 g Cholesterol: 95 mg Total Fat: 9.7 g Protein: 8.1 g Sodium: 130 mg

Seafood Strata With Pesto

Serving: 8 | Prep: 30m | Ready in: 3h30m

Ingredients

- 12 slices day-old sourdough bread, crusts removed
- 1 cup basil pesto
- 3 tbsps. butter
- 1 (10 oz.) package sliced fresh mushrooms
- 1 cup chopped green onion
- 1/4 cup dry sherry
- 8 oz. medium shrimp - peeled and deveined
- 8 oz. fresh crabmeat
- 2 cups shredded Swiss cheese
- 6 eggs
- 3 cups half-and-half cream
- 1/2 tsp. salt
- 1/8 tsp. cayenne pepper
- 1/2 cup panko bread crumbs
- 1 medium tomato, cut into wedges
- 1 tbsp. chopped fresh basil or chives for garnish

Direction

1. Preheat an oven to 175°C/350°F. Cut every bread slice to 4 triangles. Put on a baking sheet; bake till toasted for 10 minutes. Cool. On one side of every bread piece, spread pesto. Put aside.
2. Melt butter in a big skillet on medium heat. Add mushrooms; mix and cook till all liquid evaporates. Add onions; mix and cook for a few minutes. Put sherry in; simmer for a minute.
3. Put 1/2 bread triangles in a 9x13-in. greased baking dish, pesto side facing up. Sprinkle 1/2 cheese on bread. Spread crabmeat and shrimp on cheese. Put onion and mushroom mixture on top. Sprinkle all except 1/2 cup of leftover cheese on mushrooms. Use other 1/2 bread to cover, pesto side facing down. Whisk cayenne pepper, salt, half and half and eggs in a big bowl. Put over entire casserole. Refrigerate, covered, for at least 2-24 hours. Take out of fridge an hour prior to serving.
4. Preheat an oven to 175°C/350°F. In a plastic bag, mix panko crumbs and 1 cup reserved cheese. Shake to blend. Sprinkle on top of casserole.
5. Bake for 55-60 minutes in preheated oven, uncovered, till an inserted knife in middle exits cleanly. Before serving, let stand for 15 minutes. Use basil/chives and fresh tomato to garnish.

Nutrition Information

Calories: 790 calories; Total Carbohydrate: 39.5 g Cholesterol: 310 mg Total Fat: 51.2 g Protein: 45.5 g Sodium: 1078 mg

Spicy Edam Shrimp Quiche

Serving: 8 | Prep: 20m | Ready in: 1h30m

Ingredients

- 1 tbsp. butter
- 1/2 cup diced onion
- 1/2 cup diced mushrooms
- 1/2 tsp. chopped fresh parsley
- 2 tbsps. red wine
- 3 eggs
- 1/2 cup fat free sour cream
- 1/4 tsp. red pepper flakes

- 1 pinch salt
- 1 cup shredded Edam cheese
- 1 cup cooked salad shrimp
- 1 (9 inch) unbaked pie shell

Direction

1. Preheat oven to 175 degrees C (350 degrees F).
2. Over medium heat, melt the butter in a skillet and then mix in onion. Cook until translucent and softened. Mix in the mushrooms. Let it cook for 3 more minutes. Add red wine and let it simmer until liquid has almost evaporated.
3. Whisk together salt, red pepper flakes, sour cream and eggs until smooth. Mix in the cheese. Put the shrimp in an even layer into the pie shell. Sprinkle the mushroom mixture all over the top. Add custard and spread it evenly.
4. Bake for 50 minutes in preheated oven until set. Let it cool for ten minutes prior to serving.

Nutrition Information

Calories: 244 calories; Total Carbohydrate: 14 g Cholesterol: 116 mg Total Fat: 15.1 g Protein: 12.3 g Sodium: 343 mg

Traditional Layered French Croissants

Serving: 24 | Prep: 2h20m | Ready in: 1day6h45m

Ingredients

- 2 tbsps. all-purpose flour
- 1 1/2 cups unsalted butter, at room temperature
- 4 cups all-purpose flour, divided
- 1/2 tsp. salt
- 3 tbsps. sugar
- 2 (.25 oz.) packages active dry yeast
- 1/4 cup lukewarm water
- 1 cup milk
- 1/2 cup heavy cream
- 1 egg
- 1 tbsp. water

Direction

1. Sprinkle 2 tbsps. flour on butter; mix with your hands on a work surface/in a mixing bowl. Put butter on a length of parchment paper/foil; pat to 6-inch square. Fold foil up to create a packet; refrigerate for 2 hours till chilled.
2. Mix sugar, salt and 2 cups flour in a mixing bowl. Melt yeast in 38°C/100°F lukewarm water; put aside for 10 minutes till foamy. Meanwhile, warm heavy cream and milk to lukewarm. Put cream, milk and yeast in flour mixture; mix well. The dough will get a batter-like consistency.
3. Mix in leftover 2 cups flour to make a soft dough, approximately quarter cup at a time; it shouldn't be sticky anymore. Turn dough on lightly floured work surface; knead for 5 minutes till smooth. Put dough into a mixing bowl; use plastic wrap to cover. Refrigerate dough for 1 hour.
4. To start folding and rolling processor, both dough and butter should be at cool room temperature. Put dough onto floured surface; roll to 10-inch square. Diagonally put block of butter on square dough; bring every dough point towards the middle of butter square; the dough edges should overlap. Press edges together to enclose.

5. Roll dough out to a rectangle with a rolling pin beginning from middle of square then working outward; butter should be pliable enough to smoothly roll with dough. Wrap dough in plastic then refrigerate before proceeding if dough is too soft and begins to ooze out of corners. Roll dough to a long 8x18-inch rectangle. Fold length of dough to thirds, similar to a business letter.

6. You can continue with another fold in case dough is still cool. If not, wrap in plastic then refrigerate for 45-60 minutes. Take dough from fridge; allow it to warm up for 10 minutes prior to rolling it out.

7. Place the dough making open ends at 6 and 12 o'clock. Roll dough to rectangle, working from middle of dough then pressing outwards. As needed, reposition dough to fit the workspace. You should get a long rectangle for "book fold." Fold both ends of dough into center; the ends should be close, they don't require to touch. Fold the already-folded dough into half; it'll resemble a thick book. Wrap dough thoroughly in plastic; refrigerate dough for 1-2 hours.

8. Take dough from fridge; rest for 20 minutes in room temperature. Roll dough to a rectangle once more; fold to thirds, similar to a business letter. Wrap dough in plastic; refrigerate it for 4-6 hours – overnight.

9. Shape croissants: Roll dough to, 10x38-inch rectangle with 1/4-inch thickness on the lightly floured work surface. Trim dough edges with a sharp paring knife/pizza wheel. Halve rectangle to get 2 5-inch wide dough strips. Mark each strip to triangles with 5-inch wide at the bases using clean yardstick. Cut triangles; put on the parchment-lined baking sheets; if needed, chill them for 15-20 minutes.

10. Roll up dough to a log beginning at triangle's base; the triangle's tip should be under the croissant's body to keep it from unraveling. Bend in corners to make the usually crescent shape. Repeat using leftover dough.

11. Put croissants onto parchment-lined baking sheets; rise for 1-2 hours till doubled in size.

12. Preheat the oven to 220°C/425°F. Beat 1 tbsp. water and egg to make egg wash. Brush egg wash on croissants; in preheated oven, bake for 22-25 minutes till deep brown. Cool on the rack; serve.

Nutrition Information

Calories: 213 calories; Total Carbohydrate: 18.8 g Cholesterol: 45 mg Total Fat: 14 g Protein: 3.2 g Sodium: 140 mg

Trishie's Chocolate And Orange Bread Pudding

Serving: 6 | Prep: 30m | Ready in: 2h

Ingredients

- 2 tbsps. white sugar
- 1/4 cup packed brown sugar
- 1/4 cup unsalted butter, softened
- 2 tbsps. grated orange zest
- 1/4 cup orange juice
- 1 tsp. ground cinnamon
- 8 slices white bread
- 2 oz. dark chocolate, grated
- 1 cup milk
- 1 cup heavy cream
- 3 eggs

Direction

1. Mix brown and white sugars together in small bowl.

2. Put 1/2 sugar mixture in another mixing bowl; blend with cinnamon, orange juice, orange zest and butter; spread butter mixture on 1 side of every bread slice. Diagonally, cut every bread slice in half. Put bread triangles in 8x8-in. baking dish, buttered side down, in an overlapping fashion.
3. Blend eggs, cream, milk, grated chocolate and leftover sugar till mixed thoroughly in blender; put chocolate mixture on bread, evenly covering bread. Cover; refrigerate prepped dish for an hour.
4. Preheat oven to 175°C/350°F.
5. Bake bread pudding for 30-40 minutes till set and golden brown.

Nutrition Information

Calories: 458 calories; Total Carbohydrate: 40.7 g Cholesterol: 171 mg Total Fat: 29.8 g Protein: 8.6 g Sodium: 298 mg

Vanilla Crepes

Serving: 12 | Prep: 10m | Ready in: 30m

Ingredients

- 1 1/2 cups milk
- 3 egg yolks
- 2 tbsps. vanilla extract
- 1 1/2 cups all-purpose flour
- 2 tbsps. sugar
- 1/2 tsp. salt
- 5 tbsps. melted butter

Direction

1. Combine together in a large bowl the vanilla, egg yolks, and milk then mix. Add in the melted butter, salt, sugar and the flour until well combined.
2. Place a crepe pan onto medium heat until it's hot. Use a cooking spray or vegetable or oil to coat. Place about 1/4 cup of batter into the pan and tip to scatter to the edges. Once the edges are dry and bubbless appear on top, turn over and cook until the other side is slightly brown in color and edges are golden in color. Do again with left batter.
3. Pack crepes with your desired cheese, ice cream, caramel, cream or favorite fruit then serve.

Nutrition Information

Calories: 142 calories; Total Carbohydrate: 15.9 g Cholesterol: 66 mg Total Fat: 6.7 g Protein: 3.3 g Sodium: 146 mg

Bacon-wrapped Filets With Scotched Mushrooms

Serving: 2 servings. | Prep: 20m | Ready in: 30m

Ingredients

- 2 bacon strips
- 2 beef tenderloin steaks (5 oz. each)
- 1/4 tsp. salt
- 1/4 tsp. coarsely ground pepper
- 3 tsps. olive oil, divided
- 2 cups sliced baby portobello mushrooms
- 1/4 tsp. dried thyme
- 2 tbsps. butter, divided

- 1/4 cup Scotch whiskey
- 1/2 cup diet ginger ale
- 1 tbsp. brown sugar
- 1-1/2 tsps. reduced-sodium soy sauce
- 1/4 tsp. rubbed sage

Direction
1. Cook bacon in a small skillet on moderate heat until cooked slightly yet still not crispy. Transfer to paper towels to drain.
2. Set the oven to 375 degrees to preheat. Sprinkle pepper and salt over steaks, then use a strip of bacon to wrap around the sides of each steak and use toothpicks to secure.
3. Cook steaks in a small ovenproof skillet greased with cooking spray with 1 1/2 tsp. of oil on moderately high heat for 2 minutes per side.
4. Bake without a cover until meat achieves desired doneness (for medium-rare, a thermometer should reach 145 degrees, medium, 160 degrees and 170 degrees for well-done), about 8 to 12 minutes.
5. In the meantime, sauté thyme and mushrooms together in a big skillet with 1 tbsp. of butter and leftover oil until soften, then take away from the heat. Put in whiskey while stirring to loosen any browned bits from pan. Stir in sage, soy sauce, brown sugar and ginger ale.
6. Bring to a boil then lower heat and simmer without a cover until reduce by 1/2, about 3 to 5 minutes. Stir in leftover butter and serve together with steaks.

Nutrition Information
Calories: 581 calories Total Carbohydrate: 10 g Cholesterol: 108 mg Total Fat: 37 g Fiber: 1 g Protein: 35 g Sodium: 729 mg

Bacon-wrapped Stuffed Tenderloins
Serving: 3 stuffed tenderloins (4 servings each). | Prep: 45m | Ready in: 55m

Ingredients
- 3 pork tenderloins (1 lb. each)
- 2 cups crumbled blue cheese
- 3/4 cup slivered almonds, toasted
- 1/2 cup finely chopped red onion
- 2 tbsps. minced fresh rosemary or 2 tsps. dried rosemary, crushed
- 2 garlic cloves, minced
- 1/2 tsp. crushed red pepper flakes, optional
- 1/2 tsp. salt
- 1/4 tsp. pepper
- 6 bacon strips

Direction
1. Cut through the center of each tenderloin with a lengthways slit to within 1/2 inch of bottom. Open tenderloin to make it lie flat, then use plastic wrap to cover and flatten it to the thickness of 1/2 inch. Take off plastic.
2. Mix together pepper flakes, if wanted, garlic, rosemary, onion, almonds and blue cheese in a small bowl, then split between tenderloins. Close tenderloins and sprinkle pepper and salt over top. Use 2 strips of bacon to wrap each tenderloin and use toothpicks to secure.
3. Brown all sides of pork, in batches, in a big skillet until bacon is nearly crispy. Put on a rack in a shallow roasting pan.

4. Bake at 425 degrees without a cover until a thermometer reaches 145 degrees after being inserted into pork, about 8 to 12 minutes.
5. Allow to stand about 5 minutes, then get rid of toothpicks prior to slicing.

Be-my-valentine Pizza

Serving: 2 servings. | Prep: 10m | Ready in: 30m

Ingredients

- 1 tube (13.8 oz.) refrigerated pizza crust
- 1/4 cup shredded Italian cheese blend
- 1/4 cup shredded part-skim mozzarella cheese
- 2 slices provolone cheese, cut in half
- 1/4 cup pizza sauce
- 18 slices pepperoni
- 1/4 cup chopped onion
- 1/4 cup sliced ripe olives

Direction

1. Unfold pizza dough onto a greased baking sheet; flatten the dough. Cut into a 10-inches heart using kitchen scissors. (Make breadsticks using dough trimmings if wished.) Bake for 8 minutes at 425 degrees.
2. Mix the mozzarella and Italian cheeses; reserve. Arrange provolone cheese on top of crust to within 1/2-inch edges.
3. Smear with pizza sauce. Layer with pepperoni, onion, olives, and cheese mixture. Bake for 8 to 10 minutes longer or until cheese melts and crust is golden brown.

Nutrition Information

Calories: 666 calories Total Carbohydrate: 75 g Cholesterol: 57 mg Total Fat: 28 g Fiber: 4 g Protein: 30 g Sodium: 2043 mg

Beef Filets With Portobello Sauce

Serving: 2 servings. | Prep: 5m | Ready in: 20m

Ingredients

- 2 beef tenderloin steaks (4 oz. each)
- 1-3/4 cups sliced baby portobello mushrooms (about 4 oz.)
- 1/2 cup dry red wine or reduced-sodium beef broth
- 1 tsp. all-purpose flour
- 1/2 cup reduced-sodium beef broth
- 1 tsp. ketchup
- 1 tsp. steak sauce
- 1 tsp. Worcestershire sauce
- 1/2 tsp. ground mustard
- 1/4 tsp. pepper
- 1/8 tsp. salt
- 1 tbsp. minced fresh chives, optional

Direction

1. Heat a large nonstick skillet greased with cooking spray over medium-high heat; cook steaks until

both sides are browned. Take steaks out of the pan.

2. Add wine and mushrooms to the pan; heat over medium heat until mixture comes to a boil, whisking to loosen any browned bits from the pan. Cook for 2 to 3 minutes until pan liquid is reduced by 1/2. Stir together broth and flour until smooth; whisk into the pan. Mix in the rest of ingredients (without chives); bring mixture to a boil.
3. Place steaks back into the pan; cook without covering, about 1 to 2 minutes on each side, until desired doneness of meat is reached (a thermometer should register 135° for medium-rare, and 140° for medium). Sprinkle on top with chives before serving, if desired.

Nutrition Information

Calories: 247 calories Total Carbohydrate: 7 g Cholesterol: 51 mg Total Fat: 7 g Fiber: 1 g Protein: 27 g Sodium: 369 mg

Cheesy Chicken Pizza

Serving: 4 servings. | Prep: 10m | Ready in: 30m

Ingredients

- 1 tube (13.8 oz.) refrigerated pizza crust
- 1 can (8 oz.) pizza sauce
- 1/2 cup diced cooked chicken
- 1 small onion, sliced
- 1/4 cup sliced green pepper
- 1/4 cup sliced sweet red pepper
- 1 cup shredded cheddar cheese
- 1 cup shredded mozzarella cheese

Direction

1. Unfold the pizza crust onto a greased baking sheet; form into a 12-inch circle or a heart shape. Spread with pizza sauce. Place peppers, onion, and chicken on top. Scatter with cheese.
2. Place on lowest racks and bake for 16 to 20 minutes at 425 degrees or until the crust turn golden brown.

Nutrition Information

Calories: 427 calories Total Carbohydrate: 41 g Cholesterol: 67 mg Total Fat: 18 g Fiber: 2 g Protein: 24 g Sodium: 921 mg

Chicken Rolls With Raspberry Sauce

Serving: 4 servings. | Prep: 25m | Ready in: 60m

Ingredients

- 4 boneless skinless chicken breast halves (6 oz. each)
- 1/2 cup crumbled blue cheese
- 4 strips ready-to-serve fully cooked bacon, crumbled
- 2 tbsps. butter, melted, divided
- Salt and pepper to taste
- 2 cups fresh raspberries
- 1/4 cup chicken broth
- 4 tsps. brown sugar
- 1 tbsp. balsamic vinegar

- 1/2 tsp. minced garlic
- 1/4 tsp. dried oregano

Direction

1. Pound the chicken to 1/4 inches in thickness to flatten; sprinkle with bacon and blue cheese to within 1/2 inch of edges. Beginning with a short side, roll up each jelly-roll style; use toothpicks to secure.
2. Arrange in an 8-inch square baking dish that's greased. Brush it with a tbsp. of butter. Sprinkle with pepper and salt. Bake without cover at 375 degrees until meat is not pink anymore or 35-40 minutes.
3. At the same time, in a small saucepan, blend oregano, garlic, vinegar, brown sugar, broth, and raspberries. Boil. Turn down the heat; bring to a simmer, uncovered, until thick or 5 minutes.
4. Press on a sieve and discard the seeds. Pour in the remaining butter and stir until smooth. Remove the toothpicks. Serve together with raspberry sauce.

Nutrition Information

Calories: 230 calories Total Carbohydrate: 13 g Cholesterol: 51 mg Total Fat: 14 g Fiber: 4 g Protein: 15 g Sodium: 448 mg

Classic Beef Wellingtons

Serving: 4 servings. | Prep: 20m | Ready in: 45m

Ingredients

- 4 beef tenderloin steaks (6 oz. each)
- 3/4 tsp. salt, divided
- 1/2 tsp. pepper, divided
- 2 tbsps. olive oil, divided
- 1-3/4 cups sliced fresh mushrooms
- 1 medium onion, chopped
- 1 package (17.3 oz.) frozen puff pastry, thawed
- 1 large egg, lightly beaten

Direction

1. Sprinkle a quarter tsp. of pepper and half a tsp. of salt onto the steaks. Brown steaks in 1 tbsp. of oil in a large skillet for 2 to 3 minutes per side. Take steaks out of the skillet and leave in the fridge until chilled.
2. Sauté onion and mushrooms in the oil remaining in the same skillet until softened. Whisk in pepper and salt; allow to cool to room temperature.
3. Set oven to 425 degrees and start preheating. Roll each puff pastry into a 14x9 1/2" rectangle on a surface lightly dusted with flour. Slice into two 7" squares (if preferred, take advantage of scraps to make decorative cutouts). Set a steak into the middle of each square; add mushroom mixture to the top. Lightly brush water onto pastry edges. Fold the opposite corners of pastry over the steak; pinch seams to enclose tightly.
4. Bring into a greased 15x10x1" baking pan. Slice 4 small slits on pastry's top. If preferred, place cutouts on top. Brush egg over.
5. Bake for 25 to 30 minutes until pastry is golden-browned and meat achieves desired doneness (the thermometer should register 135 degrees for medium-rare, 140 degrees for medium and 145 degrees for medium-well).

Nutrition Information

Calories: 945 calories Total Carbohydrate: 74 g Cholesterol: 127 mg Total Fat: 51 g Fiber: 10 g Protein:

48 g Sodium: 866 mg

Cornish Game Hens

Serving: 6 servings. | Prep: 20m | Ready in: 01h20m

Ingredients

- 6 Cornish game hens (20 to 24 oz. each)
- 1/2 tsp. salt
- 1/4 tsp. pepper
- 1/4 cup butter, melted
- 1/4 cup orange juice
- 1/4 cup honey

SAUCE:

- 1/2 cup orange juice
- 2 tbsps. honey
- 1/2 tsp. cider vinegar
- 1 tbsp. cornstarch
- 1 tbsp. cold water

Direction

1. Put hens on a rack in a shallow baking pan. If needed, use kitchen string to truss the legs. Drizzle with pepper and salt. Mix honey, orange juice and butter; pour on top of the hens. Bake at 350° without a cover for an hour or until a thermometer indicates 165° and the juices come out clear, basting every 15 minutes.
2. Mix vinegar, honey and orange juice in a small saucepan. Blend water and cornstarch until smooth; pour in orange juice mixture and stir. Boil, cook while stirring for 1 minute or until thickened. Serve this with the hens.

Cornish Hens With Almond Stuffing

Serving: 4 servings. | Prep: 25m | Ready in: 01h25m

Ingredients

- 1 celery rib, chopped
- 1/4 cup chopped onion
- 3 tbsps. butter, divided
- 2 cups crushed seasoned stuffing
- 1/2 cup chicken broth
- 2 tbsps. slivered almonds, toasted
- 1 tbsp. minced fresh parsley or 1 tsp. dried parsley flakes
- 1/2 tsp. poultry seasoning
- 1/4 tsp. salt
- 1/8 tsp. pepper
- 4 Cornish game hens (20 to 24 oz. each)
- 1 garlic clove, minced
- 1/8 tsp. paprika

Direction

1. Sauté onion and celery in one tbsp. of butter in a large skillet until tender. Mix in pepper, salt, poultry seasoning, parsley, almonds, broth and stuffing. Ladle about one cup of the stuffing mixture

into every hen. Then use a kitchen string tie the legs together.
2. Put the hens in a shallow roasting pan on a rack with the breast side up. Encase with foil. Bake for 40 minutes at 375°. Liquify the rest of the butter with paprika and garlic in a small microwave-safe bowl. Peel off the foil from the hens and baste with the butter mixture.
3. Bake without covering for about 20 to 30 minutes more or until the juices run clear and a thermometer registers 165° for stuffing and 180° for hens.

Nutrition Information

Calories: 878 calories Total Carbohydrate: 25 g Cholesterol: 362 mg Total Fat: 56 g Fiber: 3 g Protein: 64 g Sodium: 1066 mg

Cornish Hens With Veggies

Serving: 4 servings. | Prep: 5m | Ready in: 01h20m

Ingredients
- 4 Cornish game hens (20 to 24 oz. each)
- 1/3 cup butter, melted
- 1-1/2 tsps. minced fresh rosemary or 1/2 tsp. dried rosemary, crushed
- 1 tbsp. minced fresh parsley
- 1 tsp. salt
- 1/2 tsp. pepper
- 2 lbs. small red potatoes
- 1 lb. carrots, cut into 2-inch slices, optional

Direction
1. Put hens in a rack in a roasting pan, breast side facing up, then tie their drumsticks together. Mix together pepper, salt, parsley, rosemary and butter, then scoop mixture over hens. Bake at 375 degrees without a cover about an hour.
2. In the meantime, peel around the center of each potato with one 1-inch strip. Put into a saucepan with potatoes and, if wanted, carrots, then add water to cover; boil. Lower heat and simmer with a cover about 15 minutes, then drain and transfer into roasting pan.
3. Use pan drippings to baste vegetables and hens, then bake until vegetables soften and a thermometer reaches 180 degrees, about 15 to 20 minutes. Strain pan drippings and thicken it to make gravy, if you want.

Crab-stuffed Filet Mignon

Serving: 2 servings. | Prep: 15m | Ready in: 30m

Ingredients
- 1/2 cup lump crabmeat, drained
- 2 tbsps. shredded Parmesan cheese
- 1 tbsp. chopped green onion
- 1 tsp. butter, melted
- 2 beef tenderloin steaks (6 oz. each)
- 1/4 tsp. salt
- 1/8 tsp. pepper

Direction
1. Mix butter, onion, cheese and crabmeat in a small bowl.
2. Use pepper and salt to sprinkle over steaks. Cut horizontally through each steak as a slit to within 1/2

inch of the opposite side to make a pocket. Fill 1/2 cup of the crab mixture, then use a kitchen string to secure, if needed.

3. Broil steak 4 inches away from the heat source until gets preferred doneness (for medium-rare, a thermometer should read 145 degrees; 160 degrees for medium and 170 degrees for well-done), or about 7 to 9 minutes. Before serving, allow to stand about 5 minutes.

Nutrition Information

Calories: 318 calories Total Carbohydrate: 0 g Cholesterol: 113 mg Total Fat: 14 g Fiber: 0 g Protein: 45 g Sodium: 506 mg

Crispy Scallops With Tarragon Cream

Serving: 4 servings. | Prep: 15m | Ready in: 25m

Ingredients

- 1 egg
- 2 tsps. water
- 2/3 cup Italian-style panko (Japanese) bread crumbs
- 1/3 cup mashed potato flakes
- 1 lb. sea scallops
- 1/4 cup olive oil
- 2 tbsps. butter
- 1 tbsp. all-purpose flour
- 1/4 tsp. salt
- 1/8 tsp. pepper
- 3/4 cup heavy whipping cream
- 2 tbsps. minced fresh tarragon or 2 tsps. dried tarragon

Direction

1. Whisk water and egg in a shallow bowl. Mix together potato flakes and bread crumbs in a separate shallow bowl. Dip into the egg mixture with scallops, then roll into crumb mixture to coat well.
2. In a big skillet, heat oil on moderately high heat. In batches, cook scallops until it turns golden brown, about 2 minutes per side.
3. In the meantime, melt butter in a small saucepan. Stir in pepper, salt and flour until smooth, then add in cream slowly. Bring the mixture to a boil, then cook and stir until thickened, about 1 to 2 minutes. Stir in tarragon, then serve together with scallops.

Nutrition Information

Calories: 503 calories Total Carbohydrate: 13 g Cholesterol: 166 mg Total Fat: 40 g Fiber: 0 g Protein: 23 g Sodium: 544 mg

Cupid's Chicken 'n' Stuffing

Serving: 8 servings. | Prep: 15m | Ready in: 01h05m

Ingredients

- 1 package (6 oz.) seasoned stuffing mix
- 8 boneless skinless chicken breast halves (4 oz. each)
- 1 tsp. canola oil
- 1/4 tsp. salt
- 1/4 tsp. pepper

- 4 Swiss cheese slices (2 oz.), halved
- 2 tbsps. butter
- 1 can (10-3/4 oz.) condensed cream of chicken soup, undiluted
- 1/4 cup water

Direction

1. Follow package directions to prepare stuffing mix. Remove to a 9-inch x13-inch baking dish coated with grease. Brown chicken in a big skillet with oil, then sprinkle pepper and salt over. Put on top of stuffing and place cheese on top. Use butter to drizzle over.
2. Mix water and soup, then scoop over stuffing. Place a cover and bake at 350 degrees about 40 minutes. Uncover and bake until juices from chicken run clear, about 10 to 15 more minutes.

Nutrition Information

Calories: 331 calories Total Carbohydrate: 19 g Cholesterol: 92 mg Total Fat: 14 g Fiber: 0 g Protein: 29 g Sodium: 734 mg

Curry Chicken With Mixed Berries

Serving: 4 servings. | Prep: 15m | Ready in: 30m

Ingredients

- 1 medium onion, chopped
- 2 tbsps. olive oil
- 1 lb. boneless skinless chicken breasts, cut into 1-inch cubes
- 1 garlic clove, minced
- 2 tbsps. all-purpose flour
- 1 tsp. chicken bouillon granules
- 1 tsp. curry powder
- 1/2 tsp. salt
- 1/4 tsp. pepper
- 1-1/2 cups water
- 1/2 cup heavy whipping cream
- 1/4 tsp. minced fresh thyme
- 1 cup fresh blueberries
- 1 cup fresh blackberries
- 1 cup fresh raspberries
- 2 tbsps. butter
- 2 cups hot cooked long grain rice

Direction

1. Sauté onion with oil in a big frying pan until soft. Put in chicken and sauté until not pink anymore, about 4-6 minutes. Put in garlic, cook for another 1 minute.
2. Mix together pepper, salt, curry powder, bouillon, and flour; mix into the frying pan until smooth. Slowly pour in water. Boil it, cook while stirring until thickened, about 1-2 minutes. Mix in thyme and cream, thoroughly heat.
3. Sauté berries with butter in a second frying pan until fully heated. Enjoy the chicken mixture with berries and rice.

Nutrition Information

Calories: 522 calories Total Carbohydrate: 43 g Cholesterol: 119 mg Total Fat: 27 g Fiber: 6 g Protein:

28 g Sodium: 615 mg

Elegant Pork Marsala
Serving: 6 servings. | Prep: 10m | Ready in: 30m

Ingredients
- 1/3 cup whole wheat flour
- 1/2 tsp. pepper
- 6 boneless pork loin chops (4 oz. each)
- 1 tbsp. olive oil
- 2 cups sliced fresh mushrooms
- 1/3 cup chopped onion
- 2 turkey bacon strips, chopped
- 1/4 tsp. minced garlic
- 1 cup Marsala wine or additional reduced-sodium chicken broth
- 5 tsps. cornstarch
- 2/3 cup reduced-sodium chicken broth

Direction
1. In a shallow bowl, combine the pepper and flour. Dip the pork chops into the flour mixture to coat both of the sides; shake off the excess flour.
2. In a big non-stick skillet that is coated with the cooking spray; heat the oil on medium heat. Put in the pork chops; cook till a thermometer reaches 145 degrees or for 4 to 5 minutes per side. Take out of the pan; keep them warm.
3. In the same skillet, put the bacon, onion and mushrooms into the drippings; cook and whisk till the mushrooms soften or for 2 to 3 minutes. Put in the garlic; cook for another 60 seconds. Pour in the wine; raise the heat to medium high. Cook, whisking to loosen the browned bits from the pan.
4. In a small-sized bowl, stir the broth and cornstarch till becoming smooth; put into the pan. Boil; cook and whisk till becoming thick slightly or for 2 minutes. Serve along with the pork.

Nutrition Information
Calories: 232 calories Total Carbohydrate: 7 g Cholesterol: 60 mg Total Fat: 10 g Fiber: 1 g Protein: 24 g Sodium: 161 mg

Fancy Skillet Steaks
Serving: 2 servings. | Prep: 15m | Ready in: 30m

Ingredients
- 2 beef top sirloin steaks (6 oz. each)
- 3 tsps. olive oil, divided
- 1/4 cup chopped onion
- 1/4 cup oil-packed sun-dried tomatoes, chopped
- 2 tbsps. balsamic vinegar
- 1 tsp. sugar
- 1 garlic clove, minced
- 1/2 tsp. lemon-pepper seasoning

Direction
1. Cook steaks in 1 tsp. oil in a big skillet on medium high heat for about 4-5 minutes per side till meat

gets desired doneness; 170° well-done, 160° medium and 145° for medium rare on a thermometer. Remove; keep warm.

2. Put leftover oil, lemon-pepper, garlic, sugar, vinegar, tomatoes and onion in skillet; mix and cook till onion is tender for 4-5 minutes; put on steaks.

Nutrition Information

Calories: 331 calories Total Carbohydrate: 10 g Cholesterol: 94 mg Total Fat: 17 g Fiber: 1 g Protein: 33 g Sodium: 226 mg

Flavorful Lemon Garlic Shrimp

Serving: 4 servings. | Prep: 20m | Ready in: 30m

Ingredients

- 1 package (6-1/2 oz.) broccoli au gratin rice and vermicelli mix
- 1 lb. uncooked medium shrimp, peeled and deveined
- 1 medium sweet red pepper, julienned
- 3 green onions, cut into 1/2-inch pieces
- 1 tsp. minced garlic
- 1/2 tsp. Italian seasoning
- 1 tbsp. butter
- 2 tsps. cornstarch
- 1/2 cup chicken broth
- 1 tbsp. lemon juice
- 1 tsp. grated lemon peel, divided

Direction

1. Follow package directions to prepare rice mix. In the meantime, sauté Italian seasoning, garlic, onions, red pepper and shrimp in a big skillet with butter, until shrimp become pink.
2. Mix together lemon juice, broth and cornstarch in a small bowl until smooth, then stir into shrimp mixture. Bring to a boil, then cook and stir until thicken, about 1 to 2 minutes. Stir into prepped rice with 1/2 tsp. of lemon peel, then serve together with shrimp mixture. Sprinkle leftover lemon peel over top.

Nutrition Information

Calories: 321 calories Total Carbohydrate: 35 g Cholesterol: 186 mg Total Fat: 10 g Fiber: 2 g Protein: 24 g Sodium: 907 mg

Fruit-stuffed Pork Roast

Serving: 12-14 servings. | Prep: 15m | Ready in: 01h15m

Ingredients

- 3/4 cup diced pitted dried plums
- 3/4 cup diced dried apricots
- 1 tbsp. minced fresh gingerroot
- 1-1/2 tsps. ground cumin, divided
- 1 tsp. grated orange zest
- 1/2 tsp. ground cinnamon
- 1/4 tsp. salt
- 1/8 tsp. pepper

- 1 boneless pork loin roast (3 to 4 lbs.)
- 1/4 cup packed brown sugar
- 2 tsps. all-purpose flour
- 1 tsp. cornstarch
- 1 tsp. ground mustard
- 2 tsps. cider vinegar

Direction

1. Combine the plums, pepper, salt, cinnamon, orange zest, 3/4 tsp. cumin, ginger, and apricots in a bowl; put aside. Untie the roast and separate the pieces. Next, scoop the fruit mixture onto 1 piece. Lay the second piece on top; use kitchen string to retie. Arrange on a rack in a shallow roasting pan.
2. Combine the remaining cumin, vinegar, mustard, cornstarch, flour, and brown sugar until smooth; rub over the roast. Bake while uncovered for 60-75 minutes at 350°, or until inserting a thermometer in the pork and it states 145°. Allow to sit for 10 minutes before slicing.

Nutrition Information

Calories: 182 calories Total Carbohydrate: 16 g Cholesterol: 48 mg Total Fat: 5 g Fiber: 1 g Protein: 19 g Sodium: 77 mg

Greek-style Ribeye Steaks

Serving: 2 servings. | Prep: 5m | Ready in: 25m

Ingredients

- 1-1/2 tsps. garlic powder
- 1-1/2 tsps. dried oregano
- 1-1/2 tsps. dried basil
- 1/2 tsp. salt
- 1/8 tsp. pepper
- 2 beef ribeye steaks (1-1/2 inches thick)
- 1 tbsp. olive oil
- 1 tbsp. lemon juice
- 2 tbsps. crumbled feta cheese
- 1 tbsp. sliced ripe olives

Direction

1. Mix together the first 5 ingredients in a small bowl, then rub mixture over steaks, on both sides. Cook steaks in a big skillet with oil until meat achieves desired doneness (for medium-rare, a thermometer should reach 145 degrees, medium, 160 degrees and 170 degrees for well-done), about 7 to 9 minutes per side. Sprinkle olives, cheese and lemon juice on top, then serve instantly.

Grilled Beef Tenderloins

Serving: 2 servings. | Prep: 10m | Ready in: 20m

Ingredients

- 1/4 cup dry red wine
- 1/4 cup reduced-sodium soy sauce
- 1/2 tsp. garlic powder
- 1/2 tsp. dried oregano
- 1/4 tsp. ground cumin

- 1/4 tsp. ground ancho chili pepper
- 1/4 tsp. pepper
- 2 beef tenderloin steaks (6 oz. each)

Direction

1. Mix all the initial 7 ingredients together in a big Ziplock plastic bag. Put in the steaks then seal the Ziplock bag and turn to coat the steaks with the marinade. Keep in the fridge for a maximum of 4 hours.
2. Drain the marinated steaks and throw away the marinade mixture. Use tongs to lightly rub an oiled paper towel on the grill rack. Put the marinated steaks on a grill over medium heat then cover and grill or put the marinated steaks in a broiler and let it broil 4 inches away from heat for 4 to 6 minutes on every side until the preferred meat doneness is achieved (a thermometer inserted on the meat should indicate 170°F for well-done, 160°F for medium and 145°F for medium-rare).

Nutrition Information

Calories: 263 calories Total Carbohydrate: 1 g Cholesterol: 75 mg Total Fat: 10 g Fiber: 0 g Protein: 37 g Sodium: 402 mg

Grilled Lamb Chops With Wine Sauce

Serving: 4 servings. | Prep: 25m | Ready in: 55m

Ingredients

- 2 tbsps. finely chopped sweet onion
- 3 tsps. olive oil, divided
- 1 cup dry red wine
- 1 tsp. butter
- 1 tsp. minced fresh thyme or 1/4 tsp. dried thyme
- 1 cup cherry tomatoes
- 6 whole unpeeled garlic cloves
- 2 garlic cloves, minced
- 1/4 tsp. salt
- 1/4 tsp. pepper
- 4 lamb rib or loin chops (6 oz. each)

Direction

1. Put 1 tsp. of oil in a small saucepan, then add in the onion and let it cook until the onion has softened; pour in the wine. Let the mixture boil and allow it to cook until the wine has reduced to just 2 tbsps.. Add in the thyme and butter and give it a mix. Remove the pan away from the heat source and let it stay warm.
2. In a double thickness durable foil, put in the tomatoes. Pour 1 tsp. of oil evenly on top of the tomatoes. Fold the foil over the tomatoes to keep it inside then seal it tightly; put it aside. Do the same for the remaining oil and whole garlic cloves. Put the enclosed garlic clove in a covered grill and let it grill for 30 minutes over medium heat.
3. While the garlic is grilling, mix the salt, pepper and minced garlic together and massage it onto the chops. Put the coated lamb chops and tomato packet onto the grill over medium heat then cover and let it grill for 6 to 8 minutes on every side until the preferred meat doneness is achieved (a thermometer inserted on the meat should indicate 170° for well-done, 160° for medium and 145° for medium-rare).
4. Gently open the grilled tomato packet to let out the steam then put the tomatoes in a small bowl.

Crush the grilled softened garlic on top of the grilled tomatoes once the garlic is cool enough to the touch; mix everything together. Serve the grilled lamb chops together with the prepared wine sauce and the tomato-garlic mixture.

Nutrition Information
Calories: 262 calories Total Carbohydrate: 6 g Cholesterol: 70 mg Total Fat: 11 g Fiber: 1 g Protein: 22 g Sodium: 221 mg

Hearty Lasagna
Serving: 12 servings. | Prep: 01h45m | Ready in: 02h30m

Ingredients
- 1-1/2 lbs. ground beef
- 1 medium onion, chopped
- 1 garlic clove, minced
- 3 tbsps. olive oil
- 1 can (28 oz.) Italian diced tomatoes, undrained
- 1 can (8 oz.) tomato sauce
- 1 can (6 oz.) tomato paste
- 1 tsp. dried oregano
- 1 tsp. sugar
- 1 tsp. salt
- 1/4 tsp. pepper
- 2 carrots, halved
- 2 celery ribs, halved
- 12 oz. lasagna noodles
- 1 carton (15 oz.) ricotta cheese
- 2 cups shredded part-skim mozzarella cheese
- 1/2 cup grated Parmesan cheese

Direction
1. Cook garlic, onion, and beef in oil using a large skillet, until the onion is tenderized, and the meat turns brown. Strain. Add tomato paste, tomato sauce, tomatoes, oregano, salt, pepper, and sugar and mix evenly. Add in celery and carrots into the sauce. Simmer without covering for 1-1/2 hours, periodically stirring the sauce. In the meantime, follow package instructions to prepare the lasagna noodles. Strain and run under cold water. Dispose celery and carrots. Grease a 13x9-inch baking tray and layer as follows; 1/3 of noodles, 1/3 of meat sauce, 1/3 ricotta cheese, 1/3 mozzarella cheese, and 1/3 Parmesan cheese. Repeat the arrangement again. Cover with excess noodles and meat sauce. Cut a piece of aluminum foil into a heart and place at the center of the sauce. Distribute remainder of ricotta around the heart. Scatter remaining Parmesan and mozzarella. Bake while uncovered for 45 minutes at 350 degrees. Dispose the heart-shaped foil. Let the dish sit for 10-15 minutes before slicing.

Nutrition Information
Calories: 391 calories Total Carbohydrate: 36 g Cholesterol: 56 mg Total Fat: 16 g Fiber: 3 g Protein: 25 g Sodium: 790 mg

Lemon Chicken And Peppers
Serving: 4 servings. | Prep: 20m | Ready in: 20m

Ingredients

- 2 packages (10 oz. each) lemon-pepper marinated chicken breast fillets
- 1/2 tsp. paprika
- 1/4 tsp. dried thyme
- 1 tbsp. butter
- 1 medium green pepper, cut into 1/4-inch strips
- 1 medium sweet red pepper, cut into 1/4-inch strips

Direction

1. Sprinkle thyme and paprika over chicken. Cook chicken in a big nonstick skillet with butter until juices run clear, about 4 to 6 minutes per side. Drain chicken and put aside. Sauté peppers until soft, about 3 to 4 minutes. Place chicken back to pan and heat through.

Nutrition Information

Calories: 207 calories Total Carbohydrate: 8 g Cholesterol: 77 mg Total Fat: 7 g Fiber: 1 g Protein: 28 g Sodium: 1157 mg

Lemony Grilled Salmon Fillets With Dill Sauce

Serving: 4 servings (3/4 cup sauce). | Prep: 20m | Ready in: 30m

Ingredients

- 2 medium lemons
- 4 salmon fillets (6 oz. each)

LEMON-DILL SAUCE:

- 1-1/2 tsps. cornstarch
- 1/2 cup water
- 1/3 cup lemon juice
- 4 tsps. butter
- 3 lemon slices, quartered
- 1 tbsp. snipped fresh dill
- 1/4 tsp. salt
- 1/8 tsp. dried chervil
- Dash cayenne pepper

Direction

1. Trim two ends from every lemon and chop the lemons into thick pieces. Use cooking oil to moisten a paper towel with the help of long-handled tongs and then coat the grill rack lightly. Grill the salmon and slices of lemon while covered on high heat or broil for about 3 to 5 minutes per side with 3-4 in. away from the heat source or until the lemons are browned lightly and the fish easily flakes with a fork.
2. For the sauce, mix the lemon juice, cornstarch, and water in a small saucepan. Place in butter. Cook while stirring on medium heat until bubbly and thickened. Take out from the heat source and mix in the seasonings and quartered lemon slices. You can serve together with grilled lemon slices and salmon.

Nutrition Information

Calories: 320 calories Total Carbohydrate: 6 g Cholesterol: 97 mg Total Fat: 20 g Fiber: 1 g Protein: 29 g Sodium: 266 mg

Light Chicken Kiev

Serving: 2 servings. | Prep: 25m | Ready in: 45m

Ingredients

- 1 tbsp. butter, softened
- 1/4 tsp. each dried thyme, parsley flakes and rosemary, crushed
- 1/4 cup all-purpose flour
- 1/4 tsp. salt
- 1/4 tsp. pepper
- 1 egg white
- 1/2 cup soft bread crumbs
- 1 tbsp. grated Parmesan cheese
- 1/4 tsp. paprika
- 2 boneless skinless chicken breast halves (4 oz. each)

Direction

1. Mix together rosemary, parsley, thyme and butter, then form into 2 cubes. Place a cover and freeze for 10 minutes, until firm.
2. In the meantime, mix together pepper, salt and flour in a shallow bowl. Whisk egg white gently in a separate shallow bowl. Mix together paprika, Parmesan cheese and bread crumbs in a third bowl.
3. Flatten chicken to the thickness of 1/4 inch. Put down the center of each with a cube of butter, then roll up and tuck in ends. Use toothpicks to secure. Cover chicken in flour mixture, then dunk in egg white, and dredge in crumb mixture.
4. Put coated chicken in an 8-inch square baking dish greased with cooking spray, seam-side facing down. Bake at 425 degrees without a cover until a thermometer reaches 170 degrees, about 20 to 25 minutes. Get rid of toothpicks.

Nutrition Information

Calories: 231 calories Total Carbohydrate: 8 g Cholesterol: 80 mg Total Fat: 9 g Fiber: 1 g Protein: 27 g Sodium: 315 mg

Makeover Beef Stroganoff

Serving: 6 servings. | Prep: 20m | Ready in: 30m

Ingredients

- 1/2 cup plus 1 tbsp. all-purpose flour, divided
- 1/2 tsp. pepper, divided
- 1 beef top round steak (1-1/2 lbs.), cut into thin strips
- 2 tbsps. canola oil
- 1 cup sliced fresh mushrooms
- 1 small onion, chopped
- 1 garlic clove, minced
- 1 can (14-1/2 oz.) reduced-sodium beef broth
- 1/2 tsp. salt
- 1 cup (8 oz.) reduced-fat sour cream
- Chopped fresh parsley, optional
- Coarsely ground pepper, optional
- 3 cups cooked yolk-free noodles

Direction

1. In a big resealable plastic bag, mix together the 1/4 tsp. of pepper and 1/2 cup of flour, then add the beef, several pieces at a time and shake until coated.
2. Heat the oil in a big nonstick frying pan on medium-high heat. Cook the beef by batches until no visible pink color. Take it out and keep it warm. Sauté the onion and mushrooms in the drippings in the same frying pan until it becomes tender, then add the garlic and cook for 1 minute more.
3. Whisk the leftover flour with broth until it becomes smooth and mix it into the frying pan, then boil. Let it cook and stir for about 2 minutes until it becomes thick, then add the leftover pepper, salt and beef. Mix in sour cream and heat it through (don't boil). Sprinkle coarsely ground pepper and parsley if preferred, then serve it with the noodles.

Nutrition Information

Calories: 349 calories Total Carbohydrate: 25 g Cholesterol: 78 mg Total Fat: 12 g Fiber: 2 g Protein: 33 g Sodium: 393 mg

Mozzarella-stuffed Italian Meatballs

Serving: 8 servings. | Prep: 40m | Ready in: 01h05m

Ingredients

- 2 eggs, lightly beaten
- 1 tbsp. Worcestershire sauce
- 2 large onions, finely chopped
- 2/3 cup seasoned bread crumbs
- 1/3 cup grated Parmesan cheese
- 3 tbsps. minced fresh parsley
- 2 tbsps. minced fresh basil
- 1 tbsp. minced fresh oregano
- 8 garlic cloves, minced
- 1/2 tsp. kosher salt
- 1/4 tsp. pepper
- 1/8 tsp. crushed red pepper flakes
- 1 lb. lean ground beef (90% lean)
- 1/2 lb. ground pork
- 1/2 lb. ground veal
- 16 fresh mozzarella cheese balls, drained and patted dry
- Hot cooked spaghetti
- Marinara or spaghetti sauce, warmed

Direction

1. Blend Worcestershire sauce and eggs in a large bowl. Add in red pepper flakes, pepper, salt, garlic, oregano, basil, parsley, Parmesan cheese, breadcrumbs, and onions. Crumble veal, pork, and beef on top of the mixture; combine thoroughly.
2. Divide into 16 parts. Form each part around mozzarella ball.
3. In a shallow baking pan, arrange meatballs on a greased rack. Bake at 400 degrees until a thermometer registers 160 degrees or 25-30 minutes. Transfer to paper towels to drain.
4. Serve together with marinara or spaghetti sauce.

Nutrition Information

Calories: 281 calories Total Carbohydrate: 12 g Cholesterol: 131 mg Total Fat: 14 g Fiber: 1 g Protein: 26 g Sodium: 418 mg

Peppered Filets With Cherry Port Sauce For 2

Serving: 2 servings. | Prep: 15m | Ready in: 30m

Ingredients

- 2 beef tenderloin steaks (8 oz. each)
- 2 tsps. coarsely ground pepper
- 1 cup dry red wine
- 1/2 cup chopped red onion
- 1/3 cup golden raisins
- 1/3 cup dried cherries
- 2 tbsps. sugar
- 1-1/2 tsps. cornstarch
- 1/4 tsp. ground mustard
- Dash salt
- 2 tsps. cold water
- 1/4 cup crumbled blue cheese

Direction

1. Season the steaks with pepper and grill them covered over medium heat. You can also cook it inside the broiler, 4-inches away from heat source until the meat reaches 145°F for medium-rare, 160°F for medium, or 170°F for well-done meat, depending on the desired doneness.
2. Mix raisins, sugar, wine, cherries, and onion in a small saucepan and boil. Simmer the mixture until the liquid reduces by half.
3. Whisk mustard, salt, cornstarch, and water in a bowl until smooth. Pour the cornstarch mixture into the small saucepan gradually and boil. Simmer the sauce for 2 minutes until thickened. Top the steak with cheese and serve together with the sauce.

Nutrition Information

Calories: 710 calories Total Carbohydrate: 59 g Cholesterol: 112 mg Total Fat: 19 g Fiber: 3 g Protein: 54 g Sodium: 319 mg

Peppered Filets With Horseradish Cream Sauce

Serving: 4 servings. | Prep: 15m | Ready in: 25m

Ingredients

- 4 beef tenderloin steaks (6 oz. each)
- 1 tbsp. plus 1/8 tsp. coarsely ground pepper, divided
- 3/4 tsp. salt, divided
- 5 tbsps. butter, divided
- 2 tsps. all-purpose flour
- 2/3 cup heavy whipping cream
- 2 tbsps. horseradish
- 1 tsp. Dijon mustard

Direction

1. Sprinkle 1/2 tsp. salt and 1 tbsp. pepper on steaks; cook steaks in 1 tbsp. butter in a big skillet on

medium heat for 4-5 minutes per side till meat gets desired doneness; 170° well done, 160° medium and 145° for medium-rare on a thermometer.

2. Meanwhile, melt leftover butter in a small saucepan. Mix in leftover pepper and salt and flour till smooth; add cream slowly. Boil; mix and cook till thick for 1-2 minutes. Mix in mustard and horseradish; serve with steaks.

Nutrition Information

Calories: 525 calories Total Carbohydrate: 4 g Cholesterol: 167 mg Total Fat: 39 g Fiber: 0 g Protein: 38 g Sodium: 589 mg

Quick Honey-mustard Chicken

Serving: 2 servings. | Prep: 10m | Ready in: 30m

Ingredients

- 1/4 cup honey
- 2 tbsps. butter, melted
- 2 tbsps. Dijon mustard
- 1 tbsp. orange juice
- 1/8 tsp. curry powder
- 2 boneless skinless chicken breast halves
- 1 tbsp. vegetable oil
- 1/8 tsp. salt
- 1/8 tsp. pepper

Direction

1. Mix together curry powder, orange juice, mustard, butter and honey in a small bowl, then scoop half of the mixture into an 8-inch square baking dish coated with grease.
2. Brown chicken in a skillet with oil, then sprinkle with pepper and salt. Put over sauce and turn to coat.
3. Bake at 350 degrees without a cover about 15 minutes. Drizzle leftover sauce on top, then bake until a thermometer reaches 170 degrees, about 5 to 10 minutes more.

Nutrition Information

Calories: 454 calories Total Carbohydrate: 38 g Cholesterol: 104 mg Total Fat: 23 g Fiber: 0 g Protein: 28 g Sodium: 707 mg

Shrimp In Herbs

Serving: 4 servings. | Prep: 25m | Ready in: 35m

Ingredients

- 2 lbs. uncooked medium shrimp, peeled and deveined
- 2 tbsps. olive oil
- 3 garlic cloves, minced
- 1-1/2 cups chopped fresh tomatoes
- 1 tbsp. minced chives
- 1 tbsp. minced fresh flat-leaf parsley
- 1 tbsp. minced fresh tarragon or 1 tsp. dried tarragon
- 1 tsp. dried chervil
- 3/4 tsp. salt

- 1/4 tsp. pepper
- 2 tbsps. butter, cubed

Direction

1. Cook the shrimp in oil for two minutes in a large nonstick skillet that is sprayed with cooking spray. Place in garlic and then cook for 1 minute. Mix in seasonings and tomatoes. Let cook for 3 to 5 minutes or until the shrimp turns pink. Mix in the butter until it melts.

Nutrition Information

Calories: 304 calories Total Carbohydrate: 5 g Cholesterol: 351 mg Total Fat: 15 g Fiber: 1 g Protein: 37 g Sodium: 894 mg

Shrimp Pasta Primavera

Serving: 2 servings. | Prep: 5m | Ready in: 15m

Ingredients

- 4 oz. uncooked angel hair pasta
- 8 jumbo shrimp, peeled and deveined
- 6 fresh asparagus spears, trimmed and cut into 2-inch pieces
- 1/4 cup olive oil
- 2 garlic cloves, minced
- 1/2 cup sliced fresh mushrooms
- 1/2 cup chicken broth
- 1 small plum tomato, peeled, seeded and diced
- 1/4 tsp. salt
- 1/8 tsp. crushed red pepper flakes
- 1 tbsp. each minced fresh basil, oregano, thyme and parsley
- 1/4 cup grated Parmesan cheese

Direction

1. Follow package directions to cook pasta. In the meantime, sauté asparagus and shrimp together in a big skillet with oil until shrimp are pink, about 3 to 4 minutes. Put in garlic and cook for another minute. Put in pepper flakes, salt, tomato, broth and mushrooms, then simmer without a cover about 2 minutes.
2. Drain pasta and put seasoning and pasta in skillet, tossing to coat. Sprinkle cheese over top.

Nutrition Information

Calories: 581 calories Total Carbohydrate: 49 g Cholesterol: 89 mg Total Fat: 32 g Fiber: 3 g Protein: 24 g Sodium: 783 mg

Simple Chicken Cordon Bleu

Serving: 4 servings | Prep: 15m | Ready in: 30m

Ingredients

- 4 small boneless skinless chicken breast s (1 lb.)
- 8 slices OSCAR MAYER Deli Fresh Black Forest Ham
- 4 KRAFT Slim Cut Swiss Cheese Slice s
- 1 cup HEINZ HomeStyle Classic Chicken Gravy
- 1 Tbsp. chopped fresh parsley

Direction

1. In large ovenproof skillet, cook each side of the chicken on medium heat until evenly browned on both sides, for 4 min per side. (Chicken will not finish cooking.)
2. Add the remaining ingredients on top.
3. Bake until chicken is done, or for 15 min (at 165°F).

Nutrition Information

Calories: 210 Total Carbohydrate: 3 g Cholesterol: 85 mg Total Fat: 8 g Fiber: 0 g Protein: 30 g Sodium: 510 mg Sugar: 0 g Saturated Fat: 3 g

Southwestern Scallops

Serving: 4 servings. | Prep: 10m | Ready in: 20m

Ingredients

- 2 tsps. chili powder
- 1/2 tsp. ground cumin
- 1/4 tsp. salt
- 1/8 tsp. pepper
- 12 sea scallops (1 to 1-1/2 lbs.)
- 2 tbsps. butter, divided
- 1/2 cup white wine or chicken broth

Direction

1. Combine seasonings together in a small bowl. Use paper towels to pat scallops dry then sprinkle seasonings over while pressing to coat.
2. Heat 1 tbsp. of butter in a big skillet on moderately high heat then put in scallops and cook until firm and golden brown, about 2 to 3 minutes per side. Take out of the pan and keep warm.
3. Put wine into pan and cook on moderate heat while stirring to loosen any browned bits from pan. Bring to a boil and cook until the liquid is reduced halfway. Stir in leftover butter until melted and serve together with scallops.

Nutrition Information

Calories: 180 calories Total Carbohydrate: 4 g Cholesterol: 52 mg Total Fat: 7 g Fiber: 1 g Protein: 19 g Sodium: 386 mg

Special Strip Steaks

Serving: 2 servings. | Prep: 10m | Ready in: 25m

Ingredients

- 2 boneless beef top loin steaks (8 oz. each)
- 1 garlic clove, halved
- 1/4 tsp. salt
- 1/4 tsp. pepper
- 1 tbsp. butter
- 1/4 cup sherry or beef broth
- 1/4 tsp. Worcestershire sauce
- 2 tbsps. chopped green onion

Direction

1. Use garlic to rub over steaks, then sprinkle with pepper and salt. Put aside. In a big skillet, melt butter, then put in onion, Worcestershire sauce and broth or sherry. Bring mixture to a boil, then lower heat and simmer about 5 minutes without a cover.
2. Put in steaks and cook on moderate heat until meat attains the desired doneness (for medium-rare, a thermometer should reach 145 degrees, medium, 160 degrees and 170 degrees for well-done), about 3 to 7 minutes per side.

Nutrition Information

Calories: 389 calories Total Carbohydrate: 6 g Cholesterol: 115 mg Total Fat: 16 g Fiber: 0 g Protein: 48 g Sodium: 807 mg

Steaks With Molasses-glazed Onions

Serving: 2 servings. | Prep: 5m | Ready in: 30m

Ingredients

- 2 bacon strips, diced
- 2 beef top sirloin steaks (6 oz. each)
- 1/2 tsp. salt, divided
- 1/2 tsp. pepper, divided
- 1 large sweet onion, thinly sliced
- 1-1/2 tsps. balsamic vinegar
- 1/2 tsp. molasses

Direction

1. Cook bacon in a big skillet on moderate heat until crispy. Use a slotted spoon to transfer to paper towels and drain, saving 1 1/2 tsp. of drippings each in a skillet as well as a small bowl, then put bowl aside.
2. Sprinkle 1/4 tsp. of pepper and 1/4 tsp. of salt over steaks. Cook steaks in a skillet on moderate heat until meat obtains desired doneness (for medium-rare, a thermometer should reach 145 degrees, medium, 160 degrees and 170 degrees for well-done), about 4 to 6 minutes per side. Take steaks out and keep warm.
3. Put reserved drippings and onion in skillet, then sauté until soften. Put in leftover pepper and salt, molasses and vinegar, then heat through. Serve steaks together with onion mixture and a sprinkling of bacon over top.

Nutrition Information

Calories: 370 calories Total Carbohydrate: 15 g Cholesterol: 82 mg Total Fat: 16 g Fiber: 2 g Protein: 40 g Sodium: 837 mg

Steaks With Peppery Onions

Serving: 4 servings. | Prep: 10m | Ready in: 25m

Ingredients

- 3 medium onions, sliced
- 1 tsp. salt
- 1 tsp. pepper
- 2 tbsps. olive oil
- 1 tbsp. butter
- 1 tsp. minced garlic
- 4 beef ribeye steaks (6 oz. each)

Direction

1. Cook pepper, salt and onions in butter and oil till onions are golden brown for 15-20 minutes in a big skillet on medium heat, frequently mixing. Add garlic; cook for 1 minute.
2. Meanwhile, broil steak for 6-8 minutes per side 3-4-in. from heat till meat gets desired doneness; 170° well done, 160° medium and 145° medium-rare on a thermometer. Serve with onion mixture.

Stuffed Flank Steak With Mushroom Sherry Cream

Serving: 6 servings (1-1/2 cups sauce). | Prep: 45m | Ready in: 01h25m

Ingredients

- 1 beef flank steak (1-1/2 lbs.)
- 1/3 cup garlic-herb spreadable cheese
- 2 tbsps. prepared pesto
- 3/4 lb. whole fresh mushrooms, thinly sliced, divided
- 2 cups fresh baby spinach
- 1 jar (7 oz.) roasted sweet red peppers, drained and julienned
- 1 tsp. coarsely ground pepper
- 1/2 tsp. salt
- 2 tbsps. olive oil, divided
- 1 shallot, sliced
- 2 cups reduced-sodium beef broth
- 1 cup sherry
- 1 cup heavy whipping cream

Direction

1. From a long side, horizontally split steak within 1/2-in. from opposing side. Flip steak so long side faces you; so it lies flat, open steak. Cover in plastic wrap; flatten to 1/4-inch thick. Remove plastic.
2. Within 1/2 in. from edges, spread cheese on steak; layer with salt, pepper, red peppers, spinach, 1 3/4 cups mushrooms and pesto. Roll up, rolling the steak away from you, jellyroll style. Tie in 1 1/2-in. intervals with kitchen string; rub 1 tbsp. oil.
3. Brown all sides of steaks in a big ovenproof skillet; bake in skillet for 40-50 minutes at 375° till meat gets desired doneness; 170° well done, 160° medium and 145° medium rare on thermometer. Remove from pan then cover; keep warm.
4. Sauté leftover mushrooms and shallot in leftover oil till tender in same skillet. Put sherry and broth in pan; boil. Cook for 15 minutes till liquid reduces by half. Add cream; boil. Cook for 10 minutes till liquid reduces by half; serve with sliced beef.

Nutrition Information

Calories: 489 calories Total Carbohydrate: 8 g Cholesterol: 127 mg Total Fat: 36 g Fiber: 1 g Protein: 27 g Sodium: 681 mg

Tenderloin Steak Diane

Serving: 4 servings. | Prep: 15m | Ready in: 30m

Ingredients

- 4 beef tenderloin steaks (6 oz. each)
- 1 tsp. steak seasoning
- 2 tbsps. butter

- 1 cup sliced fresh mushrooms
- 1/2 cup reduced-sodium beef broth
- 1/4 cup heavy whipping cream
- 1 tbsp. steak sauce
- 1 tsp. garlic salt with parsley
- 1 tsp. minced chives

Direction
1. Sprinkle steak seasoning on steaks. Heat butter on medium heat in a big skillet. Add steaks; cook till meat gets desired doneness for 4-5 minutes per side. Take steaks from pan.
2. Put mushrooms in skillet; mix and cook till tender on medium high heat. Add broth; mix to loosen browned bits from the pan. Mix in garlic salt, steak sauce and cream; boil. Mix and cook till sauce is slightly thick for 1-2 minutes.
3. Put steaks in pan; flip to coat. Heat through; mix in chives.

Nutrition Information
Calories: 358 calories Total Carbohydrate: 2 g Cholesterol: 111 mg Total Fat: 21 g Fiber: 0 g Protein: 37 g Sodium: 567 mg

Tenderloin Steaks With Cherry Sauce

Serving: 4 servings. | Prep: 5m | Ready in: 25m

Ingredients
- 1/3 cup dried tart cherries
- 3/4 cup port wine
- 2 tsps. butter
- 3/4 tsp. salt, divided
- 1/8 tsp. plus 1/4 tsp. coarsely ground pepper
- 4 beef tenderloin steaks (4 oz. each)
- 1 green onion, chopped

Direction
1. Place cherries and wine in a large saucepan. Boil; cook until liquid is reduced to 1/4 cup, about 5 minutes. Mix in 1/8 tsp. pepper, 1/4 tsp. salt, and butter.
2. Season steaks with the rest of pepper and salt. Broil about 4 inch away from the heat source until desired doneness of meat is reached, about 4 to 6 minutes per side (a thermometer should achieve 145° for medium-rare, 160° for medium, and 170° for well done)
3. Serve steaks with cherry sauce and garnish with green onion.

Nutrition Information
Calories: 291 calories Total Carbohydrate: 15 g Cholesterol: 55 mg Total Fat: 9 g Fiber: 1 g Protein: 25 g Sodium: 461 mg

Veal With Mushroom-wine Sauce

Serving: 4 servings. | Prep: 15m | Ready in: 30m

Ingredients
- 4 veal cutlets (4 oz. each)
- 1/2 tsp. canola oil
- 1 lb. sliced fresh mushrooms

- 1 small onion, chopped
- 1 garlic clove, minced
- 1/2 cup white wine or reduced-sodium chicken broth
- 4 tsps. all-purpose flour
- 1/4 cup water
- 2 tbsps. minced fresh parsley
- 1/4 tsp. salt
- 1/8 tsp. pepper

Direction

1. Cook the veal in a big nonstick skillet greased in cooking spray with oil on moderate heat until not pink anymore, about 2 to 3 minutes per side. Take veal out and keep warm.
2. Put garlic, onion and mushrooms into skillet, then cook on moderately high heat until soften, about 5 to 8 minutes. Put in wine while stirring to loosen any browned bits from pan.
3. Mix together water and flour until smooth, then stir into mushroom mixture. Bring to a boil, then cook and stir until thicken, about 2 minutes. Stir in pepper, salt and parsley, then serve over veal.

Nutrition Information

Calories: 231 calories Total Carbohydrate: 9 g Cholesterol: 74 mg Total Fat: 12 g Fiber: 2 g Protein: 23 g Sodium: 281 mg

White Wine Coq Au Vin

Serving: 2 servings. | Prep: 25m | Ready in: 01h05m

Ingredients

- 4 cups water
- 1 cup pearl onions
- 4 bacon strips, cut into 1-inch pieces
- 2 bone-in chicken breast halves (8 oz. each)
- 1/4 tsp. salt
- 1/8 tsp. pepper
- 3/4 cup sliced fresh mushrooms
- 2 garlic cloves, minced
- 4-1/2 tsps. all-purpose flour
- 3/4 cup chicken broth
- 3/4 cup white wine or additional chicken broth
- 1 bay leaf
- 1/2 tsp. dried thyme
- Hot cooked noodles

Direction

1. Boil water in a big saucepan. Put in onions and let boil for about 3 minutes. Strain and rinse using cold water then remove peel; put aside.
2. Cook bacon in a big skillet on moderate heat until crispy. Transfer bacon to paper towels with a slotted spoon.
3. Sprinkle pepper and salt over chicken, then brown chicken in the drippings. Take chicken out and keep warm. Put mushrooms and onions into drippings, then sauté until tender-crisp. Put in garlic and cook for another minute.
4. Mix broth and flour together, then stir into onion mixture. Put in thyme, bay leaf and wine, then

bring to a boil. Turn bacon and chicken back to the pan, then lower heat and simmer with a cover until a thermometer reaches 170 degrees, about 25 to 30 minutes.

5. Take chicken out and keep warm. Cook the sauce until somewhat thicken on moderate heat. Get rid of bay leaf then serve chicken, noodles and sauce together.

Nutrition Information

Calories: 672 calories Total Carbohydrate: 22 g Cholesterol: 141 mg Total Fat: 37 g Fiber: 1 g Protein: 47 g Sodium: 1093 mg